TO La____,

God Bless you!

Bob Buh

7-19-94

Heb. 13:1

Like a
PRAIRIE FIRE

*A History of the
Assemblies of God
in Oklahoma*

BY   BOB   BURKE

FOREWORD BY THOMAS E. TRASK

LIKE A PRAIRIE FIRE
A History of the Assemblies of God in Oklahoma

Copyright © 1994 by
The Oklahoma District Council of the Assemblies of God
P.O. Box 13179
Oklahoma City, Oklahoma 73118

Edited by Robert C. Cunningham and David A. Womack
Cover Design by 2W Design Group

Library of Congress Catalog Card Number 94-66820
ISBN 0-9641325-0-8

Printed in the United States of America

∴Contents∾

∿ *Preface* ∿

In 1914, 300 Pentecostals gathered in Hot Springs, Arkansas, to form a cooperative fellowship. Little did they realize the impact of their gathering. Eighty years later, 25 million people gather in Assemblies of God churches in 133 countries. There can be no logical, human explanation for what has happened. It was God's doing. He promised to pour out His Spirit on all flesh—and that is exactly what He did and what He continues to do.

Like a Prairie Fire is an appropriate name for the exciting saga of the birth and spread of the Assemblies of God in Oklahoma. Eighty years ago, Pentecostal preachers stepped into the void in American religion and sparked a spiritual wildfire on a drought-stricken prairie.

The story you are about to read is the result of a massive research effort. Thousands of pages of church and district records were reviewed. Hundreds of early newspapers and magazines were carefully scanned for references to Oklahoma. More than 130 persons were interviewed. And 120 Assemblies of God churches responded with photographs and local church histories.

There are literally thousands of inspiring stories to be told of the formation and growth of the Assemblies of God in our state. The wealth of information often overwhelmed me as I tried to put the bits and pieces of the history together. I apologize in advance for surely missing some of the wonderful events and individuals that shaped our heritage.

I could not have completed this gargantuan project without the help of many people. District Superintendent Armon Newburn and other district officials cooperated superbly. Wayne Warner and his staff at the Assemblies of God Archives in Springfield, Missouri, provided outstanding support in research and old photos. I could not have had a better research staff behind me. Eric Dabney, Darlene Ax, Chimene Wood, Cindy Wilson, and Glenn Gohr scheduled interviews, conducted interviews, reviewed mountains of paper, spent hours and days looking at microfilm and old magazines, and typed hundreds of pages of interview transcripts.

Thanks to my office manager Linda Danker for keeping my law office running while the rest of us were off writing a book.

I was blessed with a dedicated and talented group of manuscript editors: Robert Cunningham, who faithfully served our movement for 35 years as editor of *The Pentecostal Evangel*, Louise Jeter Walker, Bert Webb, Armon and JoAnn Newburn, James Dodd, Ron McCaslin (my pastor and friend who always encourages me in my book projects), Greg Whitlow, Ryan Wilson, W.G. and Doris Baker, Leroy Hawkins, Dan Shaeffer, and Jim and Faye Bertelmann.

Joseph Kilpatrick and his team at the Gospel Publishing House made the technical end of this project smooth. David Womack and Doug and Sandi Welch worked with me closely to assure that the final product was one of quality.

A special tribute is due Leroy Hawkins, who laid the groundwork 30 years ago for this present book with his thoroughly researched graduate paper on the early history of the Assemblies of God in Oklahoma.

This history needed to be written. In fact, the 1955 Oklahoma District Council passed a resolution approving such a project. I am honored to have been chosen almost 40 years later for the task.

I have reserved the greatest tribute for the men and women who gave up fame and fortune—and often everything—to spread the Pentecostal message to every village and hamlet in the state. To them, Pentecost was not just another religion; it was a whole way of life. The pioneers of the Assemblies of God fellowship in Oklahoma deserve every accolade we can ever offer. Because of them, the Assemblies of God and Pentecost are alive and well in Oklahoma.

Bob Burke
1994

∽ *Foreword* ∽

This book is a historical look at the Oklahoma District Council of the Assemblies of God, the first district to organize following the formation of the Fellowship in Hot Springs, Arkansas. Established in July of 1914 just three months after the Hot Springs meeting, the district has afforded our Fellowship a rich heritage. The Oklahoma District has distinguished itself as a strong district. It is in the forefront in advancing the kingdom of God.

Many outstanding Assemblies of God leaders, such as former General Superintendents J.W. Welch and W.T. Gaston, could trace their ministry to the Oklahoma District. Its present district superintendent, Armon Newburn, serves as a General Council non-resident executive presbyter, is a member of the Evangel College and Southwestern Assemblies of God College Boards of Directors, and serves on various national committees. Another leader in our Fellowship, Bert Webb, was saved in 1922 in a year-long revival in Wellston, Oklahoma. The contributions he has made to the Assemblies of God as pastor, presbyter, district leader, and assistant general superintendent are inestimable.

The Oklahoma District has been and continues to be a leader in many areas of our Fellowship. Its vision to see churches planted in every community has made it one of the largest district councils in its number of churches. It is interesting to note that one of the greatest periods of church growth came during the Great Depression.

While Southwestern Bible School was located in Enid, Oklahoma, P.C. Nelson served as its capable leader. It was in Enid that Brother Nelson wrote *Bible Doctrines*, a book that has been such a blessing to our Fellowship. We shall be eternally grateful for his contribution. The strong emphasis on missionary training by President Nelson resulted in such men as J.W. Tucker, Hugh Jeter, and Klaude Kendrick, who were mightily used of God for the cause of world missions. Oklahoma continues to be a strong missions district. Its giving to world ministries has placed Oklahoma among the leading districts of the Fellowship.

7

The past is rich with evidences of God's blessing upon the Oklahoma District. I am confident the future, should Jesus tarry, will be one of continued blessing to Christ's Church and its great mission.

I welcome this opportunity to commend the Oklahoma District and its leadership for a task well done.

Thomas E. Trask
General Superintendent
The Assemblies of God
Springfield, Missouri

Chapter 1

⸭

Oh, What Singing! Oh, What Shouting!

It's Sunday night in the Oklahoma hills. Down by the creek—in a brush arbor dimly lit by a kerosene lantern—new converts are singing. A rousing anthem pierces the night air:

Lord, send the old-time pow'r, the Pentecostal pow'r!
Thy floodgates of blessing on us throw open wide!
Lord, send the old-time pow'r, the Pentecostal pow'r,
That sinners be converted and Thy name glorified.

The singing is unlike anything else on earth, for this is a Pentecostal meeting. It's the early part of the twentieth century. The people have been baptized in the Holy Spirit and they are pouring their overflowing joy about the newfound baptism into their happy songs. Before Pentecost came, sacred music was slow, cold, and reserved. Only the "worldly" would dare sing a fast song. Pentecost changed that forever. The new Pentecostal songs—and even the old Holiness hymns—were sung at a break-neck speed. It was as if the joy of the Lord was so built up in them, they exploded during the song service. Howard Goss observed those song services:

9

"This crescendo of joyous, happy people singing unto the Lord was infectious. The sound of victorious Christian living wrapped you around. It seemed to slip down gently into the deeps of your affections, to tap at your heart's door, and...spread warmly through your entire being... People who had never attempted to sing before felt free to sing along with us. Some could not manage a tune, but they could accompany us without fear of being conspicuous."[1]

If you passed by a Pentecostal brush arbor or tent meeting in 1913 you would probably hear songs like "Just Over in the Gloryland," "I am Thine, O Lord," "The Lily of the Valley," "Victory Ahead," "The Hallelujah Side," "Oh, This Is Like Heaven to Me," "The Meeting in the Air," or a favorite song of the new convert, "He Took My Sins Away"—

> I came to Jesus weary, worn, and sad,
> He took my sins away, He took my sins away,
> And now His love has made my heart so glad,
> He took my sins away.
>
> He took my sins away,
> He took my sins away,
> And keeps me singing every day!
> I'm so glad He took my sins away,
> He took my sins away.

Pentecost would probably not have had such a sweeping effect on America's heartland had it not been for the anointed singing.

Not only was the singing different; the preaching was different, too. Many of the Pentecostal evangelists and pastors of those days had no formal education for the ministry. All they had was on-the-job training under the tutelage of the Holy Spirit. Often they used too many Hallelujahs, Praise the Lords, Amens, to make up for a possible lack of study. But what they said made sense. They preached from their hearts with such sincerity and warmth that critics could not seriously question their motives.[2]

There were exceptions to the limited educational level of the early preachers. For example, Samuel Jamieson had preached in Presbyterian churches for 25 years when he received the baptism and jumped into the ranks of Pentecostal preachers. Jamieson, who later became the second pastor of the Assembly of God at Fifth and Peoria in Tulsa, was highly educated, but he said that God told him to throw away all his written sermons and depend completely upon the Holy Spirit.[3]

Two characteristics possessed by all successful Pentecostal preachers were a life of prevailing prayer and a holy boldness. Opponents of Pentecost could not understand the lack of fear displayed by pioneer ministers. Their consecration was so deep that there was no room for anything other than God and His will in their lives.[4]

The Pentecostal preacher gladly went anywhere God sent him, leaving entirely to Him the supplying of every need. The seriousness of that early ministry was explained by Howard Goss:

"The Lord's work in those days was not child's play... Wherever we happened to meet...there was prayer, Bible-reading or singing... Those baptized in the Holy Ghost lived in this atmosphere as naturally as fish live in water. Hence, there was almost no teasing or joking...little of ordinary visiting... We were looking for Jesus only, and we found Him."[5]

The Pentecostal fire was spread everywhere by traveling bands of workers. They depended entirely upon the Lord for direction as to where they should go or where they should stay. Usually there was one preacher in each band. The rest were "workers." Real workers they were, too. They would pray, study, visit, testify, sing, play any instrument, paint signs, do all the janitorial work, scrub, cook, sew, wash, iron, and clean. Above all else, everything was done to save souls.[6]

Transportation was primitive. Early workers sometimes traveled by train but more often they used bicycles, rode in lumber wagons, went horseback, or walked. They waded creeks and rivers. How they got to where God wanted them wasn't important. They just wanted to get there as quickly as they could, often starting a meeting the same night they arrived. They had a burning desire to see people saved, healed, and baptized in the Spirit. The time was short.

The fire in their souls came with the baptism in the Holy Spirit. Howard Goss received the baptism on a train during a prayer meeting. His experience was typical of thousands:

"Soon the power and fire of God came heavier and heavier upon me, until it seemed that I must really be on fire. This fire...seemed to melt all my natural strength, leaving me lying helplessly back in my seat. With every compartment of my mind fully surrendered to God, I told Him to have His way with me,...and He did. I had never dreamed it could be. Soon my English stopped, and I could talk and praise no more. As I lay back limply against my seat, the Spirit of God took possession of my fully surrendered body, and lastly took hold of my throat and vocal cords in what to me was a new and strange way... When another great bolt of God's lightning struck me, thereby loosening me still further, I began to speak in strange tongues."[7]

BRUSH ARBORS AND PALLET QUILTS

Pentecostals didn't invent brush arbors—but they certainly made good use of them. A couple of small trees would be cut and stripped to make poles and cross members. Branches of the trees were laid across the framework to keep out the sun. People came in their wagons or jalopies. The women packed baskets of food or box suppers. At dark, youngsters were put to bed on a "pallet" quilt either in the wagons or underneath the rough-hewn benches in the brush arbor.

The preaching was strong and straight. People responded by rushing to the altar with tears streaming down their faces. Doubters so felt the presence of God that they often threw themselves on to the ground and begged for forgiveness. Neighbors and friends sometimes gave mixed signals to the seekers by shouting, "Hang on, Sister," or "Turn loose, Brother."

The Holy Spirit was completely in charge in early Pentecostal services. To the outsider it looked as if no one was in control. There was no individual directing the service. One man would stand to testify, another would give a message in tongues, a little lady in the corner would interpret, and the lady next to her might begin singing. There was a spirit of unity that cannot be present without the Holy Spirit simply "taking over" a service.

Another supernatural element of some of those Pentecostal services was the "heavenly anthem," singing by the entire congregation directed by the Spirit. Maria Woodworth-Etter, a leading healing evangelist, gave a vivid description:

"It didn't sound at all like human voices, but seemed much more like the tones of some wonderful instrument of music... It began on the right side of the audience and rolled...over the entire company of baptized saints in a volume of sounds resembling...the rolling waves of the ocean... It filled me with such holy awe, worship and praise to the Lord, that before I was able to realize the fact fully, the Holy Ghost led me to join in that heavenly song of praise with the rest."[8]

The Pentecostal movement was a "youth" movement. Six out of every seven leaders, pastors, and evangelists were young. They had no loyalties to mainline denominations or doctrines. Their loyalty was to Christ alone. No sacrifice was too great, no duty too hard to perform. No indignity they could suffer could compare with what Jesus had suffered for them.[9] These Holy Ghost-filled preachers, having no earthly means of support and living by faith alone, laid the foundation for the vast Pentecostal movement that has produced an estimated 360 million professing Pentecostals and charismatics—21 percent of the world's Christians.[10]

Chapter 2

How It All Began

Within the American church world in the late nineteenth century there was an increased fervor to take the gospel to the whole world. Great revivals led by evangelists such as Charles G. Finney and Dwight L. Moody created a spiritual paradox. Thousands were being saved, but the traditional Protestant church did not provide an atmosphere to sustain the focused Christian life of the new believer. American Protestant churches were wealthy, cultured, and influential. Their spiritual state was low, their worship was formal and unemotional.[1] One religious writer of the day commented that "elaborately dressed and ornamented choirs...go through a cold artistic or operatic performance... Under such worldly performance, spirituality is frozen to death."[2] The average Protestant did not know the meaning of the phrase "separated from the world."

The Holiness movement in the northeastern United States was the lone voice of protest to worldliness in America. Holiness revivalists taught separate living and strict standards of conduct. As a result of its focus and divergence from traditional churches, the Holiness revival led frequently to the organization of independent churches. By 1895 Holiness groups spread into the Midwest and the South. As the twentieth century approached, it became increasingly evident that the older denominations would not be able to contain the fresh anointing that had fallen like rain upon America.

15

The modern Pentecostal revival had its start in Kansas. Charles Parham, a minister with a Methodist background, had opened Bethel Bible College in an old Topeka mansion known locally as "Stone's Folly."

Parham had asked his students to study diligently what the Bible said about the evidence of receiving the baptism in the Holy Spirit. On the first day of 1901, the Holy Spirit came upon one of the students. Agnes Ozman, the first to receive the baptism at Topeka, tells her story:

"The presence of the Lord was with us in a marked way, stilling hearts to wait upon Him for greater things. The spirit of prayer was upon us in the evening. It was nearly eleven o'clock when it came into my heart to ask that hands might be laid upon me that I might receive the gift of the Holy Ghost. As hands were laid upon my head, the Holy Spirit fell upon me, and I began to speak in tongues, glorifying God... It was as though rivers of living water were proceeding from my innermost being."[3]

Agnes Ozman later became a credentialed Assemblies of God minister.

Howard Stanley was another student who received the Pentecostal baptism in Topeka. He said he saw fire come from heaven into the corner of the room:

"Suddenly our vocal cords and tongues changed so that we began to speak in other tongues and praise God... And those who could speak English stood to their feet and sang the old song: 'The Comforter Has Come.'"[4]

> *The Comforter has come,*
> *The Comforter has come!*
> *The Holy Ghost from heav'n,*
> *The Father's promise giv'n;*
> *O spread the tidings 'round,*
> *Wherever man is found,*
> *The Comforter has come!*

School was suspended as the power of God swept through the student body of 40. After Parham also was filled with the

Spirit, the news spread quickly. Reporters came from Kansas City and St. Louis. Soon Parham and his followers carried the news about Pentecost to the surrounding states, including Oklahoma.

J. Roswell Flower, an executive officer of the Assemblies of God for many years, explained what happened at Topeka this way: "It was as though a spiritual atom had been exploded, which produced a spiritual mushroom effect, the activated particles spreading...to all parts of the earth."[5] Every Pentecostal group in America can trace its history back to the humble beginning at "Stone's Folly" in Topeka.

Parham's most successful revival was in Galena, Kansas, in October, 1903. Hundreds were saved, healed, and filled with the Spirit. The Galena revival had a significant impact on Pentecost in Oklahoma. Several future leaders of the Assemblies of God in Oklahoma came in contact with Parham as a result of the Galena crusade.

A young high school football star, Howard A. Goss, was gloriously saved:

"God had surely changed my life. I was so happy that everything around me seemed scintillating with joy. God had changed my outlook on life so completely that even the old mine dumps around Galena suddenly seemed beautiful."[6]

Early in 1905, Goss held a tent revival in Tahlequah. That revival resulted in the formation of a local church, probably Oklahoma's first Pentecostal congregation.

Parham took his revival band to Joplin, Missouri, in 1904. Many people from northeast Oklahoma came and accepted Pentecost. Historian Klaude Kendrick wrote that "many persons in an area from Carthage, Missouri to Miami, Oklahoma, accepted the 'full gospel', and numerous conversions and healings were reported."[7] The influence of Parham and his converts made northeast Oklahoma (still Indian Territory at that time) a hotbed of Pentecost almost from the very beginning of the movement.

Howard Goss joined Parham and future Oklahoma Assemblies of God District Chairman Oscar Jones on a landmark trip to Houston, Texas, in July, 1905. Also in the Parham band was Will Pennock, an early Pentecostal preacher in the Norman, Okla-

17

homa, area. By winter, 25,000 people had been saved at Parham's revival in Houston. One convert, a black Holiness preacher, W. J. Seymour, would provide the link between Parham's ministry and the Pentecostal "explosion" that would soon occur on Azusa Street in California.

THE BEULAH COLONY

Pentecost came to western Oklahoma in 1906—the year before Oklahoma joined the union as the 46th state. A colony of Holiness believers truly wanted to be separated from the world and settled in Beckham County on the site of the present town of Carter. They called their community "Beulah," from Isaiah 62:4. The settlement was a cooperative. There was no individual ownership of land. An orphanage and a hotel were built. And in 1907 Frank T. Alexander founded the Emmanuel Bible School, which occupied a three-story brick building in the center of town.[8]

The "Holiness" colony soon became a "Pentecostal" colony. Ironically, a Holiness evangelist called Uncle Tom was summoned to hold a campmeeting to stamp out the Pentecostal fire that was taking over the colony. Before Uncle Tom could begin preaching, however, a Sister McClung began shouting and dancing in the Spirit. Several people were slain in the Spirit. Pentecost had arrived at Beulah to stay, even though many of the members of the colony wanted nothing to do with the Pentecostal experience. That division would finally result in the closing of the colony by 1910.[9]

Revival at Beulah was continuous. In the winter, nightly meetings were held in the Bible school. In the summer, tents were pitched to accommodate the large crowds coming from west Texas and western Oklahoma.[10]

Several families in the Beulah colony later became part of the Assemblies of God. Mary Bernice Ferguson and her sons, Clyde and Paul would serve more than a combined 170 years as Pentecostal preachers.

The first Pentecostal songbook in the world was published in Oklahoma—in Beulah, by R.E. Winsett, one of the Bible teachers at the school. Winsett called his collection of Pentecostal songs *Old Time Power*. The songbook's price of just twenty-five cents resulted in widespread distribution. Paul Ferguson recalls the difficulty of the publishing effort:

"The typesetting and handpress work were largely done by older students at the school... In some cases a song would be partly on one page with the rest of the song on another page or elsewhere. However, the book became a very powerful tool in those early days."[11]

Even the titles in the new song book changed people's ideas about God. Some of the songs were "Honey in the Rock," "This World is Not My Home," "The Old Account Was Settled," "Come and Dine," and "Dwelling in Beulah Land." Howard Goss remembered the impact of the first Pentecostal hymnal:

"When I went into a new house and saw one of our hymn books, usually on the piano where someone had been using it, I knew it was a home which would be Pentecostal before long, without any further help from me."[12]

Beulah produced possibly Oklahoma's first Pentecostal missionary. Daniel P. Awrey, a teacher at the Bible school, so strongly felt the call of God to go to southern Asia that he left town with only a dime in his pocket. God miraculously provided transportation to the other side of the earth—to India—where Awrey faithfully served for many years in a Pentecostal orphanage. Awrey was one of the early proponents of cooperation among Pentecostals worldwide. In 1909 he attended an international Pentecostal conference in England.[13]

By 1906, it was estimated that 13,000 persons called themselves "Pentecostal" in Oklahoma, Missouri, Texas, Kansas, and Arkansas. The Pentecostal message was taken to all towns, large and small by young preachers who "testified" more than they preached. Pentecostal newspapers, such as the *Apostolic Standard* in Beulah, spread the news about the outpouring of the Holy Spirit, even before the revival on Azusa Street in California.

Chapter 3

Azusa Street and Beyond

As though hit by a bolt of lightning, the entire company was knocked from their chairs to the floor. Seven began speaking in other tongues. The shouts were so fervent—and so loud—that a crowd gathered outside, wondering, "What meaneth this?" Soon the news spread throughout the city that God was pouring out His Spirit. It was April 9, 1906; and the Pentecostal baptism had suddenly come to Los Angeles, California, where William J. Seymour was conducting a service among Baptists who hungered for a deeper experience with God.[1] Seymour, a convert of Charles Parham's revival in Houston, soon moved his meetings to an old, two-story frame structure on Azusa Street in the industrial section of Los Angeles. There was constant revival at the mission on Azusa Street for three years. An eyewitness described a typical service:

"As soon as it is announced that the altar is open...for pardon, sanctification, the baptism in the Holy Ghost, and healing for the body, people rise and flock to the altar. There is no urging. What kind of preaching is it that brings that? The simple declaring of the Word of God. There is such power in the preaching of the Word in the Spirit that people are shaken on the benches. Coming to the altar many fall prostrate under the power of God and often come out speaking in tongues."[2]

21

There was no doubt that the visitation of the Holy Spirit on Azusa Street was real, though unexplainable in human terms. Another witness to the events said:

"The how and why of it is to be found in the very opposite of those conditions that are usually thought necessary for a big revival. No instruments of music are used. None are needed. No choir. Bands of angels have been heard by some in the Spirit and there is heavenly singing inspired by the Holy Ghost. No collections are taken. No bills have been posted to advertise the meetings. All who are in touch with God realize as soon as they enter the meeting that the Holy Ghost is the leader."[3]

The exciting news about Azusa Street spread eastward across the country to Oklahoma and beyond. Seymour's monthly newspaper, *The Apostolic Faith*, was distributed free of charge to thousands of ministers and laymen. In December, 1906, G. A. Cook stopped in the northern Oklahoma town of Lamont in Grant County on his way home to Indiana from Azusa Street. His letter was printed in the January, 1907, edition of *The Apostolic Faith*:

"Left Los Angeles Dec. 4 and arrived in Oklahoma just one week later... Quite a number were tarrying and waiting for Pentecost when I arrived, but much had to be done before God could pour out His Spirit. The people had been in much bondage. Eating pork, wearing neckties, drinking coffee, and wearing a moustache were taught to be very sinful... After about ten days of prayer and holding up the Blood, God began to break them up...and in a short time, in a cottage prayer meeting, God poured out His Spirit in slaying power and nearly all went down, one woman coming through speaking in tongues... The country was stirred for miles around. Some came 100 miles to get Pentecost and healing."[4]

In the same edition of the newspaper was a report from Arthur Grimshaw in Pawhuska, Oklahoma, that "the wonderful power is not only in the mission in cities, but also among the cowboys and farmers in the country. We have got the Pentecost here and it is glorious."[5]

By 1908 the Pentecostal influence was widespread in Oklahoma. *The Pentecost*, a newspaper edited by J. Roswell Flower, listed the Beulah colony in Doxey, Oklahoma (near Beulah, later Carter, Oklahoma), and the Holiness Mission in Oklahoma City as "Pentecostal" missions. And *The Apostolic Standard*, published at the Beulah colony, was one of two dozen Pentecostal newspapers being published from New York to California.[6]

PARHAM IN TULSA

Charles Parham held a tent revival in Tulsa at the corner of Third Street and Cincinnati Avenue in August, 1908. The revival was financed in an unusual way. Vandalia Fry, a petite and soft-spoken saint, had started a Pentecostal prayer meeting and Bible study in her home in 1907. She had been healed of cancer and received the baptism in Parham's great Galena, Kansas, revival. By 1908 she felt God wanted the Pentecostal message brought to Tulsa. She sold her diamond ring for $1,500, more than enough money to ship Parham's tent to Tulsa.

Fannie and Mabel Hughes, Willa Lowther, Mr. and Mrs. A.J. Welker, Martha Baxter, E.K. Gray, Oscar Wolfe, Frank Carter, Mr. and Mrs. John Reddout and Mrs. Sam Dague were listed among the 100 converts of the revival. All would become charter members of one of the oldest Assemblies of God churches in Oklahoma—Central Assembly of Tulsa, which was commonly known as "Fifth and Peoria." The church is said to be the first Pentecostal group in the state to build a permanent place of worship.[7]

The February, 1909, edition of the *Latter Rain Evangel* carried the story of a miraculous healing in the Parham tent revival in Tulsa. Mrs. J. C. Ament testified that God perfectly restored her sight and healed her of stomach, spinal, and head problems:

"During these meetings I learned that our blessed Savior had made provision in His precious atonement to heal our bodies as well as to save us from sin. Prayer was offered for me with the laying on of hands, and my body was instantly healed. I have been perfectly well ever since."[8]

Assemblies of God pioneer Pastor E.L. Newby attended a Pentecostal tent revival held by A.G. Jeffrey in Ryan, in Jefferson County, in southern Oklahoma in 1908. The following year

23

Newby received the baptism experience at a meeting in Waurika that was conducted by Archie and Pearl Adams:

"In one of the morning services, the evangelist spoke a few words in tongues. It was the first time I had ever heard anyone speak in tongues, and since my own heart was prepared and hungry, the Spirit of God came upon me also and I began to speak in tongues."[9]

Newby and his brother-in-law, J.J. Grubbs, were the only persons to receive the baptism at that meeting. Both were later called to preach.

In September, 1909, Lillian Thistlewaite, a sister-in-law of Charles Parham, conducted a revival in Tulsa. Only one young man, Willard H. Pope, was saved. However, Pope later became a charter member of the Assemblies of God and the second chairman of the Oklahoma District. He held numerous meetings in Chelsea, Catale, Claremore, Wellston, Tahlequah, Shawnee, Pawhuska, Broken Arrow, and at Fifth and Peoria in Tulsa.[10]

PENTECOST IN LINCOLN COUNTY

Lincoln County, in central Oklahoma, was a hotbed of Pentecost by 1910. In the year before, Alonzo Horn held a campaign in a schoolhouse about four miles southeast of Davenport. He had been saved in Galena, Kansas. The Davenport revival lasted nine weeks with many people being saved and filled with the Holy Spirit. Among the new converts were F.W. Pryor and a Mrs. Minson who helped form the local Pentecostal group after the revival.[11]

Aggie and Lottie James were saved in a revival conducted by Horn and A.E. Humbard (father of famed television preacher Rex Humbard) in May, 1912, at the Pleasant Grove school near Sparks in Lincoln County. James was left in charge of the mission when the revival team moved on. He received the baptism while plowing. He played the guitar, and he and his wife Lottie sang together. Teenagers, on their way home late at night, often heard James praying in his orchard, calling out to God the names of people of his community who needed salvation. Aggie James later became one of the most effective evangelists and pastors in the

Assemblies of God fellowship in Oklahoma. He pastored the church at Sparks for 40 years.[12]

W.T. Gaston spread the full gospel to Fallis, Carney, and Wellston in 1913. Later that year, Alonzo Horn returned and conducted a series of meetings in an old store building on Wellston's Main Street:

"Folks began coming, most who came expected to see a show, not to worship God. A common saying was, 'Well, are you going to the show tonight, down where they shout, sing, and dance in the Spirit?' Some found the service amusing, others attempted to intimidate the worshipers with rotten eggs. Nevertheless, God began to move, and folks were saved, baptized in the Holy Spirit, and healed. At the close of the revival, over 500 people met on the banks of the Deep Fork river for the area's first baptismal service."[13]

THE TATHAM FAMILY

One of the most rousing stories of early-day Pentecost in Oklahoma is found in Dan Morgan's book, *Rising in the West: The True Story of an Okie Family from the Great Depression through the Reagan years*. The book chronicles the Tatham family and Pentecost arriving with itinerant Evangelist John Himer on Drake's Prairie, six miles west of Sallisaw, in 1909. Himer floated down the Arkansas River on a raft, put up a tent and began holding meetings. Morgan describes the Holy Ghost revival that swept through Drake's Prairie:

"Baptism by the Holy Spirit was not only a spiritual event but also a rite of passage through which younger people entered the tightly knit fellowship of the church-going circle... The church bound together families and linked generations through an almost daily round of meetings that were alive with the anticipation of unexpected conversions, healings, tongue speakings, and admonishments by the preacher of some brother or sister who had strayed from the strict code. The Holy Spirit changed lives."[14]

Morgan tells of Cora Tatham's conversion at a "holy roller" meeting at a country church on Brushy Mountain near Sallisaw:

25

"This preacher was different... He was full of the power of God and he preached a sermon to make your hair raise on your head. Made you examine yourself to see if you were really, truly, born again... He had the Holy Ghost and spoke in tongues. Banjo lamps with long stems and round globes full of kerosene cast a dim, yellow glow over the interior of the church... She felt the Holy Spirit drawing her down to that altar to repent of her sins, and so when all the rest of the people laughed, she knew that's what she needed."[15]

Some people called Drake's Prairie the "prayin'-est place in all Oklahoma."

Chapter 4

The Fire Spreads in All Directions

Revival broke out in southwest Oklahoma in 1909. Oscar Jones, a Kansas preacher who had followed Charles Parham to Houston and received the baptism, traveled by two-horse buggy with his wife to Frederick in Tillman County. It was probably the first revival for Jones, who later became district chairman of the Assemblies of God in Oklahoma during the 1920's. The trip to Frederick took three days. Jones had only 32 cents in his pocket and knew no one between Texas and Frederick.

The revival began in a small schoolhouse. By the second night, the schoolhouse was packed; and all but one person was converted, and that one holdout later was saved. The meeting shook up the local economy. Bootleggers ran from the schoolhouse and destroyed their stills. Stolen pigs, chickens, and cattle were returned to their owners as thieves were convicted of their sins.

Jones held a second revival in Tillman County and suffered persecution from some of the local cowboys who rode around the building shooting their guns during the service. A lighted cigarette was dropped down Jones' shirt as he knelt in prayer by a window. Jones and his wife lived with a large family in a dugout and existed on "water gravy" during the revival.[1]

Famed Evangelist Daniel C.O. Opperman also left his footprints on Tillman County in the summer of 1909. Opperman preached a campmeeting in the small town of Manitou. He was a pioneer Pentecostal educator who "trained and put hundreds of workers in the Pentecostal harvest field."[2]

David Wilson Savage was an ordained Holiness preacher in Wise County, Texas, when he underwent surgery in 1912 by a country doctor for what he thought was appendicitis. The doctor found a large cancer and gave Savage only three months to live. But Savage had heard about a group of Pentecostal people at Cordell, Oklahoma, who preached divine healing. He was weak and hemorrhaging badly when he took the train to the campmeeting at Cordell. The saints laid hands on him and prayed. His son, H.M. Savage, reported the results:

"Ten days later we looked out the door and saw him walking up the road with his suitcase. He had been healed, returned on the train, and walked the four miles from the depot. There was not a trace of weakness or disease. Some skeptical neighbors didn't believe he was healed until they saw him out in the field picking cotton and dragging a heavy cotton sack behind him."[3]

Savage didn't stay in the cotton patch for long. He was soon filled with the Holy Spirit and pioneered several new churches over the next 19 years in Oklahoma. His son, grandchildren, and great grandchildren have continued the David Savage tradition as Assemblies of God ministers.[4]

Ethel Musick preached her first sermon in 1913 at age 17 at the Payne schoolhouse 18 miles east of Duncan. Her magnificent career as a woman evangelist began in Velma later that year. In a three-week meeting, 60 were saved and 30 filled with the Holy Spirit. She and her husband Marcus began a long, fruitful ministry in a very humble way:

"I made speaking appointments at nearby schoolhouses. I would work in the field all week till Saturday at noon, then I would take my dear old Bible and go to the woods where I would bury my face in its pages and seek the Lord for wisdom. There I took a course in 'knee'-ology... We went out of one meeting right into another, and the Lord blessed by saving souls and filling them with the Spirit of Promise."[5]

Ethel Musick made a significant impact on southwest Oklahoma. Her revivals resulted in the formation of Assemblies of God churches in several towns over a period of 20 years.

REVIVAL FIRES IN EASTERN OKLAHOMA

By 1910 the Pentecostal colony at Beulah ceased to exist. Mary Bernice Ferguson and her family headed to eastern Oklahoma where she took the Pentecostal message by horseback or wagon to such places as Spade Mountain, July Springs, Bidding Springs, and Stilwell. Sister Ferguson's meetings produced tremendous results, but not without persecution. Many services were disturbed by showers of rotten eggs. Paul Ferguson recalled one incident:

"One night in a brush arbor, I, being about nine years old, answered the call of nature and retreated to the nearby woods. Upon my return I heard my father, who was leading singing, suddenly say, 'Let us all pray now.' And as it was our custom to pray kneeling, all of the saints, who were sitting on the two front benches (planks placed on nail kegs) fell to their knees. Instantly, rotten eggs were thrown into the meeting striking the spectators who had come to see the 'show'... Not one of the kneeling saints had even a splatter upon them."[6]

Pentecostal services began at Lee School near Muldrow in 1909. The Lee's Chapel Church met in a new school building built in August, 1909. It contained one large school room, two large cloak rooms, and a library. The church continued meeting in the school until the late 1930's.[7]

Arkansas Evangelist Powell Youngblood held a revival at the schoolhouse in Turkey Ford in Delaware County in 1912. Two Holiness men and a Baptist had asked him to bring the Pentecostal message to the area. Bertie Roberts was 14 and had resisted the urging of the Holy Spirit to get saved out of fear that her unsaved father would disapprove. In 1993, 81 years later, Mrs. Roberts wept as she remembered her conversion experience at the Turkey Ford school:

"I was so under conviction that I cried all during the service. A sweet sister came and talked to me about salvation, but I still wouldn't go. I knew Daddy would be mad. Then suddenly God told me that it wasn't a matter between me and my father...it was between me and God. He made that so plain to me that I knew I had to settle the matter with God, no matter what Daddy thought. I felt that if I didn't get saved that night, I would never be saved. I ran to the altar and God saved me. I was so carried away in the Spirit that I was completely unaware of the large crowd that had gathered in and around the schoolhouse."[8]

W.T. GASTON

The Pentecostal group in Tahlequah had been struggling for existence for five years when the Hargis family and other leaders in the church called W.T. Gaston to be their pastor in late 1910 or 1911.[9] The Hargis' son, Vache A., later became the first secretary of the Oklahoma District of the Assemblies of God.

Gaston pastored in Tahlequah for two years before he became the first full-time pastor of the famed Fifth and Peoria Church in Tulsa. He was known as "the walking preacher," having hiked hundreds of miles over "the worst roads that God ever let afflict the earth" in order to spread the Word. Gaston was universally acknowledged to be one of the most forceful and anointed preachers in the entire Pentecostal movement. For decades he preached to some of the largest crowds in Pentecost. Eventually he was elected as the first Oklahoma District chairman, and later (1925) as general chairman to head the entire Assemblies of God movement.[10]

JOHN WILLIAM WELCH

Oklahoma continued to have a major impact upon the future formation of the Assemblies of God with the arrival of John William Welch to the state in 1910. At age 50, Welch was sent to Oklahoma by the Christian and Missionary Alliance. Soon he discovered he was the only Alliance minister in the state. He held services every night for six months in Muskogee and saw a great harvest of souls.

But Welch longed for a deeper experience with God. He attended a Pentecostal revival led by Arthur B. Cox in Muskogee and was convinced of his need of the baptism in the Holy Spirit. When he received the baptism a few months later, he was invited by W.T. Gaston to preach a revival in Tahlequah. From that time, Welch was a Pentecostal preacher and had a "steadying influence" upon the movement. He was at the core of the leadership at the Hot Springs meeting in 1914, which resulted in the organization of the Assemblies of God, and served as general chairman from 1915 to 1920.[11]

THAT OKLAHOMA WEATHER

Howard Goss held another tent revival in Tahlequah in 1911. He never forgot the impression the Oklahoma weather had on him:

"We entered the tent for a Sunday afternoon service at 2:30 p.m. The thermometer was high—around 90 degrees. Soon, a wind came up from the northwest, bringing rain. Believe it or not, within a half hour the temperature had dropped from 90 degrees to below freezing. The rain froze over everything; the landscape looked as though it had been carved in ice."[12]

The Tulsa Pentecostal congregation that later became the church at Fifth and Peoria took a major step in 1911 in providing a permanent place of worship. The group leased a lot on Brady Street at Cincinnati Avenue and built a 20 by 40-foot frame structure. The worshipers sat on plain, rough benches but accepted the situation gladly, cheered by the reality of a meeting place of their own.[13]

Pentecost came to McCurtain in Haskell County in 1911 when Jacob "Jake" Miller held a revival. In 1912, Miller returned to McCurtain and conducted a six-week campaign in which 32 people were baptized in water.[14]

WILLARD H. POPE

Also in 1912, Willard H. Pope pioneered the church that became Broken Arrow Assembly of God. Pope took a train from Tulsa to Broken Arrow. The Southern Methodist congregation had closed a tent revival, and the tent they used was now available for lease. Pope, in his book *Your Radio Pastor*, recalls the Broken Arrow revival:

"Within two weeks God gave us such a spiritual awakening that the whole country for miles around was stirred mightily for God. It was in the midst of the threshing season, and the crews would come in on their old hayracks from every direction. At the close of the second week, I found myself again confronted with the problem of material for sermons... I had preached everything from Genesis to Revelation the first two weeks... The whole country was on fire with a revival such as they had never had in the history of that section, and the 'boy preacher' had run out of sermons."[15]

Pope sent for Evangelist M.M. Pinson, who was conducting revivals in Arkansas. Pinson, a former Holiness preacher from Tennessee, was a "fighter, not for personal advantage, but for principles in which he believed."[16] He later delivered the keynote address at the Hot Springs convention in 1914.

Pinson's meeting in Broken Arrow resulted in hundreds of conversions. The local newspaper reported, "The Pentecostal band is holding forth at the tent near the Southern Methodist Church. They have had quite a good many converts. Some of them make a good deal of noise, and the meetings continue into the night."[17]

The Broken Arrow revival ended in late August, 1912. The newspaper reported: "The Pentecostal band closed their meeting at the tent last Sunday night. In the afternoon they repaired to the Haskell pond east of town, and 13 were immersed. They will hold meetings at the Public School building on Wednesday evenings and on Sunday."[18] Pope pastored the independent church at Broken Arrow for four years.

Chapter 5

Pentecost Everywhere

The growth of Pentecost in Oklahoma is well documented in the pages of *Word and Witness*, a newspaper published by M.M. Pinson (and later by E.N. Bell, who would become the first chairman of the Assemblies of God). Pentecostal leaders wrote to the newspaper with reports of their successes and failures. The following are excerpts from letters received by *Word and Witness*:[1]

October 20, 1912

"Praise God for victory through the blood. Our meeting here under Bro. J.E. Osborne was very good. Some saved and sanctified and some seeking Pentecost."

—W.M. Dobbs, Carter, Oklahoma.

"In a 10-day meeting God saved 23 and baptized 24 in His Spirit... The house was shaken by the power of God. One man afflicted 45 years was healed instantly."

—J.A. Corbell and band, Pleasant Grove.

"Held a 15-day meeting here. The local banker gave us a building rent free. During one of the services, a man fell to the floor as dead. After prayer, he immediately revived and was a great witness in the town."

—J.A. Corbell, Davenport.

"Had meeting the night we arrived here. The power falling. People getting saved in their seats, during preaching. Four baptized in the Spirit while there, and we promised to return for a regular meeting."
—J.A. Corbell, Panama.

(Dora Barlow, a charter member of the First Assembly of God in Panama confirms the stories of the marvelous revival in the summer of 1912. In July, 1913, A.J. Anderson, W.T. Adkins, and W.D. Massey, trustees of the Apostolic Faith Church, led the effort to build a frame structure with a sheet iron roof in Panama.)[2]

December 20, 1912
"Seven baptized in the Spirit with Bible signs in schoolhouse near here. The power of God is still falling."
—S.D. Goldsmith, McAlester.

"The good work of 68th mission still going. Bro. and Sis. Corbell were with us in October. We have had glorious meetings. It is wonderful how God is pouring out His Spirit in these last days."
—E.M. Pinson, Elder, Chandler.

February 20, 1913
"Several blessed, saved, and filled lately."
—W.T. Gaston, Tulsa.

"Quite a meeting here."
—O.J. Knight, Clinton.

"We can report victory from these parts through the blood of the Lamb."
—W.T. Laughlin, Marlow. (Laughlin was an early Pentecostal evangelist across southern Oklahoma.)

"God still blessing, crowds increasing."
—F. Romines, Shawnee.

"Hardly a meeting but what from two to three get saved and about the same get the baptism.
—W.H. Pope, Broken Arrow.

"The devil is stirred over the moving of the Spirit."
—G.W. Harrison, Ft. Towson.

"Near Stroud at the Stone school, four saved and two baptized.
—F.C. Marsh, Chandler.

May 20, 1913
"We are out here alone in this faith, and we are getting so hungry to hear the gospel preached again. Our house is open for a good preacher and good worker to hold a meeting for us.
—Mrs. G.S. Mills, Frederick.

"Bro. Romines and I are here in a battle for the Lord."
—J.H. James, Hitchita.

"Three saved and baptized."
—Jacob Miller, Claremore.

"God is blessing in the meeting five miles from here. The 30 baptized saints are being built up and mean to go on."
—R.L. Fowler, Heavener.

"Since our band came here from Tulsa last August, God has baptized 50 or 60 with the Holy Ghost."
—W.H. Pope, Broken Arrow.

"Great meeting with a small band of saints."
—W.G. Dunlap, Marlow.

June 20, 1913
"Nine saved, seven baptized. The country is stirred. J.H. James is helping in the meeting."
—Sam Berryhill, Middle Creek.

"Considerable interest here among the saints."
—Earl Borgan, Box.

"Some being hindered here by the doctrine of Jess Finton, which is causing a great deal of trouble. He is teaching a fourth blessing called perfection."
—Sam Berryhill, Hitchita. (Not all the reports were positive.)

"We are only in school with the Holy Ghost. Our tuition was paid for at Calvary and the school is open to all classes."
—W.T. Gaston, Tulsa.

August 20, 1913
"God is blessing in our tent meeting. Souls are weeping their way to the cross every night."
—W.T. Gaston, Tulsa.

September 20, 1913
"Baptized four in water, some wonderfully saved."
—F.G. Barker, Wetumka.

"On Sunday, four saved, two baptized."
—J.A. Corbell, Shawnee.

"We have just completed a meeting at this place. Fifteen received the baptism."
—F.M. Montgomery, San Bois.

"Good meeting, seven filled."
—Robert Smith, Covington.

"The battle is hard. Two saved, two filled."
—J.S. Jones, Turkey Ford.

"50 saved, 30 baptized."
—N.R. Adams, Chandler.

"We came over here from Tahlequah, 15 miles. Six saved. Much interest among the people. One sister lay under the power four hours."
—W.R. Amiot, Spring Creek.

"We have been in a meeting in Lono Valley. Members of the Methodist Protestant Church are very hungry. 22 baptized."
—J.E. Combs, Quinton.

October 23, 1913
"The devil is roaring here. Pray for me. Our trial has been put off. The Spirit seems to say to me that I will be a foreign missionary."
—Wm. Click, Whitefield.

"Twenty saved, one filled."
—W.R. Amiot, Christie.

"Bro. Mitchell and band from Ft. Worth closed a meeting at Wray's Chapel. First Pentecostal meeting ever in this part of the country. People came from several communities. 40 saved, 25 baptized in water. Others healed.
—E.G. Bailey.

"Bro. Herbert Buffum has been helping since Pinson left. I'm leaving for needy fields in Kansas. Bro. Peter Davies is taking charge here."
—W.H. Pope, Broken Arrow.

"Since leaving Los Angeles camp meeting, God has given us good times. We stopped in San Diego for three weeks, in Santa Ana for three weeks, in Phoenix for three weeks and now Cruce, Oklahoma. 18 days God has been with us, 21 baptized in water last Sunday. At the baptismal service the power fell and three got saved and were baptized in the same service. Altogether 31 baptized in water. My next address will be Malvern, Arkansas."
— A.E. Humbard, Cruce

(Humbard had been gloriously filled with the Spirit in the revival that was still going in California as a result of Azusa street. He stopped over in Oklahoma on his way home to Arkansas. He was headed for Malvern to team up with E.N. Bell, who was also interested in getting many of the Pentecostal groups together.)

November 20, 1913

"At Coplin schoolhouse, 41 saved, 8 filled with the Holy Ghost. One sister healed who had not walked by herself in 12 years."

—Elder S.D. Fairchild, Blaine.

March 20, 1914

"Souls are being saved and baptized in almost every meeting. We never meet in the name of the Lord without the power falling and the saints getting blessed."

—R. Minson, Fallis.

"God has given us a blessed meeting at Neff's schoolhouse. Four were baptized in the Spirit... Several had visions of heaven and the glory of God while under the power of the Spirit."

—C. Fairbanks, Webbers Falls.

THE NEED FOR UNITY

The many local independent Pentecostal groups in Oklahoma saw the need for fellowship and association. An annual campmeeting had been held in Tulsa since 1909. W.T. Gaston reported on the 1913 campmeeting:

"The saints rallied to the call to come together and seek the Lord... There was a blessed spirit of unity and love, the best I have ever seen in a campmeeting. The day of 'scrapping' over doctrine is drawing to a close, and the glorious simple gospel of the crucified and glorified Christ is to be the theme for every believer. The power of God increased from day to day until the ninth day when the glory of the Lord overshadowed the camp, and wave after wave of power and glory swept over the vast audience."[3]

Howard Goss recognized that Oklahoma was becoming a leader in believing that unity was necessary if the Pentecostal movement was to have a lasting impact upon America. Goss wrote, "Hope this blessed spirit will increase all over the country."[4]

Chapter 6

Oklahomans at Hot Springs

Oklahoma's influence on organizing the General Council of the Assemblies of God in 1914 was tremendous. Although the state was only seven years old, it contained some of America's strongest and largest Pentecostal churches. Oklahoma's Pentecostal preachers were among the best known in the land.

For a decade prior to 1914, attempts had been made to unite the thousands of Pentecostal churches that sprang up throughout the South and the Midwest. Campmeetings played a major role in bringing together Pentecostals from several states. By 1913 at least 15 campmeetings were annually announced in the Pentecostal newspapers around the country. Interestingly enough, most of the campmeetings were centered in Oklahoma, Texas, Arkansas, and Missouri.[1]

Most Pentecostal ministers belonged to one of four regional associations of independent churches. Oklahoma ministers joined a group headed by Howard Goss and E.N. Bell of Malvern, Arkansas. In 1911 the Goss-Bell group adopted the name "Church of God in Christ," with the permission of the leader of a major black Pentecostal organization of the same name that still exists today.

The white Church of God in Christ listed 352 credentialed ministers in June, 1913. From Oklahoma were Forrest and Clara Barker of Wetumka, J.A. and Myrtle Corbell of Oklahoma City, A.B. Cox of Oklahoma City, Wilson Dobbs of Carter, Henry Dunlap of Canute, W. T. Gaston of Tulsa, Howard Goss, J.C. Hawkins of Doxey, F.D. Hall of Carter, W.L. Lambert of Elk City, Fred and Elva Marsh of Oklahoma City, George Nichols of Sayre, W.H. Pope of Broken Arrow, R.T. Smith of Cowlington, John W. Welch of Tahlequah, W.D. Wilkins of Fort Cobb, and Powell Youngblood of Turkey Ford. Also listed were evangelists from surrounding states who spent much of their time in Oklahoma holding revivals.[2]

Leaders like Goss and Bell saw the need for organization. By 1914 Pentecostals had been driven outside the framework of traditional American Protestant churches. Missionary efforts were splintered because of a lack of cooperation among independent churches. Publication of newspapers, tracts, and other literature was so widespread that a central printing plant was seen to be a necessity.[3]

THE CALL FOR A MEETING

The December 20, 1913, issue of *Word and Witness* carried a formal invitation to Pentecostals to meet in Hot Springs, Arkansas, in April, 1914, to explore the potential for unity and cooperation. E.N. Bell, D.C.O. Opperman, M.M. Pinson, A.P. Collins, and Howard Goss signed the invitation. Opperman, Pinson and Goss had strong Oklahoma ties and were thoroughly familiar with the wishes of Pentecostal saints in Oklahoma.

The March 20, 1914, edition of *Word and Witness* contained a final call for the organizational meeting. The notice contained practical advice like "Bring your own bed clothing" and "No dead beats allowed." The notice listed 33 Pentecostal leaders who had promised to come. Eight of the 33, including W.T. Gaston and W.H. Pope, were either living or preaching in Oklahoma at the time.[4]

Three hundred workers and saints convened in the Hot Springs opera house on April 2. They came from 17 states, primarily in the Midwest, and from Egypt and South Africa. After days of prayer, worship, preaching, and discussion, they formed a "voluntary cooperative fellowship" and adopted as its official name, "The General Council of the Assemblies of God."

There are a dozen stories or legends about how the name was chosen. Some history books claim T.K. Leonard of Findlay, Ohio, suggested the name.[5] Allie Hughes, a 21-year-old new convert from the Pentecostal church in Wellston, Oklahoma, said her group, after a night of prayer, proposed naming the new organization after the local church in Wellston—"The Assembly of God."[6] The one undisputed fact is that a committee was appointed to pray for God's direction in the choice of a name. Oscar Jones, later chairman of the Oklahoma District, led the prayer meeting on the mountain behind the opera house the night before the convention finally chose the name, "The Assemblies of God."[7]

The convention elected E.N. Bell as the first General chairman (later the name was changed to general superintendent) of the Assemblies of God. J.R. Flower was named the first secretary. An Executive Presbytery of eight men was elected. Four of the eight (J.W. Welch, M.M. Pinson, D.C.O. Opperman, and Howard Goss) had spent much of their ministry in Oklahoma.

Among those present at the Hot Springs convention were five men who would later head the Assemblies of God movement: J.W. Welch (from Tahlequah, Oklahoma), E.N. Bell, A.P. Collins, W.T. Gaston (from Tulsa), and Ralph M. Riggs. The fact that two of the first five national leaders of the Assemblies of God were pastors from Oklahoma underlines the significant impact that Oklahoma had on the movement that would spread around the world by the end of the twentieth century.

The following is a glimpse of the residents of or frequent visitors to Oklahoma who attended the 1914 organizational meeting in Hot Springs:

W.T. Gaston was pastoring the Pentecostal church that became the Fifth and Peoria Church in Tulsa. He later was general chairman of the Assemblies of God.

J.W. Welch, the former Christian and Missionary Alliance preacher, was pastoring in Tahlequah in 1914. He too served later as general chairman.

Willard H. Pope was the first pastor of the church that became Broken Arrow Assembly of God.

41

James Hutsell, a resident of Oklahoma, and two non-residents, Oscar Jones and S.A. Jamieson, later joined Pope, Welch, and Gaston as district chairmen or superintendents of the Oklahoma Assemblies of God.

Mary Bernice Ferguson, W.H. Boyles, Forrest Barker, John W. Hudson, C.M. Riggs, Joseph R. and Effie Russell (who pastored the Collinsville church from 1924 to 1940), Joshua F. and Willie Miller, and A.P. and Mrs. Bryan, and C.O. Haymaker were Oklahoma delegates at Hot Springs.[8]

Vache A. Hargis, later the first secretary of the Oklahoma District, and his father, came from Tahlequah to the convention.

Allie Hughes was a young Christian at the Pentecostal church in Wellston. She and two young couples from the church traveled by wagon to Hot Springs and slept on quilts laid on the ground. The author interviewed Mrs. Hughes about the trip just 13 days before her death at age 100 in 1993. Her eyes sparkled with excitement as she talked about the glorious times of worship at Hot Springs.[9]

At the time of the writing of this book, three Oklahomans who were at Hot Springs were still alive. Versie E. Russell of Tulsa, Lola Bryan Stockton of Shawnee, and Rachel Cline of Antlers, were all young children and attended the convention with their parents.

A.B. Cox had been saved at a street meeting in 1906 in Oklahoma City. A few days later he received the baptism in the Holy Spirit and was called to preach. He held many Pentecostal revivals in Oklahoma. He has been called the "father" of the article in the General Council Bylaws that takes a strong stand against worldliness. In a 1955 interview, Cox said, "Unless we keep close to the Lord we will go like other organizations. There is a danger of forgetting the 'upper room.' There is too much pleasure and worldliness creeping into our churches."[10]

At Hot Springs were other out-of-state evangelists including F.F. Bosworth, Jacob Miller, D.C.O. Opperman, Howard Goss, and E.N. Richey who spent a lot of time in Oklahoma in the early years.

AFTER HOT SPRINGS...NOW WHAT?

Oklahomans came home from Hot Springs and immediately began promoting the new Assemblies of God organization. In July, 1914, Pentecostals gathered in Tulsa for their annual campmeeting at Midway Park about a mile west of Tulsa. It had been held each summer since 1909. W.T. Gaston was in charge. The July 22, 1914, *Tulsa Daily World* reported the event under the headline "Holy Rollers Camp Meeting On Today":

"Fifty or more tents have already been pitched on the grounds and everything is in readiness for the opening of the meeting. Rev. W.T. Gaston, whose parsonage is but a short distance from the grounds, will be in charge... Everything is taking on the appearance of a real old-fashioned campmeeting, where the glories and hallelujahs resound up to the dome of the sky... There will be shouting and praying against sin and hell until even the wood in the tabernacle will tremble."[11] (The tabernacle, costing about $3,000, and a house for Pastor Gaston had been built adjacent to the street car line by wealthy Pentecostal businessman Charles Page.)[12]

The newspaper was right. Large crowds attended the campmeeting to hear some of the great Pentecostal preachers of the day—T.K. Leonard, Howard Goss, A.P. Collins, J.W. Welch, and W.T. Gaston. The *Tulsa Democrat* described the camp site:

"The Holy Rollers have selected a beautiful camp site on the banks of the Arkansas River... A substantial platform capable of seating several hundred has been erected and filled with homemade benches, and lighted with electricity. The grove in which the camp is placed is white with the tents of the campers who have come from all parts of the state to take part in this annual religious festival... The many Rollers from Tulsa swell the audience to something like five hundred. So pleased are the leaders...with the site that arrangements have been made to buy the land and make a permanent camp to be used as a center for Holy Roller religious fervor not only in Oklahoma, but for the whole southwest."[13]

By the end of the campmeeting, the local newspapers reported 100 tents pitched on the camp grounds and 1,000 persons attending the nightly services.[14] Many were filled with the Spirit and healed:

> "Sunday, August 2, was indeed a time of refreshing. The services began about 10 a.m., lasting all day, and until late at night...the saints melted down in tears under the touching messages... The joy of the Lord was plainly seen on their faces."[15]

A DISTRICT COUNCIL FORMED

In July, 1914, during the Tulsa campmeeting, Oklahoma Pentecostals had the distinction of forming the first district council of the Assemblies of God. Such district organization had been suggested at the Hot Springs convention. However, until the Oklahoma churches organized, no other districts had been formed.

The Oklahomans passed a resolution making the Preamble and Resolution adopted at Hot Springs the constitution of the Oklahoma District Council. They chose for themselves the official name, "Oklahoma District Council of the Assemblies of God." W. T. Gaston was elected as chairman, and Vache A. Hargis of Tahlequah was chosen as secretary of the District Council. Within weeks, Texas and Iowa also formed district councils, and the fledgling movement that would become the largest Evangelical denomination in the world was alive and well and growing.[16]

Chapter 7

New Growth Despite Controversy

Satan has always launched ferocious attacks on young churches. Paul warned the first-century church at Ephesus about dissension among the believers: "Even from your own number men will arise and distort the truth in order to draw away disciples after them" (Acts 20:30, NIV). The same kind of controversy threatened the infant Assemblies of God organization with disaster in 1914 and 1915.

The "New Issue" began in California even before Hot Springs. Several evangelists began preaching about a "new revelation" that Christians should be baptized in the name of Jesus only, not in the name of the Father, the Son, and the Holy Ghost. The "New Issue" movement went on to teach that Jesus was the only member of the Godhead.

The "New Issue" or "Oneness" movement spread eastward across the country and caused a great debate among Pentecostals by the summer of 1915. The leadership of the Assemblies of God had maintained an editorial policy stoutly defending the Trinitarian position. However, many leaders within the Assemblies of God defected. E.N. Bell, the first general chairman, who served until A.P. Collins was elected at the second General Council in the fall of 1914, was rebaptized in the name of Jesus only. (Bell later returned to the Assemblies of God and served another term as general chairman.) Preachers with solid Oklahoma contacts such as Howard Goss, D.C.O. Opperman, and G.T. Haywood fell prey to the new enthusiasm. Nearly all the Pentecostal ministers in Canada were rebaptized and all 12 Assemblies of God preachers in Louisiana were carried away in the "Oneness" wave.[1]

Oklahomans played a major role in keeping the new Assemblies of God movement intact. J.W. Welch, the former Tahlequah pastor, was elected general chairman at the General Council in St. Louis in October, 1915. Welch and J. Roswell Flower worked hard to save the Assemblies of God from dissolution. Welch served both as general chairman and editor of *The Weekly Evangel* (later the *Pentecostal Evangel*), having taken over the editorial job of E.N. Bell, who resigned. Welch, through the pages of the newspaper, called for another General Council for October, 1916, to take an official stand on the "Oneness" debate and other areas of doctrine.

Three preachers with Oklahoma connections were at the forefront of the "Oneness" debate. Howard Goss, one of the most ardent promoters of the Hot Springs convention, left the fellowship over the problem. He later became the first general superintendent of the United Pentecostal Church. Goss publicly admonished Oklahoman E.L. Newby that "if he turned down this wonderful truth" he "would miss God." Newby rejected the idea that the "Oneness" doctrine had come by "revelation." Newby said, "Well, frankly, I'm not interested. If you can't prove it in the Word, if it is not there plain and simple, I'd distrust any 'revelation' that communicated it. It's too farfetched for me."[2]

William Burton McCafferty, who later assisted P.C. Nelson in Oklahoma, was an ardent defender of the Trinity. When told at a campmeeting that E.N. Bell had been rebaptized in the name of Jesus only, McCafferty retorted, "I never was one to be stampeded into believing something that's not in the Bible. I don't care if the whole movement swallows this thing. I'm not going to, because it's wrong."[3]

It was J.W. Welch who led the effort at the 1916 General Council to adopt a "Statement of Fundamental Truths." The

Assemblies of God had been formed only as a cooperative fellowship, but Welch felt the fellowship needed to state what it believed. Welch appointed a committee to prepare the "Statement." The committee included Oklahoman S.A. Jamieson, D.W. Kerr, T.K. Leonard, longtime *Pentecostal Evangel* Editor Stanley Frodsham, and E.N. Bell (who had repented of his earlier involvement in the "Oneness" movement and returned to the fold).[4]

There was great debate as to whether the General Council had the right to draw up a statement of faith. In the end, Welch and his allies won. The Statement of Fundamental Truths was approved, thus removing any doubt how the Assemblies of God believed on such vital doctrinal issues as the Trinity, the baptism in the Holy Spirit, and divine healing. It is amazing that the 16 articles contained in the Statement adopted by the 1916 General Council have changed very little.

Chairman Welch saw tremendous growth in the Assemblies of God in 1917 and 1918. The headquarters' offices were moved to Springfield, Missouri, in 1918. At the General Council in Springfield that year, another doctrinal dispute arose. Evangelist F.F. Bosworth, who had held many revivals in Oklahoma for a decade, decided that "speaking in tongues" was not the initial evidence of receiving the baptism in the Holy Spirit, but was only one of the gifts of the Holy Spirit. Welch again met controversy head-on and successfully sponsored a resolution stating in no uncertain terms that speaking in tongues is the initial physical evidence of the baptism in the Holy Spirit.[5]

The "Oneness" and "initial evidence" debates had resulted in the withdrawal or dismissal of no less than ten executive presbyters of the movement and a total of 156 ministers in its first four years, leaving only 429 ministers. Such a turnover would spell doom for many organizations. But the loss of dissidents only strengthened the General Council. Two years later there were 819 ministers and missionaries on the denomination's list.[6]

Chapter 8

The Sick Are Healed

Many were drawn to Pentecostal churches by the miraculous healings that were witnessed. God healed men and women of all manner of sicknesses and diseases in response to the "prayer of faith."

One of the notable healings was the case of Grace Williamson of Tulsa. It occurred in 1914 during a four-week meeting conducted at Fifth and Peoria by William Booth-Clibborn, a descendant of the founder of the Salvation Army, along with his brothers Eric and Theodore and their friend Willard Pope.

Grace Williamson had been stricken with terminal spinal meningitis. She and her husband Fay were veteran vaudeville performers. For two months she struggled between life and death.

Martha Kitchen, the wife of future Fifth and Peoria Pastor William Kitchen, tried to witness to Grace, but was rebuffed. Fay Williamson was converted at the revival but Grace still resisted. After the doctor told her she could not live much longer, Grace asked to see Mrs. Kitchen. This time Grace accepted the Lord and wanted to go to one of the revival services.

The doctor said it would be suicidal to move her twisted and deformed body. But Fay Williamson disregarded the doctor's warning and hired an ambulance to carry his wife to church. Grace's screams of pain while being lifted into the ambulance could be heard a block away.

Pastor W.T. Gaston prayed over Grace, "Lord, this young woman has wasted her life; but if you can do something with this body, do it in the name of Jesus." The simple prayer worked. Gaston offered his hand to Grace. She said she couldn't stand up. Gaston insisted. He convinced Grace that God would help her. Afterward, she testified:

"Nine times I heard my back pop and with each pop I straightened up a little more. Then I stood up erect and ran the length of the building while the congregation rejoiced and praised God."

Grace and Fay Williamson began full-time ministry within 15 days of the healing. Women in the church helped them convert their gaudy theatrical clothing to "preaching" clothes. The Williamsons helped establish at least 18 Assemblies of God churches. Their daughter Charlotte later married Oklahoma and national Assemblies of God leader Bert Webb.[1]

After Pastor W.T. Gaston was elected district chairman, he worked very hard to bring Pentecostal churches into the new Oklahoma District Council. He was hampered in his efforts because of the great size of Oklahoma and his full-time job pastoring his church in Tulsa. The District Council followed the lead of the General Council in establishing rules that each local church should be "set in order" and hold a business meeting, formally pass a resolution requesting recognition of the General Council, and submit the request to the General Council of the Assemblies of God in Springfield.

Campmeetings and district councils (a name that has denoted both district organizations and annual conventions) helped get the word out. At the District Council in 1915, Willard Pope was elected district chairman. Pope saw Oklahoma as a great harvest field:

"I believe we have one of the greatest fields for labor...and one of the ripest, therefore we have a great responsibility resting upon us in bringing to the thousands of lost men and women in this great state this message of great joy... There are a number of assemblies and missions, some of which have no pastors, that are alone, and it seems that no one is taking any interest in them.

I would like to get in touch with every minister, elder, and deacon in the state, and if there is a mission or assembly that has not been set in order and you have no pastor or ordained deacon, I would be glad to hear from you... By getting better acquainted and cooperating together in this great battle against sin, I believe God can bless our efforts in a mightier way and make us more effective in His precious service."[2]

Pope was reelected chairman at the 1916 District Council in Pawhuska, which featured J.W. Welch and F.F. Bosworth as speakers. However, Pope left Oklahoma for Maryland in the summer of 1917, and J.R. Evans assumed the leadership of the district.[3] In 1917 the District Council was again held in Pawhuska, and S.A. Jamieson of Tulsa was elected district chairman, a position he would hold until the end of the decade. Also elected were Fred Eiting as assistant chairman and S. L. Shockey as secretary-treasurer. Thomas O'Neal of Wellston, Oscar Jones of Chickasha, and J.J. Grobbs of Waurika were named presbyters.[4]

Wellston was the site of the 1918 District Council. General Chairman J.W. Welch was the speaker.[5] In 1919, the Oklahoma District actually held two District Councils—in April in Claremore, and in October in Panama in southeast Oklahoma. The Panama Council was called the "largest and best Council ever held in Oklahoma."[6]

NORTHEAST OKLAHOMA

After the General Council was formed at Hot Springs, Pentecostal churches continued to flourish in northeast Oklahoma. The church at Tahlequah, which had called W.T. Gaston as pastor in 1910, was blessed with early pastors such as J.W. Welch, Robert and J.A. Freeman, V.A. Hargis, Fred Eiting, and S.L. Shockey.[7] It is assumed that Tahlequah became affiliated immediately after the meeting at Hot Springs because Welch, its pastor, became an early leader in the Assemblies of God. However, documents to support this assumption have long since been lost.

Since W.T. Gaston became the first Oklahoma District chairman, it can also be assumed that his Fifth and Peoria church in Tulsa was affiliated with the Assemblies of God as soon as he returned from Hot Springs. It was actually 1915 before the famous

51

I remember Diannie Hanes talking about services at this church many times.

church was located at Fifth and Peoria in downtown Tulsa. The church had begun shortly after the 1908 Charles Parham revival. Early pastors were David Hockersmith, W.T. Gaston (1912-1916), S.A. Jamieson (1916-1919), and E.G. Cunningham (1919-1920).

W.T. Gaston reported on another revival at Fifth and Peoria in March, 1917:

"In the last three weeks about twenty children have been saved and fifteen received the baptism... There have been some remarkable healings... The saints are united and are getting deeper in the Lord."[8]

S.A. Jamieson was pastor of Fifth and Peoria when the church hosted two Aimee Semple McPherson revivals in 1919. The first revival ran 22 days but met with only limited success. Only 25 were saved.[9] In May, McPherson returned to Tulsa where the church had rented the Convention Hall to hold the expected large crowds. They were not disappointed. People came from ten different states to the meeting. As many as 3,000 attended the nightly services, described by Pastor Jamieson:

"The people in the gallery looked upon the scene with amazement, and many said they had never seen a revival in this fashion, never heard such stirring messages, and never saw the power of God so manifested at the altar. Over 200 were saved and about 100 received the baptism."[10]

Woodlake Assembly of God in Tulsa traces its history back to 1919, when five people established the Haskell and Peoria Mission in an old house given to them by the Welker family. Brother Harmon, a Sunday school teacher from the Fifth and Peoria Church, volunteered to lead the small mission and became its first pastor. In 1941 the church moved to the Capitol Hill addition of Tulsa and was renamed Capitol Hill Assembly of God. In 1974 the church needed more room, moved again, and changed its name to Woodlake Assembly of God.[11]

Another strong Pentecostal church that became one of the anchor churches of the Assemblies of God was at Broken Arrow. Willard Pope had been the first pastor in 1912. Other pastors before 1920 were Peter Davis, George Carriger, Joe Rosselli, Will

Jones, M.N. Pinson, J.R. Evans (who later became secretary-treasurer of the General Council), and Paul Bucher. The church officially became an Assemblies of God church under Pastor J.R. Evans on July 13, 1917. Willard Pope came back to the church in 1918 and erected a new building.[12] General Council Chairman J.W. Welch was the guest at the dedication in April, 1919. Pope reported in *The Christian Evangel*:

"We are going to begin a month's revival with the dedication. The meetings will be preceded with a week of prayer, day and night... We believe God is going to visit the earth with one supreme effort to constrain men to turn to Him, and be saved before the awful storm of His wrath breaks in upon them."[13]

There were other early Assemblies of God works in Tulsa County. W.R. Amiot held a revival in Collinsville in the fall of 1914. He wrote to *The Christian Evangel* that 125 were saved and 71 baptized with the Holy Ghost.[14] R.E. Lister, his wife, and a Brother Enos held a revival at Dawson in the summer of 1915.[15] Earlier that year W.E. Hammers and Theodore Smith reported that 77 had received the baptism and 28 had been baptized in water at Skiatook. One woman who could not eat solid food, received the baptism and was healed, and then could then eat anything.[16]

In 1914 revivals were reported in Hanna in McIntosh County, at the Elm Grove school near McLain in Muskogee County, and at Gore where 25 were saved and two filled with the Spirit.[17]

Possibly the first benevolence project in Oklahoma was the establishment of the Pentecostal Rescue Mission in Sapulpa in late 1916. R.L. Cotnam, the manager, found a 10-room house on North Elm Street. He announced that the mission was for "fallen girls, indigent persons, and homeless children."[18] The May 19, 1917, edition of *The Weekly Evangel* displayed a picture of the rescue home and asked for free-will offerings.[19]

Willard Pope held a revival in Claremore in the winter of 1915. Pope saw nearly 40 saved: "When we came here there were just a few, discouraged saints. God has revived His people."[20] F.O. Burnett became pastor in 1915. The Claremore assembly was set in order shortly after A.R. Donaldson became pastor in January, 1919.[21]

The Assemblies of God church at Pawhuska traces its roots to a revival by Willard Pope in September, 1915. *Word and Witness* reported, "The Lord is blessing. Up to last night about 50 or 60 have been converted. The town is being turned upside down. Great crowds every night."[22] Immediately after the revival, Pawhuska First Assembly of God was organized. Thomas J. O'Neal and J.R. Evans were two of the first pastors. Pope held another three-week meeting in December, 1916, with F.F. Bosworth. Fifty were saved. Pope said the "work is in good shape, and we expect great victory in the future."[23]

The Pentecostal message had been brought to Okmulgee, McIntosh, and Muskogee Counties as early as 1910 when J.W. Welch received the baptism in an A.B. Cox revival in Muskogee. The church at Morris, a small town in Okmulgee County, worshiped without a pastor in the summer of 1914. W.C. Winn wrote in *Word and Witness* that "we have unity of the Spirit and the interest is good."[24]

Pioneer Assemblies of God Evangelist R.C. Nicholson was called as the Morris church's first pastor in the fall of 1914. Nicholson, his wife, and five children moved in with Elder Murrell while the church completed a two-room parsonage. In her book, *Covered Wagon Days of Evangelism*, Jewell Nicholson Cunningham recalls their first Christmas at Morris:

"Since we were poor—there were no salaries for preachers (Papa like all pastors survived off hat offerings)—the Salvation Army brought a box to the parsonage for us. There were ribbons for the older girls, a bugle for Coy, a doll for me, and a toy for baby Frances. There were also dominoes in the box, but Papa threw them away. Such games, as well as comic papers and novels, were considered worldly and were not allowed in the house."[25]

The Nicholson family soon packed up their wagon and started east. Evangelist Nicholson preached in communities along the way. They camped and trusted God for food. One Christian lady brought fresh eggs, milk, and butter for breakfast one morning. She and fellow believers had been praying for revival. The Nicholsons camped and slept in the covered wagon and on the ground in a borrowed tent. The revival was in the schoolhouse in the community of Christie in Adair County. After a loud service at the schoolhouse one night, the sheriff showed up at the Nicholson camp the next morning and arrested Brother Nicholson for disturbing the peace. He was jailed in Stilwell, where eight other Pentecostal preachers had been arrested. World War I was in full swing and tensions mounted against Pentecostals because of the teaching of "tongues."

The next day, Nicholson was hauled before the judge who explained that the actual charge was Nicholson's failure to sign a pledge card to be loyal to America. Nicholson gladly signed the card. As he was released, Nicholson turned to the sheriff and said, "Let me hug your neck. You are a big man and you could hold a lot of God." Brother Nicholson walked the 20 miles back to Christie and arrived in time for service. The crowd heard him coming, singing through the woods.[26]

Traveling by wagon had its advantages for witnessing. Jewel Nicholson Cunningham says:

"When we passed a wagon, both wagons would slow down to cautiously edge by on the narrow road. This allowed us to run up and offer the driver a gospel leaflet. No one refused. It seemed the church workers then were more reluctant to witness than the public was to receive it."[27]

Adair County was the field of labor for Mary B. Ferguson in 1915. She wrote from Bidding Springs, "Please pray that God will remove the hindering cause and give us a glorious meeting soon."[28]

Chapter 9

A Fertile Field for Pentecost

Wellston, in Lincoln County, was one of the early centers of Pentecostal activity in Oklahoma. At least five persons from the Wellston Assembly of God attended the Hot Springs meeting in 1914.

The exact date when the church became part of the District Council and General Council is unknown. However, because of its central location, the Wellston church hosted all of the early denominational leaders elected at Hot Springs. The list of evangelists who held meetings at Wellston is like a "Who's Who" of Pentecost—E.N. Bell, J.W. Welch, W.T. Gaston, S.A. Jamieson, Fred Eiting, and Aggie James. Alonzo Horn was the church's first pastor in 1913. He was followed by Vache Hargis, Joe Roselli, Thomas J. O'Neal, a Rev. Grubbs, and Calvin Riggs.

Allie Hughes, the last remaining charter member of the Wellston church, told of her early experiences in the church:

"After Hot Springs, I wanted to be baptized in water. I had tonsillitis and they told me I would have to wait until I was better. I didn't want to wait. They broke the ice in the pond and baptized me. It never hurt me, and I never had tonsillitis again."[1]

In 1914 the Wellston congregation bought a church building from the Christian Church for $1,000 just a block off Main Street. A belfry equipped with a large bell topped off the church. Pastor Alonzo Horn rang the bell every Sunday morning to call his people to church:

"The auditorium consisted of 12 pews, a home-made pulpit, four single stained glass windows on both north and south side, and a triple stained glass window in the west end... The little 'out house' stood behind the church building on the northeast corner of the lot."[2]

The Wellston Assembly of God must hold the record for staying the longest time at one location. The church is still at Third and Cedar, 80 years later.

Alonzo Horn and A.M. Humbard held a revival in Sparks in 1912. In 1916 a local farmer, Ike Long, began holding brush arbor meetings near Sparks. Hundreds were saved and received the baptism in the revival that lasted most of the summer. Veteran Oklahoma Pastor Otto Goins was only six years old, but remembers the Ike Long meeting in the summer of 1916:

"They had no sound system, but no one failed to hear every word he said. When he preached he just opened his mouth, and the volumes just rolled. The meeting lasted several weeks without ever taking an offering. Finally my grandfather went to the pulpit and told the folks that Ike had preached about every night all summer and had about lost his cotton crop. Grandfather grabbed a big black hat and asked the men to pass it around, inside and outside the arbor. When the hat came back, it was overflowing with money for Ike."[3]

In 1917 E. Vuncannon reported in *The Weekly Evangel*: "The Lord is working in Sparks, picking up the drunks, the gamblers, and saving them and baptizing them with the Holy Ghost... Bro. Long is our pastor, and a strong assembly is being built up here."[4] Aggie James was pastor of the church when the members voted unanimously on March 28, 1919, to join the Assemblies of God officially. C.M. Riggs presided over the meeting.

Alonzo Horn took the Pentecostal message to Chandler in 1916 where believers were meeting in homes. People from the church at Davenport came to Chandler on Saturday nights to help in cottage prayer services. It was 1940 before the Chandler church officially entered the District Council.[5]

A Henry Goff revival birthed the Carney Assembly of God in 1914. Amos "Preacher" Chase became the first pastor in 1915. The congregation bought an old schoolhouse and was set in order in 1926.[6]

Shawnee was also a strong local church in the Assemblies of God movement. Forrest and Ethel Barker pastored the church in 1914 and 1915 before they became missionaries to Peru. William Booth-Clibborn came to Shawnee in April, 1915, for a meeting. He was expecting a move of God: "We will labor for an old-time Pentecostal fresh wind of revival. This is sorely needed in many of our Assemblies where the human touch is more noticeable than the sweeping power of God."[7]

F.O. Burnett pastored the Shawnee church in 1917.[8] Jesse I. Miller was holding a revival there in June, 1919, when the church was set in order. Jesse Miller left town in style: "On Wednesday night the meeting closed with a farewell to Brother Casey and a Godspeed, and we followed him to the depot singing songs on the platform while the train was waiting."[9]

Other towns in central Oklahoma saw early revivals. Mrs. Hattie Trussel went to Lexington in October, 1914, and W.H. Whelchel began a meeting in a schoolhouse six miles southeast of Tecumseh in March, 1917.[10]

SOUTHEAST OKLAHOMA

The local church in Panama actually began in 1912 but probably did not affiliate with the General Council until 1917 when C.E. Arnold was pastor. In October, 1919, R.E. Shrader was pastor when the church hosted the Oklahoma District Council—a great honor for a small church in a remote part of the state. Early pastors of the Panama church were Ed Williams, Orvall Painter, and Robie Harrison.[11]

The church in Broken Bow began a few months after the Hot Springs meeting in 1914. Willie Jones established a local assembly and reported 40 saved and 25 filled with the Holy Spirit.[12]

W.H. Whelchel held a revival in Broken Bow in July, 1915, and wrote, "A large crowd of people were saved and baptized with the Holy Ghost."[13] D.K. Murphy also preached a revival there in the fall of 1915.[14]

The Assembly of God at McCurtain dates back to recognition from the General Council on June 13, 1917. The church had begun in 1912 after a Jacob Miller revival. Members planted cotton, made quilts, and sold chickens and eggs to build the first church building in 1919. Miller's son Joe followed his father as pastor.[15]

H.O. Hogan sounded the alarm for his hometown of Sulphur in 1915:

"I want to call the saints' attention to a place that needs help, my hometown. The population is over 4,000 and it is in gross darkness. There are only two baptized saints here...the people have ceased assembling and I fear we will grow cold. Please pray for God to open up a work here."[16]

Trouble was present in the local assembly in Wilburton when William Booth-Clibborn and Alonzo Horn arrived there for a meeting in September, 1915:

"We took the Opera House and have preached every evening... God has melted the hearts of many. The history of this assembly is deplorable. A great revival, many interested, work flourished with leaps and bounds, a hair-splitting dispute on doctrines, a separation, a decline, and four years of indifference and neglect... I would rather establish one good work with one revival and steady advance than 20 momentary strawfire revivals."[17]

In McAlester, Fred Eiting, later an Oklahoma District chairman, began a revival in May, 1917. Charley Peppers ended a revival in McAlester in April, 1919, and wrote, "The saints are wonderfully encouraged to fight the battle on for Jesus."[18] Two months later Peppers reported that seven received the baptism in a meeting near Scipio in Pittsburg County.[19]

J.M. Murray took his Pentecostal band to Boswell in Choctaw County in October, 1914. Crowds of seven or eight hundred from miles around packed into or around a tent after their curiosity was aroused by two mysterious occurrences.

Dozens of people in the community saw smoke pouring out of the tent one night. They feared the tent was on fire. However, when they arrived, the only fire was the fire of God settling down on the Pentecostal service inside.

On another night, as people were returning from the meeting, the heavens were suddenly lit up as bright as day. The light went toward the north and the report that followed said it jarred the ground and shook the houses.[20]

Another strange event occurred near Boswell in 1915. Murray reported that a star appeared in the east one night in July after church and went out of sight and came back seven times. Murray wrote, "Several sinners were with the saints and were all impressed that it was a sign of Jesus' coming."[21]

Famed pioneer Evangelist A.C. Bates first arrived in Oklahoma at Boswell in 1918. He and his wife had sold their furniture and left Texas for the Sooner state. They began preaching under the shade trees near Boswell. They slept in the brush arbor where their nightly services were held. God gave Bates a gracious revival:

"Many of those people were bootleggers, hog thieves, and many had never heard a sermon in their lives. But, oh, the shouts and praises that ascended from their souls as they found the Saviour precious to their hearts."[22]

Revival was in progress at nearby Fort Towson as early as June, 1915. Mrs. L.E. Cundiff said, "Some at this place are beginning to see the light of the glorious Latter Rain and are taking a stand for it. Some have been healed and saved."[23]

Evangelist W.H. Whelchel reported 60 saved and 43 filled with the Holy Ghost at Seminole in August, 1917. He called Seminole "a new field." One thousand people attended an unusual evening service:

"While the altar service was going on, a doctor came in and attacked a blind man that was healed. He told him that he was committing sin by telling the people that God had healed him... By looking at the man you cannot tell he ever was blind...

I cannot fill the calls that are coming in for meetings. If there are any who want work, tell them to come down here, and I can find them something to do for the Lord. Pray that the power of God may sweep this country like a tidal wave."[24]

In December, 1919, Whelchel was still going strong in a revival in Fanshawe, Oklahoma.[25]

In Wetumka, S.J. Berryhill had a successful meeting in October, 1914: "At the baptismal service yesterday, the power of God fell...and during the service some were saved by the water's side."[26]

SOUTHWEST OKLAHOMA

Lawton received Pentecost shortly after the Hot Springs convention. The October 24, 1914, *Weekly Evangel* contained a letter from F.O. Burnett indicating that 10 or 11 had received the baptism and that the church was "set in better order and people are becoming interested."[27] A major Assemblies of God thrust in Lawton came the next year in 1915 when R.C. Nicholson and Will T. McLaughlin held a tent revival.[28] Valeria Lee Hammond spent several months in revival in Lawton in 1915. In 1918, Roy L. Steger and Clarence Evans preached at schoolhouses a few miles west of Lawton.[29]

Beckham and Washita Counties had been early sites of Pentecostal works because of the nearby Beulah Colony. C.E. Shields and Robert Smith established a Pentecostal group at Bessie in December, 1915, and invited any workers passing that way to "spend a few days with us."[30] O.J. Knight of Dill also announced in *The Weekly Evangel* in September, 1915, his community's need for a preacher.[31]

Pentecost was new in Kiowa County in 1915 when Beulah Monroe in Roosevelt reported: "There are few here who have ever heard a Pentecostal sermon... Truly the harvest is white. Pray that I may be a soul-winner for Jesus."[32] A.W. Gold of Lone Wolf wrote that he and his family were the only Pentecostal people in town in July, 1915.[33]

Near Hinton, T.J. O'Neal, former pastor at Wellston, held a brush arbor revival in September, 1917. Fifteen were saved and one filled with the Spirit.[34]

L.S. Purdue found the community of Martha an open field where Pentecost had not been preached in December, 1915.[35] And from Elmer came O.L. Pitkin's call for workers:

"We have a fine place for meeting—a nice shady grove. If we could not get a preacher with a tent, we could easily make an altar... We want one who preaches salvation from all sin, and confession, and the baptism..."[36]

In November, 1917 E.F. Williams turned his hotel in Bradley into a church:

"I came to this place and found it to be a wicked town. God sent along Bro. G.W. Brown and he surely preached the Bible... God has saved 42 and baptized several with the Spirit... We are taking steps to build a big church here."[37]

J.J. Grobbs had established an Assemblies of God church in Waurika by February, 1918, and was serving as presbyter for southwest Oklahoma. The local group had begun during a John H. James camp meeting in 1914. J.A. Woods sent a "preacher wanted" letter to *The Christian Evangel* in October, 1914. Woods said, "We want to have the meeting go on all winter and need a good shepherd to take charge of the work."[38]

A small group of believers at Ringling was "set in order" in 1918. Roy L. Steger called it the "third church 'set in order' south of Oklahoma City."[39] Steger and his wife, affectionately known as "Pa" and "Ma" Steger, would serve the Oklahoma District for more than a half century. They pioneered the church at Cement and pastored at Wilson, Anadarko, Sapulpa, and Maud.[40]

First Assembly of God in Chickasha began in the summer of 1918 when Oscar Jones started holding tent services. People flocked to the meetings in wagons throughout the fall and winter. Jones had begun his work in Chickasha the year before by holding street meetings. It was a trying time for his family. His son, Ossie, recalls that only a 10-cent offering came in one night and his father bought popcorn for his hungry children.[41] In 1919, the local assembly bought a small one-room church from a Methodist congregation. Jones was well-respected in the District because he had already pioneered several churches in Oklahoma and Texas and was serving as district presbyter in 1918.[42]

Alma was the scene of a Will T. McLaughlin revival that began in September, 1914. Ten were filled with the Spirit.[43]

In a community southeast of Rush Springs, M.G. Dunlap reported a church with 50 or 60 saints in June, 1915. Just in the month of April that year, 15 were saved and 20 received the baptism in the Holy Spirit.[44]

NORTHWEST OKLAHOMA

The northwest part of Oklahoma was the last to see a major Pentecostal move. A search of the Pentecostal newspapers from 1914 to 1919 found only two references to Pentecost in that area. Mrs. Vista Naylor wrote from Okeene that she had received the baptism in Dallas and found no Pentecostal people in Okeene, "The darkness seems so thick that I fear."[45]

The one point of Pentecostal light in northwest Oklahoma by 1919 was in Ringwood in Major County. Evangelists Jacob Miller and C.E. Shields left G.G. Collins in charge after a major revival. Their letter to the *Evangel* said, "The country is stirred... Twenty-two received the baptism... Some of the leading farmers were saved and baptized, and are now rejoicing in the Lord."[46]

During the first five years after the Oklahoma District was organized, hundreds of revivals were held across the state. Many people were saved and baptized. However, the lack of stable pastors and leaders hindered the effort to organize the churches as part of the Oklahoma District Council. Often, when the fire subsided in a local assembly, the fragile group would disband. Few of the Pentecostal groups had a permanent building. Historian Leroy Hawkins called it "strawfire" evangelism and noted that a lack of follow-up of new converts was perhaps the greatest weakness of evangelistic endeavors. There was no organized effort to disciple new Christians into a strong and lasting local church.[47]

Oklahoma was truly a fertile field for Pentecost. However, it would still be another decade before stable local assemblies would be organized in most parts of the state.

Chapter 10

The Roaring Twenties

In the 1920's, leaders of the Assemblies of God were very serious about keeping alive the intensity of the Pentecostal revival across America. The young organization grew and matured under the stable leadership of two Oklahoma ministers, J.W. Welch and W.T. Gaston.

J. Roswell Flower, warned about compromise in *The Pentecostal Evangel*:

"Satan is luring us into a position of compromise. He would have us modify our position, to let down on the distinguishing marks of Pentecost, to avoid the reproach, to court the applause of the people. Shall we fall into this snare? To do so will be to go to sleep like Samson. Let us beware lest our locks be cut off and we be rendered powerless to do the work that God has called us to do."[1]

"Daddy Welch," as he was affectionately known, was a tower of strength during the first 15 years of the Assemblies of God. At the 1920 General Council, Welch, who had served as general chairman of the fellowship since 1915, traded jobs with Secretary E.N. Bell. When Bell died in June, 1923, Welch became general chairman again.

At the 1925 General Council, it was Welch and Flower who recommended that resolutions that had been passed at the previous councils be codified into a "constitution." There was such opposition to that suggestion that both men were voted out of office. (Interestingly, the controversy subsided and when the same suggestion was offered two years later a constitution was approved unanimously.)[2]

Welch's replacement in the top post in 1925 was another Oklahoma preacher, W.T. Gaston, the former pastor of Fifth and Peoria in Tulsa. Gaston served as general chairman until 1929. For seven years in the Twenties, Oklahoma Assemblies of God preachers were at the helm of what was becoming the most significant Pentecostal group in the world.[3]

Preachers from Tulsa County, Oklahoma, filled the two top positions within the national fellowship in 1925. James R. Evans, former pastor of the Broken Arrow church, became the general secretary at the same time Gaston was elected general chairman. Evans, who served 12 years as general secretary, was widely known for his phenomenal memory and his ability to recall the names and addresses of many ministers on the rolls.[4]

As general chairman, W.T. Gaston was very popular with his constituency. Throughout his two terms, he traveled across the country by train, speaking at campmeetings and churches from Maine to California. While Gaston was away from Springfield, Evans took over many of the day-to-day responsibilities of running the Headquarters.[5] C.M. Ward has called W.T. Gaston "tender in spirit and always broken before the Lord...a deeply spiritual man."[6]

While Oklahomans were active in the national leadership, Oklahoma became one of the strongest districts in the fellowship during the Twenties. Most old-line denominations saw an alarming decline in church and Sunday School attendance during the decade. This drought among the older denominations created an opportunity for the excitement of Pentecost to fill the spiritual vacuum. Carl Brumback observed:

"Spiritual farmers were needed: men who could plow deep, sow good seed, hoe out thorns, pray down rain, and thrust in the sickle—and God supplied the need. 'From the mountains, to the prairies, to the oceans white with foam,' the Lord thrust forth laborers into the fields, and how He blessed their earnest efforts, opening the windows of heaven upon them, rebuking the devourer, and giving His servants an abundant harvest!"[7]

Oklahoma was abundantly blessed with dedicated "spiritual farmers" in the Twenties. Phenomenal growth came under the leadership of District Chairmen Fred Eiting (1920-1921), Paul H. Ralston (1921-1922), Oscar Jones (1922-1927) and James S. Hutsell. (Elected in 1927, Hutsell would serve as the District leader until 1938, a long tenure for officials at any level of the movement in the early days.)

The district chairmanship was still a part-time position, certainly a hindrance to leading a well-oiled statewide organization. The chairman always continued to pastor a church and spent only a small portion of his time on district affairs. There was no permanent district office. Wherever the chairman happened to be pastoring, that was the District Headquarters. (It was not until 1928 that the headquarters were located elsewhere—temporarily in Enid at Southwestern Bible School, even though Chairman Hutsell continued to operate the district business out of his home in Slick, Oklahoma.)

District councils were not major meetings as they are today. Oscar Jones and his wife hosted the 1920 District Council at their church in Chickasha. The 20 or so ministers who attended slept in the church, in the pastor's small house, or in the homes of local parishioners. Sister Jones later remembered how easy it was to plan the meals for the Council: "I just prepared a big pot of beans, cooked some cabbage, fried potatoes, baked cornbread, fixed gravy, and put out some molasses."[8] The food and lodging must have set well with the Council participants. *The Pentecostal Evangel* reported the Council had closed with "a blessed feeling of fellowship and cooperation among the brethren."[9]

District councils were held in Collinsville in 1923 and in Shawnee in 1924. There was a campmeeting atmosphere in Shawnee:

"On Wednesday night as the saints marched across the platform of the convention hall...waving handkerchiefs, shouting and dancing, many were made to weep for joy, as they thought of the reality of the time 'when the saints come marching in, and when we crown Him Lord of all.'"[10]

District Councils were held in Sand Springs in 1925, in Shawnee again in 1926, in Woodward in 1927, and in Enid in 1929.

Oscar Jones was elected district chairman in 1922 when the Oklahoma District was operating on a shoestring. In 1924 delegates to the District Council raised his salary to $35 per week and asked ministers to send another $1.50 per month. Eighteen-year-old Glenn Millard was elected district secretary-treasurer in 1922 and drew no salary. He was expected to perform his functions on strictly voluntary support from the ministers.[11] Millard's salary later was raised to $15 per week.[12]

Chairman Jones had to trust completely in God for his "travel budget." Once he was called to help set a church in order in Ardmore but lacked the $2.90 for the train ticket from his home in Sand Springs to Ardmore. Before he left home, he and his wife prayed. He headed to the depot without a penny in his pocket. Just before the passenger train arrived, a stranger walked up to him and said, "I don't know who you are, don't know what you are doing here, but something is making me give you this $3.00." Jones bought the ticket and stuck the dime in his pocket. He used a nickel the next morning to buy crackers for his lunch. E.R. Winter, who had summoned Jones to Ardmore, found the district chairman eating his crackers and drinking water out of an old hydrant across from the Santa Fe depot.[13]

Oscar Jones' total dependence on prayer made an impression on young Melvin Lynn in the church at Chickasha:

"The most vivid thing I remember about Brother Jones was his prayers. When most of our church members were women, he prayed for God to send more men. God did. When people were sick, he prayed. When they were broke and hungry, he prayed. His theory of life was simple. He would say, 'Don't worry about it, just pray. God will take care of you.'"[14]

Jones had learned the importance of prayer from his association with Charles Parham and William Seymour years earlier in Houston. Ossie Jones recalls his father talking about prayer:

"Dad said Parham and Seymour taught him the 'joy' of praying. Before he met them, he thought praying was stressful and a strain. Parham and Seymour taught him that even though your heart is breaking, smile and be thrilled that you are coming into the presence of Almighty God. They used the scripture, 'Come before his presence with singing,' as their motto."[15]

Jones held services in Chickasha in an old ragged tent during the winter of 1920. Elsie McCoy was pregnant and lived across the street from the tent. She listened to Jones preach every night and promised God that as soon as she had her baby, she would get saved. She kept her word. The baby girl later married Jones' son Ossie who became nationally known as an Assemblies of God evangelist and pastor. Sister McCoy, mother of later district official Carl McCoy, celebrated her 100th birthday in November, 1993. She has attended Chickasha First Assembly for more than 70 years.[16]

In his first year as district chairman, Jones received $600 in salary but spent $800 on train and bus fares taking care of the district business.[17] A major step to strengthen the position of district chairman (changed to district superintendent in 1927) came at the District Council in 1929. The delegates approved resolutions making both the district superintendent and the district secretary-treasurer full-time positions.[18]

REVIVAL IN NORTHWEST OKLAHOMA AND THE MILLARDS

By 1920 only a handful of Assemblies of God churches existed in the 15 counties of northwest Oklahoma. One family—the Millards—changed that situation.

Glenn and Gordon Millard were saved as teenagers in a Jacob Miller meeting in Ringwood in 1919. Gordon Millard remembers "Uncle Jake" Miller well:

"He was an original hellfire and brimstone preacher. There was no compromise or frivolity allowed in his presence. He was serious about the business of winning souls. He often told the congregation, 'Get in, get out, or get run over.' He would let nothing stand in the way of his proclaiming the gospel. When he preached, people were scared, and ran to the altar to be saved from the wrath of God."[19]

Glenn Millard was called to preach at age 16. By 1920, the Millard brothers began taking Pentecost to a wide area of northwest Oklahoma. District chairman Paul Ralston reported in *The Pentecostal Evangel* in March, 1921: "Revivals are breaking out over the western portion of the state. Gordon and Glenn Millard, brothers, are being much used of the Lord at various points...at least 125 have recently received the baptism... Two assemblies have been set in order."[20] The two new churches were in the town of Quinlan and at the Mayfield schoolhouse near Quinlan. The Millards reported: "We just closed another three weeks' meeting in this new field. The country is stirred."[21]

The Millards took Pentecost to Woodward County for the first time in January, 1921, in a meeting in the Loss schoolhouse near Curtis. There were no Pentecostal churches or workers in the county but "people were interested for miles around."[22]

In Mooreland, the Millards encountered opposition when they found their meeting hall had been rented to a group opposing Pentecost. God's timing was perfect because suddenly the Millard boys came down with the measles and were forced to delay the revival until the opposing group's lease expired. A month later, the revival began and 35 were filled with the Spirit.[23]

The entire Millard family helped out in the Mooreland meeting. Gordon and Glenn were joined by their parents Charles and Helen their sister Hazel and brother Clyde. (All later became ministers or ministers' wives). The revival resulted in the formation of the Assemblies of God church in Mooreland. Otis R. Keener became pastor in 1922, followed by Glenn Millard in 1923. Other notable pastors were Alvin March, T.K. Davis, Ethel Musick, Oscar Jones, Forrest Murray, Warn Gilchrist, Gordon Millard, Charles Millard, and Virgil Mangram.[24] The church affiliated with the Oklahoma District Council in 1924.[25]

The church in Woodward was set in order the same year under the leadership of Gordon and Glenn Millard. In 1926 Gordon Millard erected the first permanent building for the Woodward church, a small frame church with a dirt floor covered with straw.[26]

Leroy Hawkins has written that the Millards were responsible for taking the Pentecostal message for the first time to Lone Star, Mutual, Sharon, Seiling, Taloga, Camargo, Vici, Fort Supply, Cestos, Waynoka, Alva, Gage, and Buffalo.[27]

The revivals conducted by the Millards usually resulted in the organization of a local assembly. Many earlier revival efforts in Oklahoma had left new churches without a leader or guidance. To avoid similar problems in towns where they ministered, the Millards continued to live in northwest Oklahoma and spent a lot of time retracing their steps to visit churches and instruct the members. Glenn Millard was a district official during much of the Twenties, and used his position to convince new churches of the importance of officially becoming part of the Assemblies of God.[28]

Chapter 11

Praying for Rain

Bruce David was the first pastor of Polk Creek Assembly in Poteau, now known as Calvary Assembly of God. The church received General Council acceptance in January, 1920, and dedicated its first building on Easter Sunday, 1920, with "all day preaching and dinner on the ground."

Very few members of the congregation owned cars, so they either rode in wagons or walked to church. The janitor, Nelson Ryden, provided a valuable service for church-goers coming from the community of Witteville; he carried a lantern at night to guide his neighbors home along the banks of Polk Creek. It was not unusual for people to hear the eerie shrills of panthers along the trail as they followed Brother Ryden home from church.[1]

The Pentecostal Evangel carried a page-and-a-half story about the Polk Creek church praying for rain during a severe drought in 1925. The people were poor and made their meager living on rented land. The lack of rain had "assumed the character of a catastrophe."

Pastor Charles Robinson promised the people that rain would come if they prayed. The way they prayed for rain was unique. The church first spent several nights determining that it was God's will for the drought to be broken. The pastor called for special prayer meetings and open confession of sins:

"Before the pastor got very far, we were weeping aloud... On and on he went, confessing our sins in a most unmanning fashion. When he had finished, and God had come and comforted our hearts, and we had gotten quiet and felt clear before God, he said we were ready to ask for rain. This we did very simply, but we were surprised in our own hearts to see how sure it seemed to us that rain would come. In the following days, we forgot about praying for rain, we were busy confessing our sins and just praising and glorifying God for rain... The weather prophets assured us there would be no rain for a long time... We went home and at five we saw the Elijah cloud, but bigger than a man's hand. It covered the heavens, and by five-thirty the rain was falling... We were so happy we could not behave ourselves; not so much because of the rain, but because we felt we now knew the way to pray through to God... After service it rained again, a long steady downpour, the only really sufficient rain in about 10 months."[2]

God continued to move in western Oklahoma during the first two years of the Twenties. In the summer of 1920, Zack Tatum from McLoud held a 40-night revival at Sickles in Caddo County. More than 100 were filled with the Holy Spirit.

After the revival, Tatum was in prayer seeking guidance for his next revival. While speaking in tongues, he used the word "Eakly" over and over. He arose from his knees and asked for an Oklahoma map to find a place called Eakly. It was a community only 10 miles away. The townspeople in Eakly were less than enthusiastic about a Pentecostal revival and refused to rent Tatum a meeting place; but eventually he received permission to use the Banner schoolhouse three miles south of Eakly. A pump organ was borrowed from Mrs. O.J. Taylor and the revival was on. By 1927 the group saved in the revival became a thriving Assemblies of God church.[3]

Valeria Lee Hammond preached brush arbor and tent revivals across Carter, Stephens, and Jefferson Counties in the early Twenties. She played a major role in establishing a church at Ragtown (now called Wirt). After the oil boom in the area quieted, the church was moved to Healdton.

Sister Hammond, who had attended the Hot Springs meeting in 1914, lost two brush arbors to members of the Ku Klux Klan during a revival in 1923. Eight Klan members tore down the arbor one night after an evangelist delivered a sermon on the Second Coming. Even though the local police offered the Pentecostals protection, Klan members returned the next night and again destroyed the arbor and stole the lumber and lights.[4]

Roy Steger reported from Cement in October, 1920, that he was building a 24 x 40 mission and expected to have it up "far enough to have a service on Sunday." Steger said, "We expect to press the battle here."[5]

In Gracemont, Mrs. Jessie Spradley wrote that 30 had received the baptism in a Pentecostal meeting in the local Baptist church and that there were now 52 Spirit-filled members of the local Pentecostal church.[6] In 1921, Oscar Jones resigned the church at Chickasha and moved to Gracemont to pastor the young church. He pastored both the Gracemont and Ninnekah churches that year.[7] The church at Gracemont was born after Arkansas Evangelist L.D. Parton held a revival on the second floor of an old downtown building early in 1920. The church was set in order during a meeting on August 22, 1924.[8]

The Assembly of God in Granite began in a prayer meeting in the home of J.W. Brisco in 1921. The church then moved to an old tool shed at the Granite rock quarry. The local Church of Christ allowed the Pentecostal congregation to hold a revival in their building. Many were saved and filled with the Holy Spirit. The crowds were so large the church could no longer hold services in the tool shed. God moved on volunteers to raise money to build a one-room structure, which housed the congregation until it was set in order in 1941.[9]

The church that became Stecker Assembly of God began during the first Pentecostal revival in the Stecker community in 1923. Blanche McClure wrote a poem about that first revival:

They readied the school basement, that was now very musty,
Where hand-made benches sat so dingy and dusty.
Gasoline lights with fragile mantles were used;
Care must be taken or your lights you would lose.
There were spider webs to sweep down and nails to drive in,
Now it was time for the meetin' to begin."[10]

According to Evangelist and historian Martin Perryman, the Stecker school board soon asked the Pentecostals to leave the schoolhouse. The revival continued in homes of believers.

Oran Ricketts and George Franklin began praying about a name for the church. They had never heard about the Hot Springs meeting or the formation of the Assemblies of God. However, God told them to name their church the "General Pentecostal Assembly of God." It officially became an Assemblies of God church in November, 1934.[11]

Pentecost came to nearby Anadarko in a downtown revival in late 1923. A Baptist woman, Ethel Jones, began to attend the revival with some of her friends because they thought the Pentecostals were "funny to watch." The congregation that formed after the revival rented a tool house adjacent to the railroad. Services were interrupted each time the train rumbled through. The first revival in the new church was preached by Guy Shields who later founded the Shield of Faith Bible School in Amarillo, Texas. The Anadarko church became affiliated with the Assemblies of God in March, 1925, after two successful tent revivals led by Ethel Musick.[12]

In 1929 the Assembly of God in Elk City was renting a tin building for $5 a month. A Brother Rutherford was the first pastor. He was followed by Oscar Jones. Other pastors of Elk City First include Jack Ogle, J.S. Murrell, Joe Calabrese, Frank Cargill, and T.D. Gifford.[13]

Ed and Vesta Bice pioneered several churches in deep southeast Oklahoma in 1920 and 1921. The Bices had been saved in 1917 in a revival in the oil fields near Healdton. Vesta Bice described the scene the night her husband got saved:

"He was kneeling at the altar when suddenly he just fell backwards on the ground. He just lay there. He couldn't talk, he just groaned. Finally, he began speaking in tongues."[14]

The Bices started Pentecostal groups at Millcreek, Soper, Hugo, and Antlers. Often they pastored four different groups at once by having weeknight services at different times and preaching the Sunday services in each church once a month. Often the offering was only 50 cents. What the people lacked in money they made up in love for their pastor. They brought food—and lots of it. Sister Bice says it was easy to depend completely upon the Lord because "there was no other way."[15]

A.E. Humbard held revivals in Shawnee, Davenport, Chandler, and Duncan in 1920. He explained how he drew a crowd in an Oklahoma town:

"I got off the train and...told the people there would be a big street meeting in front of the bank at one o'clock. When the time came...no one would stop and no one came. I said, 'I will not let the devil outdo me.' So I stepped down in the street and began to look and walk and look all around...People began to come from both sides of the street to see what I had lost...After I had about 50 people there, I stepped upon the walk and began to preach to them, telling them that I was trying to get them to find Jesus. They stayed with me until I got through preaching. Many of them were crying and asked for prayer."[16]

In August, 1921, Oscar Haymaker, Alvin March, and Bertha Keener held a revival in a schoolhouse six miles north of Luther in central Oklahoma. Mrs. Haymaker wrote: "Many warnings were given to the unsaved through the Spirit. Some fell under the power of God, while others danced in the Spirit. Even sinners would shake with the power of God on them."[17]

THE GREAT WELLSTON REVIVAL

One of Oklahoma's most remarkable outpourings of the Holy Spirit occurred in 1922-24 in Wellston. Dexter Collins had worked for a paving company in Tulsa and had been converted under the ministry of W.T. Gaston. In 1922 Collins accepted his first pastorate in Wellston—population 600.

The church at Wellston had dwindled to a dozen discouraged members. Collins felt led to call a week-long prayer meeting. Only three persons came the first morning. The prayer meeting was extended for another week. The members began to confess to each other and ask forgiveness.

Revival broke out. For three years, the Holy Spirit hovered over the Wellston church and convicted men and women for miles around of their sins. Farmers would arrive at church with stories of being convicted while plowing corn in the field. One man stopped his plowing, tied his horse to a fence post, and prayed through in a nearby grove of trees.

The fire of God fell in every service. A brush arbor was built near the church in the summer of 1923. As many as 500 jammed the arbor every night for almost a month. Evangelist Jacob Miller preached the arbor meeting and saw 120 baptized in the Spirit and many saved.

Birdie Rackley was saved during the revival and still remembers the power-packed services that lasted until two or three o'clock in the morning.[18] The power of God was so strong that two men who had never been to a Pentecostal meeting drove 40 miles to church in a wagon. When they arrived they asked how to receive the baptism. Pastor Collins told them to stay near the altar and get to the altar as quickly as they could when the call came. Within a few minutes they both were gloriously baptized.

Collins was not a great orator. Rather than preach a sermon, he basically gave his testimony in the same manner as other early-day Pentecostal preachers. He and his message could not be ignored. Every service was dominated by the holy presence of Almighty God.[19] The Wellston revival, according to Collins, was a direct result of intercessory prayer for revival. The harvest was plentiful. More than 300 were saved and 200 received the baptism in the Holy Spirit.

Nineteen young people who were saved during the revival entered the ministry as missionaries, ministers, or wives of ministers. Among them were Otis Keener, Paul Ralston, W.H. Kennemer, C.O. Haymaker, Opal Master Sprague, Ola Master Millard, and Bert Webb.[20]

Revival fires burned in Wellston for years. Pastor George Patterson reported 110 saved, 62 baptized in the Holy Ghost, and 46 baptized in water in a revival with Lottie Wilcox of Fort Worth, Texas, in August and September, 1927.[21]

BERT WEBB

Bert Webb, a product of the Wellston revival, became a giant in the Assemblies of God—serving for 65 years as youth leader, evangelist, pastor, district official, and assistant general superintendent of the national fellowship.[22] When the author interviewed Webb at his home in Springfield in 1993, Webb's excitement for the gospel seemed to be as intense as it surely was after the great Wellston revival.

76

In 1925 Webb went to enroll at Oklahoma A & M in Stillwater, but God changed his plans. He returned home for the weekend before classes began. God called him to preach, and he struggled with the call all weekend. Finally he told God, "If it's your will, have somebody ask me to preach." Later that same day he was sitting on his front porch when Glenn Millard, pastor of the Oakwood Assembly of God, drove up. He told Webb he had been praying and felt impressed to ask Webb to preach. Webb knew God had answered his request and he never looked back.[23]

Immediately, Webb began holding revivals all over western Oklahoma in schoolhouses, country churches, and brush arbors. In 1925 at age 19 he was licensed by the Oklahoma District. He quickly became a force as a leader in Oklahoma.

Still a teenager, Webb felt a burden for the young people of the state. In the fall of 1925, he was encouraged by Glenn Millard and others to write letters to churches inviting their young people to a state youth conference at Wellston. Webb joined Arthur Graves and Floyd Hawkins as preachers of the conference, which drew more than 100 youth during the week of Thanksgiving.

After the last night of the meeting, Webb, Graves, and Hawkins stayed up most of the night planning a statewide youth organization and actually designed the C.A.(Christ's Ambassador) emblem that would be used nationally for decades.[24] (The name Ambassadors for Christ had been used in California. The name Christ's Ambassadors, based on 2 Corinthians 5:20, was quickly accepted by youth leaders across the country.)[25] Webb was elected the first district president of Christ's Ambassadors in Oklahoma.

All was not peace and joy for Pentecostal preachers in the Twenties. In 1927, Bert Webb and Gordon and Glenn Millard held a revival at a schoolhouse north of Oakwood. The local community dance orchestra leader was angry because his band members were getting saved and quitting the band. When Webb came to the pulpit one night, he found a note that read:

"We've put up with your fanaticism long enough... Two or three individuals have been killed here. Start to preach, and you'll never finish your sermon."

77

After a few anxious moments, Webb preached but nothing came of the threat.[26]

Another site of revival was Dustin where a tent meeting was held by William F. Hurley in the summer of 1922. The revival resulted in the organization of the Assemblies of God church at Dustin. N.B. Rayburn was saved during the tent revival and called to preach. He began his ministry by conducting prayer meetings in homes of neighbors. He was licensed by the Oklahoma District in 1925. He and his wife Nellie pastored and evangelized for more than sixty years.[27]

Many conversions and healings were reported at a September, 1923, campmeeting in Savanna by Pastor J.W. Hudson.[28] Pastor Oscar Berryhill in Tulsa wrote the *Evangel* that his building would not hold the big crowds that had attended a four-week-revival with Luther Riley in March, 1923. Fifty-three were saved and 42 baptized in the Holy Spirit.[29]

Good revivals in 1924 were also reported in Meeker with Jesse Miller and in Pushmataha County, at Adel, with Robert Davidson. E.R. Winter preached in Ardmore and Waurika in 1925 and Thackerville in 1927.

Connie Walker remembers a revival in Custer City with Glenn Millard and N.B. Rayburn in 1928:

"We walked two miles to church. I was only twelve, but the way the people worshiped the Lord made an imprint on my life. I recall one lady dancing in the Spirit. She hit her hand against the hot stove that was red hot. Her hand was not burned at all. I was convinced that God would take care of his children."[30]

Chapter 12

Churches Springing Up Everywhere

At least 75 new Assemblies of God churches were established during the decade of the Twenties. In January, 1923, First Assembly in Miami was set in order with 34 charter members. John Linn was the first pastor of the church that had been known as the Pentecostal Mission since 1919. During the next 13 years, the Miami church would move no less than nine times before finding a permanent home.[1]

First Assembly in Okmulgee began in a tent and brush arbor meeting on South Taft Street in 1923. William Harvey was the first of a long list of pastors that had tremendous influence on the Assemblies of God in Oklahoma. Several pastors of the Okmulgee church became district officials, including three district chairmen or superintendents—Fred Eiting, G.W. Hardcastle, and F.C. Cornell. Other well-known pastors were Dexter Collins, Glenn Millard, James Hamill, H.A. Brummett, and Paul Copeland.[2]

In January, 1924, First Assembly in Drumright joined the Oklahoma District Council. A.R. Donaldson was the pastor of 26 charter members:

"At that time members met in a store-front building. The Lord blessed and saved many. The church soon became a landmark and was known across the U.S. for its stand for holiness. As God answered prayer, people were saved, delivered, and healed. The dead were raised. (Bro. Wilburn, who lived across the alley from the church, was one.) Miracles and the infilling of the Holy Ghost brought many in as signs followed believers."[3]

The church in Fairview was set in order in April, 1924. P.H. Loosier, the assistant pastor, reported in the *Evangel* that a 24 x 36-foot church had been completed. The Fairview church, actually located three miles south of Brownsboro, had its beginnings in a 1922 Willie Dunn revival. The small group met in the local schoolhouse and in homes until a permanent church was built in 1924.[4]

The history of First Assembly in Bartlesville really began in Colorado. In 1921 Adeline Godwin, a resident of Bartlesville, was saved, healed, and filled with the Spirit while visiting her brother in Colorado. When she returned to Bartlesville, she had a burning testimony and began prayer meetings in her home. Later Jack Nevills held summer revivals in 1922 and 1923 in the "Old Candy Kitchen" on Park Street. The revivals led to a building program under the leadership of Pastor James Kerr. The church officially came into the Assemblies of God in October, 1924. Among the many pastors of the church were Otis Keener and U.S. Grant, two of the national movement's most successful and best-known ministers.[5]

McCurtain, Okmulgee, and Lawton saw Assemblies of God churches established in 1925. It was actually the third time that a church had been set in order in McCurtain. Trouble had developed after the church had joined the movement in 1917, and again in 1922. The church has been a strong local church in the Assemblies of God since its reorganization in November, 1925. Sister Cooper was the pastor who engineered the successful attempt in McCurtain to join the Assemblies of God.[6]

Northside Assembly of God in Okmulgee can trace its history back to 1925. Pentecostals who had been meeting in an old building called the "chicken coop" decided to build a large brick structure and call it the Assembly of God Tabernacle. Attendance peaked at 1,000 on Easter Sunday in 1925. In the 1940's, the congregation would divide and create First Assembly and Revivaltime Tabernacle (the name was changed to Northside Assembly of God in the late 1950's under the leadership of Pastor Olen Craig). V.H. Shumway and T.A. McDonough head the list of powerful pastors of the Northside Assembly of God since 1925.[7]

Elmer Gore founded First Assembly of Lawton in January, 1925. After moving to several temporary locations, the congregation found a permanent home in an old cafe building in 1929. T.K. Davis, E.L. Newby, Roy Sprague, J.L. McQueen, and John Brown have pastored the Lawton church.[8]

Evangelist Tom Gray preached a brush arbor meeting just east of Whitesboro in 1926. A 13-week revival led to the founding of Whitesboro Assembly of God. A.V. Cummings brought his family to church in a wagon. He was a tenant farmer whose landlord got upset because he was leaving early each day to attend the Gray revival. Cummings prayed about it and was convinced that God stunted the growth of the "cuckleburs" and caused the corn and cotton to grow faster while he and his family were on their way to church.[9]

First Assembly of Ponca City was organized in 1926. The people met in homes for cottage prayer meetings. A few years later, Pastor Harold Collins moved the group into a permanent building. S.J. Scott, V.H. Shumway, Neil Webb, Leo Swicegood, John Gifford, and David Satterfield have pastored the church.[10]

Lewis Avenue Assembly of God in Tulsa was established in 1928. That was a good year for church planting with the addition of Muskogee First Assembly and the Boynton Assembly of God. At Boynton, believers met in a tin feed store building for revival services led by a Rev. Campbell and Lola Justice. The church was set in order in December, 1930.[11]

Hattie Swearingen held a brush arbor meeting at Sweetwater in northwest Oklahoma in the fall of 1929. Immediately after the revival, the church was set in order and a new building was put up on land given to the church by the C.C. Perry family. Gordon Millard, the sectional presbyter, presided over the organizational meeting in October, 1929.[12]

Broken Bow was typical of many Oklahoma communities where an awesome revival resulted in many conversions, but the Pentecostal church disappeared within a short time. Hundreds were saved in Broken Bow in 1914 and 1915, but only

81

William and Hattie Wallace professed to be full gospel in 1928. Open-air meetings were held by Mrs. S.E. Pearson from Arkansas. God added to the group of believers, and a tin store building was rented for $16 per month. Brother Wallace and two other men each paid $5 per month to keep the church open. Times were hard, and $5 was a real sacrifice.

Many times, Brother and Sister Wallace, with seven children, would write out a grocery list, then go down the list to see which items could be crossed off in order to have enough money left to keep the church going.

In July, 1929, First Assembly of Broken Bow was officially recognized as part of the General Council. Loyce Walden (later the district superintendent in Louisiana), T.C. Burkett, Lawrence Langley, Simon J. Peter, Bill Alcorn, W.G. Baker, Bernard Escalante, and LaRoi Woods have pastored the Broken Bow church.[13]

By 1930 there were 110 churches recognized by the Oklahoma District. The number of licensed and ordained ministers had grown to 272. The largest churches were Fifth and Peoria in Tulsa, Broken Arrow, Okmulgee, West Tulsa, Shawnee, Faith Tabernacle in Oklahoma City, Wellston, Duncan, Enid, Pawhuska, and Wilson.[14]

NATIONAL EVANGELISTS COME TO OKLAHOMA

Among the divine healing evangelists in the 1920's, none was more popular than Raymond T. Richey. He had been healed of an eye disorder and preached in churches, tents, civic auditoriums, and tabernacles across the nation. His revivals had tremendous impact on the Assemblies of God both in Oklahoma City and in Tulsa in the Twenties.

Richey called his seven-week campaign in Tulsa in 1923 the greatest revival he had ever held. The services were held in a building known as "Richey Tabernacle" in the heart of the Tulsa business district. The lot where the tabernacle was built had been donated by Sand Springs millionaire Charles Page. The statistics of the revival are staggering. *The Pentecostal Evangel* in August, 1923, reported that 10,400 were saved and 9,000 healed. Thousands attended the nightly services.

On the Saturday night before the revival ended, a massive parade, organized by Richey, wound through the streets of Tulsa.

The downtown area of Tulsa, normally busy and noisy on Saturday night, was shocked into silence as hundreds of people who had been healed in the meeting marched with crutches held high above their heads. In the middle of the parade was a truck filled with discarded crutches and iron braces. Those on foot and in cars in the parade held homemade signs that read: "God Heals," "10,000 converted," and "Praise the Lord!" The *Tulsa World* reported:

"Occasionally a group of marchers would sing a snatch of a revival song. Some of them still carried their right hands high as those in the healing line at the tabernacle do, and praised the Lord. A little boy passed, carrying high a crutch, his face radiant. A murmur passed through the crowd, a sound repeated again and again as some happy-faced man or woman, carrying crutch or walking stick, marched by."[15]

Famous Pentecostal blind pianist Fred Henry provided special music for the 1923 Richey campaign in Tulsa.

The *Tulsa Tribune* editorialized that Richey had come to Tulsa with nothing but faith, had not appealed for money, and is "leaving Tulsa a better community than he found it."[16]

The 1923 Richey crusade had a lasting impact on a young Presbyterian minister, W.F. Garvin. It was the first time Garvin had heard divine healing preached. He accepted the doctrine and established a nondenominational Pentecostal church in Tulsa named Faith Tabernacle. It grew from a membership of 37 to several hundred. The church, now known as Faith Assembly of God, affiliated with the Assemblies of God in 1942. W.F. Garvin and his wife pastored the church for more than a quarter century.

Edna Garvin explained the intensity of the 1923 Richey revival in a 1960 article in *The Pentecostal Evangel*:

"No one thought of having a revival with only night services. All through the Richey meeting there were morning, afternoon, and night services. There in a great frame tabernacle we first heard divine healing preached and saw with our own eyes miracles wrought. Convinced that it was of God, my husband began to preach healing. God used this meeting as the entering wedge to crack our hard Presbyterian shell."[17]

The Garvins' daughter Ruth married J. Bashford Bishop, best known for his weekly Sunday School lessons in *The Pentecostal Evangel* from 1956 to 1978 and for 30 years of teaching in Assemblies of God colleges.[18]

Richey also held a major healing crusade in Oklahoma City in 1923. Mrs. Hilburn, the mother of Rosa Ricketts, a member of Anadarko First Assembly for a half-century, was dying with cancer. As a result of her condition, Mrs. Hilburn's husband and two other men carried her to the Richey meeting. Martin Perryman chronicled the story:

"When they arrived, they found the crowds were so large, and so many people wanted prayer for healing, you had to take a card with a number on it and wait until your number was called... Brother Richey began praying for the sick at 10 a.m. and prayed all day. At the end of the service, Mrs. Hilburn's number still had not been called. All day long she had watched as people were healed by the power of God, and her faith was increased."[19]

Mrs. Hilburn heard what she described as a "nearly audible" voice telling her she was already healed, because of her faith. She accepted the message from God, went home, and threw away her medicine. She was completely healed and never suffered from cancer again.[20]

FAITH TABERNACLE, OKLAHOMA CITY

The growth of Faith Tabernacle in Oklahoma City, now one of the state's largest churches, was boosted by major revival campaigns led by nationally-known evangelists in 1927-1928. The church began with a revival in a small abandoned schoolhouse in the Mulligan Gardens section of Oklahoma City in 1925. Roy Edwin Street—not really a preacher, but having a powerful testimony of his own salvation—conducted the first service of the revival. Four persons were saved.

Street soon called for the assistance of O.W. Scott, a Pentecostal preacher. Scott became the first pastor of what became Faith Tabernacle. The church moved to a vacant Baptist church at Ninth and Phillips after outgrowing the old schoolhouse in Mulligan Gardens.[21]

The first revival to impact the growth of Faith Tabernacle was in March, 1928, with Charles Price, a Congregationalist minister who had received Pentecost and specialized in praying for the sick. The meeting at the old Merry Garden building on West Main attracted large crowds. Price wrote in his monthly magazine, *Golden Grain*:

"Our pulpit is the canvas of a boxing ring...we can even see the blood that has streamed from the nose of some pugilist who has been fighting for the devil...and here we are fighting the good fight for the Lord... Last night you could hardly be heard for weeping... I am preaching through tears... This meeting feels like a volcano getting ready to blow up."[22]

A woman who had broken her back in a parachute jump from a balloon was brought into the Price meeting on a stretcher. As was his normal practice, Price would not pray for her the first night because he wanted people to see the condition of someone who needed healing so badly. On the second night, the lady, encased in a plaster cast from her hips to her chin, was brought in a wheelchair. When she was prayed for, she suddenly leaped to her feet and cried, "I am healed!" She insisted on taking off the cast immediately. She carried the cast all over the south part of Oklahoma City where she lived. Newspapers carried big stories of the healing, and the revival crowds grew even larger.[23]

Raymond T. Richey followed Price in Oklahoma City in the summer of 1928. Many were saved and healed in the Richey revival at the Stockyards Coliseum.

AIMEE SEMPLE MCPHERSON

After Faith Tabernacle constructed a building that seated 3,000 on N.W. Second Street near downtown Oklahoma City, Aimee Semple McPherson, America's most popular female evangelist of the decade, came for a revival. The crowds were enormous. At the close of one service, people had to be let out by a side door because there were so many people waiting in line for the next service. (McPherson had been licensed with the Assemblies of God until she was divorced in 1921. She is best known for her founding of the Church of the Four Square Gospel.)

Evangelist Charles Price held two more major revivals in Oklahoma in 1928. In the summer he conducted a crusade in a theater in Tulsa. Laverne Mary Hanigan saw his ads in the newspaper. For two years following surgery on her knee, Mrs. Hanigan had constant drainage. After she was prayed for, she took the bandage off and her knee was perfectly healed.[24]

Pastor William Kitchen of the Oklahoma City Gospel Lighthouse (now Faith Tabernacle) chartered a special train to take hundreds of his members to the Price meeting in Tulsa. The train was called "The Hallelujah Special." *Golden Grain* reported:

"It was only fitting and proper that we should bid the Oklahoma City people good-bye as they boarded the train before going back to their city. About half past ten a great crowd assembled at the Rock Island depot. Preachers were there, the choir was there, saints of God from many churches were grouped... Brother Fred Henry, the famous blind musician of Tulsa, had his Hohner accordion around his neck and, very soon, the strains of the grand old hymns of the campaign were filling the air. 'In the Sweet Bye and Bye,' we sang, as the station was filled with the voices of the people, and then 'When the Trumpet of the Lord Shall Sound' thundered forth on the night air."[25]

Price returned to Oklahoma City in October, his second major campaign in the capital city in eight months. The results were the same. Hundreds were saved and healed at the revival held in the new Faith Tabernacle building.[26]

OLD GLORY STATION

Faith Tabernacle pioneered one of America's first religious radio stations in 1927 in Oklahoma City. KGFG (Keep Going for God) was licensed in January, 1927, after Charles Sheaffer built the transmitter and generator out of spare parts. The 50 watts of power generated a clear signal in the Oklahoma City area. The station broadcast Faith Tabernacle services and other religious programs. Sheaffer remembers the great response from programs on the station:

"One night we were broadcasting our service when a man came running in the front door and went directly to the altar. He was saved. He said he was sitting at home listening to the radio when the Lord convinced him of his need and he could not wait any longer."[27]

KGFG continued broadcasting religious programs for several years until the station was sold and the call letters changed to KTOK.

SMITH WIGGLESWORTH

One of the strangest "revival" stories in Oklahoma in the 1920's came from a Smith Wigglesworth healing service at the Richey Tabernacle in Tulsa in 1925. Wigglesworth was an English evangelist who was widely known for his powerful faith and legendary answers to prayer.[28] Ossie Jones, the son of Oklahoma pioneer Assemblies of God leader Oscar Jones, was only five years old, but he will never forget the night he sat on the front row and observed Wigglesworth praying for the sick:

"Minnie McAfee [the mother of Caleb and Forney McAfee, later Oklahoma Assemblies of God ministers] had been given only two weeks to live. She was so weak she could not stand in the healing line without the help of her two sons. When Wigglesworth came to her, he stopped and said, 'I can see that 'debil' of cancer in your stomach.' (Wigglesworth, with his thick English accent, could not clearly say the word 'devil.') He startled the crowd when he yelled 'Debil of cancer, leave!' and hit Sister McAfee with his fist in the stomach hard enough to kill her. He then told her to run. She leaped off the high platform and ran around the crowd shouting 'I'm healed! I'm healed! I'm healed!' She lived for another 30 years."[29]

Hundreds of Pentecostal revivals were held in Oklahoma in the 1920's. God moved powerfully and miraculously in large cities, in small hamlets, and in most towns in between. The revival atmosphere served notice on Oklahoma: Pentecost and the Assemblies of God were here to stay.

▲ *"Stone's Folly" was an old mansion in Topeka, Kansas, where the baptism in the Holy Spirit came to students of Bethel Bible College on January 1, 1901. All modern Pentecostal groups trace their history to "Stone's Folly."*

▲ *Charles Parham.*

▼ *R.E. Winsett produced the world's first Pentecostal song book at the Beulah Colony in western Oklahoma before 1908.*

▲ *A.B. and Dora Cox. Brother Cox was a fiery evangelist who took Pentecost to every corner of Oklahoma.*

Howard Goss at a 1912 ▶ campmeeting. Goss was one of Oklahoma's most popular evangelists during the years preceding and following the Hot Springs meeting which resulted in the formation of the Assemblies of God.

▲ *Evangelistic team at Hickory Grove, Oklahoma, 1912. (l to r) Della Lacy, Nellie Richey, Zora Robert, Pearl and Homer Coberly, Hocker Smith, and Sister and Brother Moody.*

▲ *Campmeeting group at Tulsa, 1912. (l to r) Willard Pope, unidentified, John H. James, unidentified, W.T. Gaston, unidentified, M.M. Pinson, Lemuel C. Hall, Jean Campbell Hall, Ethel Goss, and Howard Goss.*

W.T. Gaston sponsored the annual state Pentecostal campmeeting in Tulsa each summer. This is the 1913 event at Swan Lake in Tulsa.

300 Pentecostals gathered at Hot Springs, Arkansas, in April, 1914, to form a new fellowship, the Assemblies of God.

Oklahoma formed the first District Council of the Assemblies of God at the annual Pentecostal campmeeting in Tulsa in the summer of 1914.

94

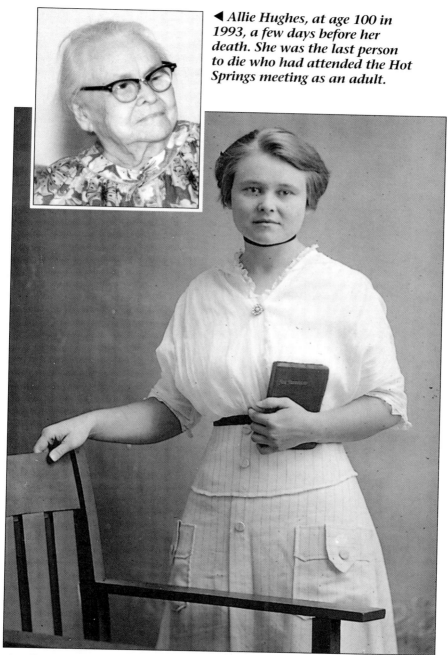

◄ Allie Hughes, at age 100 in 1993, a few days before her death. She was the last person to die who had attended the Hot Springs meeting as an adult.

▲ Allie Hughes of Wellston was a 20-year-old new Christian who attended the Hot Springs meeting in April, 1914.

▲ *The R.C. Nicholson family, 1914.*

Aggie and Lottie ▶
James, pioneer
Assemblies of God
evangelists
and pastors.

◀ *John William Welch. "Daddy" Welch left his church in Tahlequah to become General Chairman and lead the fellowship through some of its most difficult years.*

▼ *Ethel Musick's revivals resulted in many new Assemblies of God congregations in the 1910's and 1920's.*

▲ *A.E. Humbard, the father of evangelist Rex Humbard, held many early Pentecostal revivals in Oklahoma.*

▲ *Converts of a R.C.. Nicholson revival in Velma, 1914.*

▲ *Early members of the church at Fifth and Peoria in Tulsa.*
(l to r bottom) Ruth Morris, Bess Johnson Bowley, Mabel Gray,
Willa Lowther (the church's first missionary), Myrtle Morris Riddle.
(top) Homer Pendleton, Frank Bell, Kimbal Gray (the church's first
song leader), and Kenneth Riddle.

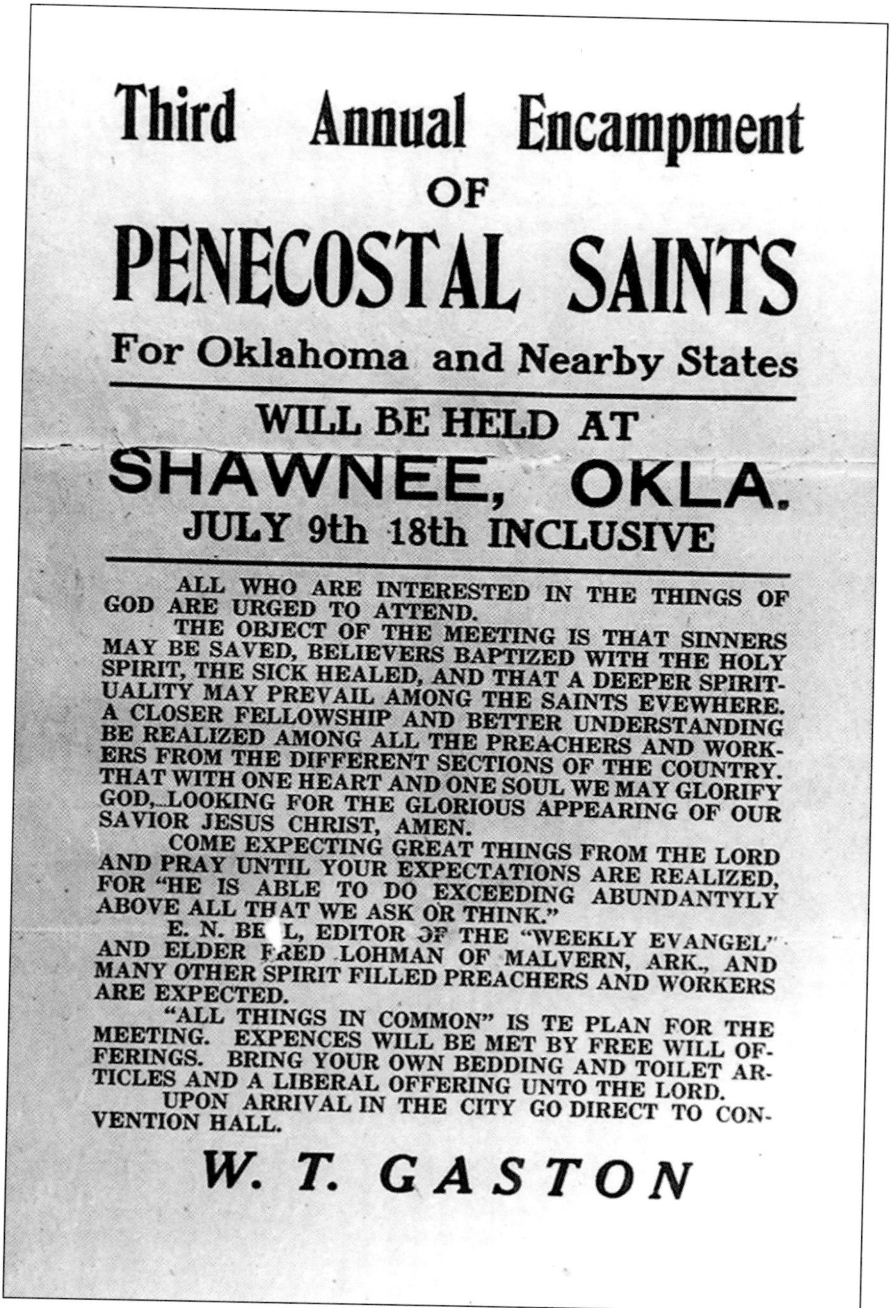

Third Annual Encampment

OF

PENECOSTAL SAINTS

For Oklahoma and Nearby States

WILL BE HELD AT

SHAWNEE, OKLA.

JULY 9th 18th INCLUSIVE

ALL WHO ARE INTERESTED IN THE THINGS OF GOD ARE URGED TO ATTEND.

THE OBJECT OF THE MEETING IS THAT SINNERS MAY BE SAVED, BELIEVERS BAPTIZED WITH THE HOLY SPIRIT, THE SICK HEALED, AND THAT A DEEPER SPIRITUALITY MAY PREVAIL AMONG THE SAINTS EVEWHERE. A CLOSER FELLOWSHIP AND BETTER UNDERSTANDING BE REALIZED AMONG ALL THE PREACHERS AND WORKERS FROM THE DIFFERENT SECTIONS OF THE COUNTRY. THAT WITH ONE HEART AND ONE SOUL WE MAY GLORIFY GOD, LOOKING FOR THE GLORIOUS APPEARING OF OUR SAVIOR JESUS CHRIST, AMEN.

COME EXPECTING GREAT THINGS FROM THE LORD AND PRAY UNTIL YOUR EXPECTATIONS ARE REALIZED, FOR "HE IS ABLE TO DO EXCEEDING ABUNDANTYLY ABOVE ALL THAT WE ASK OR THINK."

E. N. BELL, EDITOR OF THE "WEEKLY EVANGEL" AND ELDER FRED LOHMAN OF MALVERN, ARK., AND MANY OTHER SPIRIT FILLED PREACHERS AND WORKERS ARE EXPECTED.

"ALL THINGS IN COMMON" IS TE PLAN FOR THE MEETING. EXPENCES WILL BE MET BY FREE WILL OFFERINGS. BRING YOUR OWN BEDDING AND TOILET ARTICLES AND A LIBERAL OFFERING UNTO THE LORD.

UPON ARRIVAL IN THE CITY GO DIRECT TO CONVENTION HALL.

W. T. GASTON

Handbill announcing a 1915 campmeeting in Shawnee.

▲ *Early evangelist Will McLaughlin held the first two Pentecostal meetings in Lawton in 1915.*

▲ *J. Roswell Flower (l) and J.W. Welch.*

▲ *Rev. and Mrs. Samuel Jamieson, the second pastors of Fifth and Peoria in Tulsa, 1919.*

◀ *Willard H. Pope,*
Oklahoma District
Chairman, 1915-1916.

▲ *Young People's Band at Fifth and Peoria, 1919.*

▲ *Baptismal service at Panama Lake, 1917.*

Certificate and Credential of Unity

WITH

THE OKLAHOMA DISTRICT COUNCIL

OF THE ASSEMBLIES OF GOD

This Certifies That *Aggie James*

of *Sparks* State of *Okla*

being a member of the general ASSEMBLY OF GOD (Heb. 12:23), and having been divinely called according to the Word of God and in Fellowship with the GENERAL COUNCIL OF THE ASSEMBLIES of GOD in the United States of America, Canada and Foreign Lands, is hereby recognized and granted

LICENSE TO PREACH

the Gospel. We, the Presbytery of the District Council, by fervent prayer, invoke the Divine Presence, with blessing and power, upon him and hereby recognize this License so long as in Fellowship with the Assemblies of God, and while maintaining a Godly life and a Scriptural standard in teaching.

Given this *3rd* day of *October* 19*18* A.D.

C. M. Rigg Presbyter

S. A. Jamieson Sec.

E H Grey Secretary

GOOD FOR ONE (1) YEAR FROM DATE.

▲ *The "preaching" license given to Aggie James in 1918.*

Baptismal service west of Cement, 1920.

Raymond T. Richey ▶
*held major revivals in
Oklahoma in the
1920's and 1930's.*

▼ *Richey Tabernacle
in downtown Tulsa.*

▲ *General Chairman W.T. Gaston and family, 1925.*

▼ *Dr. Charles Price.*

▲ *Billboard advertising a Charles Price meeting, 1929.*

▼ *Edna Garvin.*

▲ *W.F. Garvin.*

▲ *Aimee Semple McPherson (in white dress) held numerous major meetings in Oklahoma in the 1920's.*

115

A Faith Tabernacle radio broadcast. On the left is pastor William Kitchen. Music leaders Fay and Grace Williamson are on the right.

▲ *Faith Tabernacle in Oklahoma City just after completion.*

▲ *A car that advertised Faith Tabernacle's radio station, KGFG.*

▲ *(l to r) Roxie and Dexter Collins and Bert Webb at the 1928 Oklahoma C.A. convention in Okmulgee.*

▲ *Bert Webb, Floyd Hawkins, and Arthur Graves designed the C.A. emblem at a youth meeting in Wellston in 1926. The emblem was accepted by the national C.A. leadership the following year. This is from the cover of the March 1929 Christ's Ambassadors Monthly, featuring youth in Oklahoma.*

▲ *James Hutsell and family, 1925. Hutsell served as Oklahoma District Superintendent from 1927 to 1938.*

▲ *The N.B. Rayburns stayed in this tent while holding a revival in Vici, 1927.*

▲ *Blind pianist Fred Henry and his family provided the music for many revival campaigns in Oklahoma including meetings for Raymond T. Richey, Charles Price, Smith Wigglesworth, Billy Sunday, and Aimee Semple McPherson.*

▲ *The Carl Barnes musical family, 1929.*

Chapter 13

Great Depression Brings Expansion

By 1930 the Great Depression was in full swing in Oklahoma. It began with the stock market crash in 1929 and worsened as banks failed, factories and stores closed, and millions of Americans were left jobless and homeless. Oklahoma suffered mightily.

The weather contributed to Oklahoma's farm problems. A searing drought hit the southern plains until even normally wet eastern Oklahoma was desiccated. The state was wracked with dust storms. Sand blew in such quantities that travelers lost their way, chickens went to roost at noon, airports closed, and trains stopped. Animals and humans suffered from lung disorders. George and Stella Flattery held a revival in a schoolhouse near Forgan in the summer of 1935. Recent dust storms had been so severe that Flattery had to scoop out literally bushels of dirt before he could hold services.

The drought was accompanied by blistering heat. In 1934 new high temperature records were set daily in July, records which yet stand. In the northeastern Oklahoma town of Vinita, the temperature exceeded 100 degrees for 35 consecutive days, and on the 36th day it reached 117 degrees.[1]

Oklahoma was not a wealthy state even before the Great Depression. By the end of 1931, farm foreclosures were daily events and more than one-fourth of the farmers in the state were on relief. All 77 counties were designated disaster areas and eligible for federal drought assistance. A hog farmer in northwest Oklahoma said he would give his 100 hogs to anyone who would take them so he would not have to watch them starve to death. Many Oklahomans left for California and other points west. Over the next 20 years, the state's population would decrease by almost a million.[2]

The poor suffered the most in the Great Depression. And, in the 1930's, most Assemblies of God believers, pastors, and evangelists in Oklahoma were very poor. Forrest Murray was pastoring at Mooreland and, like most Pentecostal preachers of the era, had to have a full-time job on the side to survive. Sometimes offerings would only be a dollar or two per week.[3]

Most pastors during the Depression were supported by side jobs and by food donated by farmers in their congregations. Church finances were at rock bottom. A pastor would often make a special appeal just to pay the electric bill. In 1933 First Assembly in Chickasha moved into a larger sanctuary but did not have enough money for sufficient benches. They borrowed park benches from the city for their services.[4] In Poteau, Pastor Lillie Foster used leftover bath water to scrub the floors of the church to save money.[5]

The church buildings were under-insulated—cold in winter and unbearably hot in summer. Sitting on rough-lumber seats, almost everyone spent a summer service fanning with paper fans. Most church windows were always open in the summer, resulting in the spread of the gospel to the entire neighborhood. Many a sinner was drawn to an Assemblies of God service because of the anointed singing that rang out through open windows.

An entire volume could be written about the hardships suffered by Assemblies of God pastors and church families during the Great Depression. In spite of, or perhaps because of, those difficult times, Assemblies of God people stayed together by the mercies of God.[6]

One of the few churches in the state that had the means to help poverty-stricken neighbors was Faith Tabernacle in Oklahoma City. The Frisco Railroad loaned the church an old building on South Walker Street for a "breadline" mission. News of the project spread throughout Oklahoma City. People regardless of their religious faith pitched in and sent money, clothing and provisions. In just 10 days 37,000 hot meals were served and truckloads of clothing and shoes were given away.[7]

Ironically, the Great Depression resulted in a massive expansion of the Assemblies of God movement in Oklahoma. The reason was simple. In poverty, people turned to God. There was no alternative. Since the Pentecostal experience offered a personal relationship with the Master of the universe, thousands flocked to Assemblies of God churches.

At the beginning of the 1930's there were 110 official Assemblies of God churches in Oklahoma. By 1939 the number had grown to 394. The new churches were storefront missions and roughly built tabernacles, often with nothing more than sawdust floors. Many families who had been bruised by the Depression found new hope and life in these "glory barns."[8]

Assemblies of God churches were springing up everywhere. Northwest of Waynoka, believers began meeting at the West Liberty schoolhouse in 1930. Floy Murray pastored the fledgling congregation which was formed after a J.W. DeVault revival. The group moved to a garage in Waynoka, and used the city hall and the high school auditorium as the crowds grew. Lola DeVault, the daughter of J.W. DeVault, bought an old Methodist church building in nearby Avard and moved it to Waynoka. The church was recognized by the General Council in May, 1932.[9]

E.G. Kennedy was the first pastor of the church at Erick—set in order in May, 1930.[10]

In June, 1930, the Assembly of God at Sayre was set in order under a large tent. Elgin Smith and Bert and Jessie Roberts had held a revival that resulted in the establishment of the church. P.D. Rutherford was the first pastor of the Sayre church that met during the summer and fall under a large brush arbor on 5th Street. Ethel and Allen Wade, who were among the 55 charter members of the church, recalled that difficult first year:

123

"The going was rough. When winter came it was too cold to meet at the brush arbor so we bought a sheet iron building on Railroad Hill. Cotton dust from a nearby gin and smoke from trains on the adjacent railroad tracks were a hindrance, but the revival spirit continued and the church grew."[11]

Pentecost came to Geary in 1930. Receiving the baptism cost the mother of longtime Assemblies of God Pastor Matt Goss her job. She worked for a deacon in the local Baptist church who told her if she spoke in tongues, she couldn't work for him any longer.[12]

Also in 1930, L.H. Arnold, later the secretary-treasurer of the Oklahoma District, founded the Assembly of God church at Bokoshe.[13] That same year, Dave Harris led a group of believers in an unusual fund-raising project to build the church at Porum. The faithful came on horseback, in wagons, and on foot to pick cotton that had been donated for the effort. The cotton was hauled to a gin at Webbers Falls. The money earned from the sale of the cotton was used to buy materials for the first church building in Porum. Farmers also donated their time and provided their teams and wagons to haul rocks for the foundation.[14]

Berl Dodd accepted the pastorate of the Assembly of God church in Seminole in 1930. He found only a few people worshiping in a shotgun building. Revival came and the church soon outgrew its humble quarters. Dodd bought and remodeled the local Methodist church for his growing congregation. The Seminole church became a rallying point for preachers and churches in southeast Oklahoma. Dodd sponsored some of the greatest tent revivals and campmeetings Oklahoma has ever known. He pastored the church in Seminole 24 years.

The Assembly of God in Fort Towson began in 1930 after evangelist Tomy Jacobs' car broke down at the edge of town as he was passing through. While waiting for his car to be repaired, he attended a prayer meeting conducted by Sister L.E. Cundiff. He was persuaded to stay in Fort Towson and hold a revival. At the end of the revival, the church began with 45 members.

Jacobs moved on to the Mound Grove schoolhouse near Valliant and helped set in order a church with 25 members. It was there he met his future wife, Mary Lee, who at age 16 was the first to receive the Holy Ghost in the revival. Tomy and Mary Lee Jacobs were married in 1934 and ministered together for over 50 years.[15]

Other Assemblies of God churches set in order in 1930 were in Bristow, Fairfax, Snomac, Jenks, Moravia, Soper, Hominy, Quapaw, and Erick.[16]

The 1931 District Council minutes reported new churches established that year in Sand Creek, Yeager, Maud, Sparks, Sasakwa, Geronimo, Kelleyville, Skeedee, Lone Springs and Fairview.[17]

The 1932 District Council was held in Shawnee in October. The lineup of speakers was impressive. Former General Superintendent J.W. Welch, national missions director Noel Perkin, and famous evangelist Jacob "Uncle Jake" Miller blessed the large crowds. However, there was little money for love offerings for the speakers. The offerings for Welch and Perkin totaled $14.21.[18]

First Assembly at Fort Cobb was set in order on July 2, 1932. Olen and Dora Cossey were the first pastors. They were former members of the Missionary Baptist Church who had begun holding Pentecostal meetings in the area a few years earlier.[19]

The Allen Assembly of God was founded in 1933 in the middle of the Depression. In December, 1993, newly elected General Superintendent Thomas E. Trask was the guest speaker at the church's 60th anniversary celebration.

Rural areas of northeast Oklahoma County were ripe for the planting of new Pentecostal churches in the 1930's. George and Laura McCoy began the Full Gospel Mission in a vacant store building in Jones in 1932. In November, 1934, the church affiliated with the Assemblies of God. McCoy pastored the church for 30 years until his death in 1963. After the lease on the downtown Jones building expired in 1936, the congregation worshiped in a brush arbor until a new building was completed in August, 1936. Tommy Alvarez is only the fifth pastor of the church in six decades. Previous pastors were George McCoy, J.R. Wyatt, Moody Hicks, and R.P. Corp.

Several other churches were birthed as a result of George McCoy's leadership at Jones. George Robertson founded the Assembly of God at Choctaw. Willa Lee Pendley built a new church at Spencer.

125

Bertie McCoy, at age 15, held an outdoor revival in Luther in 1934. Home prayer meetings began. By 1944 an old black-smith shop was cleaned and rented for a meeting place for Luther Assembly of God.

1936 was a great year for new churches in Oklahoma. *The Pentecostal Evangel* reported a new church set in order in November in Oilton after a four-week revival with W.A. Frazier, who was unanimously elected as the first pastor.[20]

T.E. May founded Glad Tidings Assembly in Tulsa in 1936 following another successful Raymond T. Richey crusade. One of Glad Tidings' charter members was Vivian McCormick who still attends the church almost 60 years later. She remembers the Richey meeting as though it were yesterday:

"My oldest son got lockjaw and blood poisoning after having a tooth pulled. He could not open his mouth and was in terrible pain. I took a handkerchief to the tabernacle before service and had Brother Richey and his associates anoint it and pray over it. Marvin Hartz [the pastor of Fifth and Peoria and father of Jim Hartz, later the host of the Today show on NBC Television] put the handkerchief on my son's throat and he instantly opened his mouth. He was healed completely and instantly."[21]

Maysville Assembly of God started in a little country school-house outside of town in 1936. Y.F. Fanning later led the church in a move across the creek west of the schoolhouse. The building was moved to Maysville in 1941 and the dirt floor was replaced with a wooden one.[22]

In June, 1936, several families wanted a place of worship in Fairland. They rented a lot for $1.50 per month and cut poles and brush to build an arbor. The lumber for the arbor cost $3.00. As winter approached, the meetings moved into believers' homes. After revivals with John Hopkins, Marie Keeling, and Ben Gibbons, the church moved into a newly constructed building on Easter Sunday, 1938. Two months later, the church was recognized officially by the General Council.[23]

In the fall of 1936, a nucleus of Pentecostals began meeting in an old house in Tonkawa. Cecil Smith was the first pastor and the church was set in order later that year. In 1939 the

Tonkawa church built a permanent structure with lumber bought from the dismantling of the Missionary Bible Church in Ponca City.[24]

A brush arbor revival across from the Pearl School, 17 miles east of Marlow, resulted in the organization of Pearl Assembly of God in 1936. Calvin and Reba Rogers preached to believers who sat on bridge timbers and read their Bible by the light of gas torches. A one-room church building was constructed next to the Pearl School in 1937. Woodrow and Bernice Clay were the first pastors of the church which officially joined the Assemblies of God fellowship in March, 1938.[25]

An outdoor S.W. Watterson revival resulted in the founding of Durant First Assembly in 1937. Watterson stayed on as the church's pastor. Other pastors at Durant include J.W. Reddick, Ed Bice, L.F. Ammons, Ross Davis, and H.H. Davis.[26]

In July, 1937, the Assembly of God at Claremore was set in order. The congregation of Pentecostals had existed for years at Claremore but did not affiliate with the General Council until Preston and Bertie Roberts came to pastor in 1937. Sister Roberts still attends First Assembly in Claremore.[27]

Glad Tidings Assembly in Shawnee began in November, 1939, with 33 charter members.[28] Soon, young James and Francine Dodd became pastors of the church. Brother Dodd called Raymond T. Richey to hold a revival. The Civic Auditorium in Shawnee was rented for the 10-day meeting that drew crowds as large as 6,000. Songwriter Ira Stanphil was the song leader for the revival.[29]

Chapter 14

Revivals in the Thirties

The emphasis of the Oklahoma District in the Thirties was on consolidating the growth and developing strong local churches. However, there were still great revival campaigns around the state.

Pastor T.K. Davis of Lawton wrote *The Pentecostal Evangel* in December, 1938, about "one of the most remarkable revivals that we have ever witnessed in our 25 years in the Pentecostal ministry." At that revival, scores were prostrated before God in the healing services. Many testified to definite healing. Sinners witnessing God's power fell at the altar and cried for mercy. Thirty received the baptism in two weeks. Strong men broke down, weeping like children, and rushed to the altar without a song of invitation.[1]

Great revivals were also reported in 1937 at Watonga with Edna Layton and at Harden City with F.C. Cornell.[2]

A "revival" atmosphere existed at First Assembly in Okmulgee during the Depression. The church became one of the largest Assemblies of God churches in the state, averaging 400 to 500 in Sunday School. Otto Goins served as Christ Ambassadors' President at the church in the Thirties and remembers the Wednesday night and Friday night services as "like camp-meeting." Believers had to get to church early to find a seat or be relegated to standing along the back wall during the three or four-hour service.[3]

Young Marvin McElhannon was saved in a brush arbor meeting in the community of Sharp, near Okmulgee, in August, 1937. The revival at Sharp was an outreach effort of Okmulgee First Assembly's young people. Hattie Coffey became pastor of the Sharp church. McElhannon remembers the services:

"We were just country folk. We started church 30 minutes early. The men would meet in one place and pray and women would do the same thing. We prayed under a tree somewhere. We called them 'grove meetings.' We paid the price in prayer before the service. God rewarded us with fruitful altar services. My greatest thrill ever was to see people accept Christ."[4]

Boyd Tucker was 22 when he held his first revival in Soper in 1935. In three weeks, 12 were saved and 15 filled with the Holy Spirit. Tucker and his wife received only 75 cents in offerings and had to hitchhike home from the revival. Tucker believes prayer was the key to the success of Pentecost in the Depression:

"Back then, you could hear people praying for a quarter of a mile. You could pass by a Christian's house and hear family members crying out to God for their needs. Pentecostals were not ashamed to pray. When they were hurting, they simply called upon God to help them. They prayed before church, during church, and after church. When they got home, they knew they had been to church and had met personally with God."[5]

Rufus Strange and Chester Hance put up a brush arbor on the side of the road between Sayre and Elk City in the late 1930's. People passing by would stop and listen to the preaching. When the Holy Spirit convicted them of their sin, they repented, and were immediately baptized in the creek alongside the road.[6]

In 1939 Tulsa Faith Tabernacle and its pastor W.F. Garvin united with the Mission of Redeeming Love for a major outreach to the poor and homeless in Tulsa. Ida May Graham operated the mission with the help of "practically every Assemblies of God church in Tulsa." Mrs. Graham wrote in a 1947 book that the mission was a great training ground for young preachers:

"At one of our District Councils, a young man being ordained shook my hand and said, with tears in his eyes, that he preached his first sermon in my mission. Young people from Fifth and Peoria and Faith Tabernacle who felt the call of God on their lives preached in our services. Some are now pastors and prominent evangelists. Not only were these young people a blessing to the mission but the mission proved a 'school' for them."[7]

GREAT LEADERSHIP

Oklahoma was blessed with dedicated and stable Assemblies of God leaders during the Depression. James S. Hutsell had been elected District Superintendent in 1929. In 1930 H.E. Bowley was elected District Superintendent at the District Council in Enid, but immediately resigned because he did not feel it was God's will for him to take the post.[8] Hutsell was then reelected and served until 1938 when he was replaced by George W. Hardcastle, pastor at Okmulgee. Hardcastle later served as District Superintendent in Arkansas and also as a non-resident Executive Presbyter of the national movement. The presence of Brother Hardcastle during an interview at a nursing home in Oklahoma City in the summer of 1993 was awesome. The years had dimmed his memory, but his love for Jesus continued to shine on his face.

G.W. Hardcastle was responsible for moving the Oklahoma District offices to a central location in Oklahoma City. He rented offices in downtown Oklahoma City until he could find and buy the 10 acres on North Kelley in Oklahoma City where the present District offices and campgrounds are located. The Depression was not an ideal time to raise money for a central office but Brother Hardcastle sold off lots on the back of the property to retire the debt and build a tabernacle for campmeetings.

Brother Hardcastle became one of the most respected men in the national movement. He was the only Oklahoma pastor to ever serve as a non-resident Executive Presbyter until Oklahoma District Superintendent Armon Newburn was elected to that position at the 1993 General Council.

Hardcastle did not earn this wide respect without hardship and sacrifice, however. He remembers how difficult the Depression was for ministers:

"Anyone who obeyed the call to the ministry was simply on his own to trust God for his needs. There was little or no financial support for either evangelist or pastor. Consequently, a deep consecration and a willingness to suffer for the cause of Christ were indispensable qualifications for the Pentecostal ministry...In one town, many came for salvation and the baptism...This brought the wrath of some, and a mob was formed for the purpose of whipping me and running me out of town. The message of holiness was the message most hated by the ungodly in those days."[9]

The Oklahoma District was blessed with dedicated leaders in the 1930's. R.H. Hoyer served for most of the decade as District Secretary-Treasurer. Mrs. C.A. Miles and Mrs. H.F. Beaty were presidents of the Women's Missionary Council. Berl Dodd became Assistant District Superintendent in 1939. Wallace Bragg, Earl Davis, and William Shackelford were District C. A. Presidents.

On the national leadership scene, Ernest S. Williams was reelected as General Superintendent by at least 95 percent of the vote at each General Council until he retired in 1949. Former Oklahoma pastor J.R. Evans served as General Secretary until 1935 when his failing eyesight prompted the election of J. Roswell Flower.[10]

BAD TIMES ECONOMICALLY—GOOD TIMES SPIRITUALLY

Economically the times were hard in the 1930's, but spiritually the Pentecostal churches were getting along fine. Forrest Murray, a longtime pastor, remembered:

"People were turning to God during the Depression. One night there was a terrific hailstorm near Laverne where we were pastoring. The hail was wiping out every crop in its path. One of our members knelt down by his wheat field and said, 'Lord, You promised to take care of us if we paid our tithes and honored You.' The hailstorm stopped at his fence."

Murray also recalls once when there was no money to buy kerosene for the heater in the parsonage. God stretched the kerosene and the heater burned four times longer than normal, until a man showed up at the door with 50 cents.[11]

132

Pentecost was a whole way of life. Many believers totally trusted God for healing and dared not take themselves—or their children—to the doctor. When sickness descended upon a Pentecostal household, believing neighbors came and prayed until God intervened. It was common to find saints spending the night around the bed of a sick child, petitioning God for healing. Pentecostals believed that God would honor their personal relationship with Him and keep their lives and their bodies safe from harm.

Historian William Menzies cites two other reasons for the phenomenal nationwide growth of the Assemblies of God in the 1930's: (1) Intense evangelism, largely by graduates from a growing list of Assemblies of God Bible schools, and (2) a new emphasis on world missions giving, a move that God endorsed by pouring out His blessings on missions-minded local churches.[12]

JOY UNSPEAKABLE

What Assemblies of God churches lacked in money during the Great Depression, they made up for in fellowship. Sunday School rallies became popular. Churches in a given area would come together for dinner on the ground and an old-fashioned Sunday afternoon gospel singing. Christ's Ambassadors rallies were introduced in the early Thirties. Gas and automobiles were often so scarce the young people of a church would ride a truck down dusty roads for hours to worship with other youth from the section. The dusty ride made the "foot washing" services held in some churches practical as well as spiritual.

Pentecostal family life encouraged children to follow Christ. Current Woodward First Assembly Pastor Paul Sharpe recalls his father's role in his conversion:

"I was about six and was playing with my two brothers in the dirt behind the smokehouse. My dad came around the smokehouse and said, 'Don't you boys think it's time for you to pray through?' For some reason we all agreed. We all went into the barn. I got in the cow stall and prayed in the trough, under the trough, and all over the place. I don't remember what I said, but I know the Lord saved me that day because it is as fresh today as it was then."[13]

People of every description were drawn to Pentecostal services. Robert Eskridge, a longtime member of Broken Arrow Assembly, says it is difficult to determine what brought so many people to stand outside a Pentecostal church to look in the window and listen to the gospel. Eskridge says it may have been simple curiosity, but he believes a "fear of the Lord" and the moving of the Holy Spirit were behind the phenomenon.[14]

A typical service in the Thirties began with prayer. A lively song service followed. Pentecostal music had become a tradition in the first two decades of the movement. R.E. Winsett produced popular song books that contained Pentecostal songs like "Our Lord's Return to Earth Again", "Joy Unspeakable", and "There's Power in the Blood". Black songwriter Thoro Harris joined Fred Henry and Jack Neville in publishing the famous song book *Radio Gems* at KVOO radio in Tulsa in 1934.[15]

Pentecostals were blessed with other great songwriters in the first four decades of the century: Vep Ellis, who wrote "Have Faith in God"; Cleavant Derricks, "When God Dips His Love in My Heart"; and Herbert Buffum, author of "Lift Me Up Above the Shadows" and many other songs. Buffum directed the music in several revivals in Oklahoma in the 1920's and 1930's.[16]

After the singing portion of the service, saints would testify about how God had rescued them or healed them. The testimony service was often interrupted by more singing of hymns and choruses. Special songs preceded the main part of the service—the preaching of the gospel. Sermons were never short, but the people did not seem to mind. It was as if time stood still when the presence of God totally dominated a service and "the anointing fell." The altar call brought men and women forward for repentance and renewal. People sometimes tarried for hours praying around the altars until the wee hours of the morning.

Keeping the kids up past bedtime was no problem. Pentecostal children often spent the first few hours of their sleep on a pallet under a bench. No one seemed to mind the hardships. As a result of the horrible circumstances caused by the Dust Bowl and the Great Depression, all that many Oklahomans had then was God, and cling to Him they did.

Sunday School became a priority in the 1930's. Under the leadership of General Superintendent E.S. Williams, the Gospel

Publishing House turned out tons of Sunday School materials weekly. Leaders recognized both the evangelistic and the educational potential of Sunday School.[17] Oklahoma again led the way nationally by establishing the first district Sunday School superintendent position in 1935.[18]

Chapter 15

—❦—

Heroes of the Faith

One central truth emerged from the research for this book. We owe so much to the early leaders of our fellowship—our "heroes of the faith."

During the Thirties, God raised up a mighty band of spiritual warriors in Oklahoma. Even though the Assemblies of God was growing rapidly—or perhaps because of that great growth—our leaders had to take the bitter with the sweet. They were persecuted in many ways. Preachers were jailed for disturbing the peace. Members were considered strange and crazy by their neighbors. Pentecostal meetings were pelted with rotten eggs and tomatoes.

Oscar Jones was one of the pioneers who endured great persecution:

"After giving their hearts to Christ, many men poured out their home brew and...destroyed their stills. Naturally, it made the devil mad that he was losing his crowd...so he moved upon some of his still loyal subjects to persecute the servants of the Lord... Rocks and rotten eggs were thrown at us, and a plot was made to blow up our house. Providentially, two little girls discovered the dynamite and warned us in time. Many people were healed... God worked miracles in spite of the opposition of Satan."[1]

Centuries before, Paul had warned in Acts 5:38 that those who live godly in Christ Jesus would suffer persecution. Assemblies of God people in the early days proved this to be true; but local churches were becoming established and leaders showed courage, faith, and determination to fulfill the Great Commission.

Pioneer Oklahoma pastor James W. Reddick received the baptism in October, 1937, and began preaching the Pentecostal message. His family thought he had "lost his marbles." He preached his first revival in his hometown of Weleetka and his wife was the first to receive the baptism. For the next 50 years, Reddick would preach 263 revivals at 122 different Assemblies of God churches in Oklahoma.[2] He wrote a poem about his struggles:

> It started in the early Thirties,
> On this long Gospel Road.
> Eighteen states I have traveled,
> In the heat and in the cold.
> Down in Old Mexico,
> The story I have told,
> How Jesus could save,
> Regardless how old.
>
> I have tasted of the dregs of the cup
> That Jesus gave thanks for that night,
> And on the way,
> It has made things right.
> The sealing of the wine cup,
> On Golgatha's hill that day,
> Has given me strength
> Along the way.
>
> Some days the cross was heavy,
> Oft times a groan,
> Sometimes a smile,
> Sometimes a moan.
> As I continue down
> This long Gospel Road,
> The more I serve Him,
> The sweeter life grows.[3]

Joe Stumbaugh held services in an old pool hall in Catoosa in the 1930's. The owner told him he had been praying for five years that someone would rent the building and use it for a Pentecostal church. The "pool hall" revival in Catoosa lasted for two months. Stumbaugh moved on to Stillwater and pastored for 30 years. He served several years as an executive presbyter of the Oklahoma District.[4]

WOMEN PREACHERS

In the early years women preachers played a major role in the Assemblies of God. In 1930 twenty percent of the ordained ministers in the fellowship were women, and two thirds of the women preachers were single. Mary Ruth Chamless, in her book, *Behold God's Handmaid*, describes the typical woman preacher of the day decked out in the standard all-white uniform like that of Aimee Semple McPherson:

"The uniform was quite often a nurse's uniform, with or without a colored tie under the collar... The hair was long and styled... Since many ministers and congregations did not believe in wearing jewelry, the woman minister's only adornment beyond a wedding ring was usually a lovely brooch which held a handkerchief with brightly colored crocheted edging firmly pinned to the breast pocket of the uniform."[5]

Clara Grace pastored in Wetumka after holding an 11-week revival in 1931. Thousands were saved in her meetings all over the state.[6] Etta McCaskill was a Mississippi evangelist who preached in several churches in Oklahoma. Hildreth Ethridge Brissey, known for her prayer life and music as well as her capable ministry, traveled extensively around Oklahoma in the Thirties. After her health broke, she settled down and married Dr. Brissey in Broken Arrow.[7]

Alpha Fortenberry from Tupelo began as an evangelist at age 16—traveling with her own tent. She was a veteran preacher when she came to southwest Oklahoma and held a revival in 1930 in the Beckham County town of Carter. A rodeo star, Clyde Henson, decided to go see for himself the girl evangelist preaching at the little country church. Evangelist Fortenberry, who would soon marry the rodeo star, described the altar scene:

"My eyes could not believe what I was seeing. The handsome Clyde Henson weeping at the altar of that country church. He looked as out of place as a city banker would look behind a turning-row plow. I was 19 and had traveled through several states in gospel tent meetings. Many had knelt at the altar through the short ministry of three years, but no one before had stopped me dead in my tracks."[8]

Clyde followed Alpha to a tent revival in Mangum where he received the baptism in the Holy Spirit. Sister Henson later wrote how the members of Clyde's dance band reacted:

"They stood on the worn benches looking over the shoulders of the people in the crowded building. They saw the light of a new day shine through the countenance of their buddy and they heard him speak in a language they had never heard before. It seemed as though the whole countryside gathered in one place. The newspaper reporter sat near the altar to see the great phenomenon of revival."[9]

When Alpha married Clyde, revival opportunities dried up because many pastors were disappointed that the promising young female preacher had married a rodeo star. The Hensons turned to Oklahoma oil towns for revivals where Clyde could relate to the roughnecks.[10] The Hensons later pastored for two decades and built one of America's most successful Assemblies of God churches in Sacramento, California. The chapel at the American Indian Bible School in Phoenix, Arizona bears the name of Clyde Henson. Alpha still lives in Sacramento.[11]

PREACHING TEAMS

The 1930's also produced some powerful husband-wife pastoral teams in Oklahoma. Samuel J. and Leenetta Scott were married in 1932 and pioneered nearly 20 congregations. Brother Scott was called to preach after being healed of a playground injury to his leg that resulted in 20 operations in five years. The Scotts started their first church in Okmulgee in 1932. Brother Scott describes the novel way he brought in the crowds:

"I went to a saddle shop that sold cowboy clothes. I borrowed a cowboy hat, clothes, and a saddle. Putting the saddle across the front hood of our big blue Cord car, I rode on it with a big loudspeaker calling out, 'Come out tonight and hear the cowboy preacher!' My timid wife drove the car as we went throughout the city. That night the house was filled."[12]

In 1934 the Scotts pioneered First Assembly in Norman. A Mrs. Brook had been praying for a Pentecostal church in Norman for years. She started prayer meetings in homes. Revivals led by Wesley Goodwin from Okmulgee and R.H. Hoyer of Oklahoma City planted the seed for a three-month tent revival with the Scotts on a vacant lot near the present county courthouse. The church began with 15 members.[13] Sister Scott walked the streets of Norman, asking for donations to build a permanent structure. She recalls that times were hard:

"We often ran out of groceries, we had no money or food, or materials to build the church. One morning Brother Scott was getting ready for work. There was only one piece of bread and a small jar of jelly in the house. I insisted that he eat it for breakfast. He came back at 10 and told me someone had given him 10 dollars so he could buy the building materials needed for the day. Later, about four o'clock, somebody just showed up at our door with a basket of food. We never doubted that the Lord would take care of us."[14]

The Norman church building was completed within a few months. P.C. Nelson preached the dedication service.

The Scotts' life is further evidence that God really cares about His servants. Once when Brother Scott was broke but hungry for a pie, they prayed. Within a few minutes one of his parishioners drove up with two pies.

The Scotts took over a small, struggling Assemblies of God church in Ponca City in 1934. The old building had cracks in the floor, no ceiling, and a barrel for a stove. Scott and a few faithful saints literally built a new church with their hands:

"We went hungry more than once while sacrificing to give for it. I mixed cement and laid stone for 252 days...When we had just gotten the rafters up, a storm blew them down and the insurance paid for them and let us keep them. We spliced them and were able to put them back."[15]

The Ponca City newspaper reported that 500 people were present when the cornerstone of the new church building was laid in the spring of 1935.[16]

The Scotts also played a major role in developing what is now Capitol Hill Assembly of God in Oklahoma City, currently pastored by Assistant District Superintendent Frank Cargill. The congregation had begun in 1929 after a revival by O'Neal Scott. A small frame tabernacle was erected in 1930 at S.W. 35th and Harvey. S.J. and Leenetta Scott came to the church in 1932 and began knocking on doors. The small church grew to more than 400 in attendance during their first year. Brother Scott personally hauled 80 people to Sunday School one week in a trailer behind his Ford roadster. Benches were hauled by truck to the slums of Oklahoma City for services on Sunday afternoon. God blessed, and Sunday School attendance reached 544 within a few months. A larger tabernacle had to be built. Official recognition as an Assemblies of God church came in 1938.[17]

Another strong ministry team was Eugene F. and Carol Pierce. They were married in 1927 and pastored at Elm Grove-Chester, Hominy, Nowata, and Edmond. They built churches in five states. During the Depression, Brother Pierce would drive 75 miles to preach on Sunday morning at the community of Dylan, and hold Sunday School in the afternoon in Freedom. Sister Pierce, who still attends Cathedral of the Hills (formerly First Assembly) in Edmond, loved the foot washings:

"I was so blessed when we had an old-fashioned Pentecostal foot washing. Once I danced in the Spirit all night and never fell down, even though my feet were wet and the floor was slippery. Time meant nothing to us. We lived for going to church to feel the mighty presence of God."[18]

Ed and Vesta Bice were early pioneers in southern Oklahoma. They founded what is now Lighthouse Assembly in Ardmore in 1930.[19]

142

W.C. and Katherine Drain began their ministry during the Depression. When God told them to hold a revival near Bartlesville, they stored what little furniture they had, traded their old pickup for a car, left their two oldest children with family, and headed out. Once they took the revival message to a community that had never heard about Pentecost. Sister Drain remembers the hardships:

"We slept on the floor of the tiny building and cooked on a campfire. Some of the people would bring us food at night. Cars were parked for several blocks around as people packed into the building. We prayed every day by the side of a nearby spring. God moved every night and souls were added to the Kingdom."[20]

In their first pastorate, the Drains lived on an average of $30 a month. Frequently the cupboard was bare. One Sunday the offering was only $1.50. Brother and Sister Drain used the money to buy a small amount of food for their children and decided to fast until God provided. He always did. Sister Drain recalls, "When we got down to the last meal, God always sent someone with groceries or money to rescue us. He took care of us in every situation."[21]

Leslie and Ida Moore began their ministry in 1931. They evangelized in Oklahoma and pastored in Arkansas until God called them to establish a church in Kingfisher, Oklahoma, in 1937. They arrived with $65, rented a building for a church for $10 a month and a house for $12 a month, and bought some groceries. With the remaining money, Brother Moore had handbills printed, announcing the new church to the townspeople. He started a revival the next night with 13 present, including his wife and four children.

God provided miracles to boost the new church at Kingfisher. The Moores' son Jimmy was healed on his death bed. One of the ranchers in the congregation was being ruined by a disease sweeping through his cattle herd. Brother Moore went to the ranch and laid hands on the cattle and prayed. God healed the cattle and the story spread like wildfire. The church grew and was officially recognized by the General Council in May, 1939, as Kingfisher Gospel Tabernacle of the Assemblies of God.[22]

143

Holy Ghost-filled preachers who loved God with all their hearts and feared nothing but sin spearheaded the phenomenal growth of our fellowship in the 1930's. They were successful in planting hundreds of new churches. As the decade closed, there was an Assemblies of God church in almost every city and town in Oklahoma.

▲ *Preston and Bertie Roberts and family, 1931.*

▲ *Hattie Swearingen and husband, first pastors at Sweetwater.*

145

Polk Creek Sunday School near Poteau, 1930.

Tabler, Oklahoma, Gospel Tabernacle, 1934. All-day dinner on the ground.

Handbill announcing the Seminole campmeeting, 1932.

◄ Glennie and Hobson Kennemer, early pastors.

▲ First Assembly, Anadarko, c. 1935.

149

▲ *Sunday School staff at Seminole, 1933. Burton McCafferty is at far right. Pastor Berl Dodd is to his left.*

▲ *Pastor H.L. Walker, far right, and members of his congregation during a radio broadcast in Sayre in 1934. Allen Wade is holding the guitar.*

▼ James William and Emma Lucy Reddick at age 90 in 1992.

▲ Clyde and Alpha Henson.

▲ Young people's group at First Assembly, Chickasha, 1932.

151

▼ *A.C. Bates brought his long legs and powerful Pentecostal message to southern Oklahoma.*

▲ *Herbert Buffum directed the music for revivals during the Depression. Among the many songs he wrote was "Lift Me Up Above the Shadows."*

▲ *The David Wilson Savage family has produced four generations of Assemblies of God ministers.*

▼ The first parsonage at Pearl Assembly near Foster, 1938.

◄ Rev. and Mrs. Adam Anderson, first pastors at Pearl Assembly near Foster, 1938.

▲ *The Leonard H. Arnold family, 1936. Brother Arnold was District Secretary-Treasurer from 1958 to 1972.*

▲ *The Leslie Moore family, 1937. Brother Moore later became District Sunday School Director from 1960 to 1972.*

◀ *Forrest and Evelyn Murray and children in front of the church in Colony, 1938.*

▲ *James A. Plant and family in front of Konawa Assembly of God, 1938.*

159

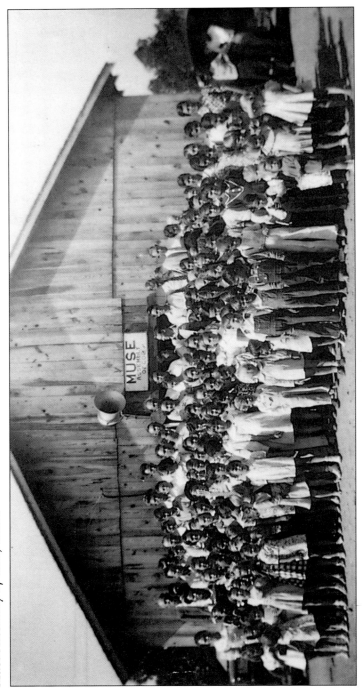

Muse Assembly of God, 1938.

▲ *1939 C.A. convention in Oklahoma City. District Superintendent G.W. Hardcastle is second from left, P.C. Nelson is fourth from left, and DCAP S.J. Scott is second from right.*

165

▲ *Lone Deer Assembly near Konawa, 1938.*

*Pastor Lillie ▶
Foster, Polk Creek
Assembly near
Poteau, 1939.*

▲ *Capitol Hill Tabernacle, Oklahoma City, 1938.*

▲ *First Assembly, McAlester, 1939.*

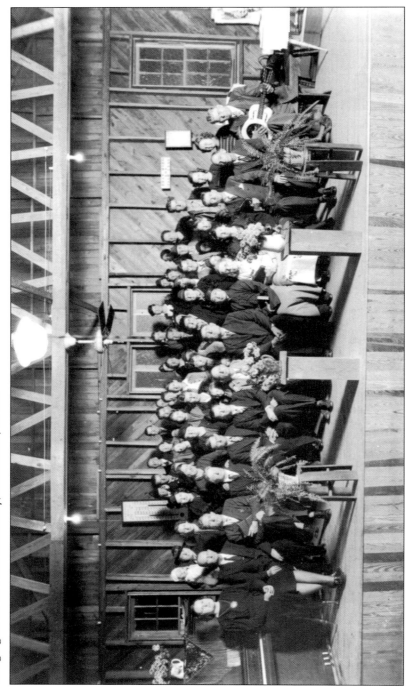

Congregation at First Assembly, McAlester, 1938.

Chapter 16

Southwestern Bible School

Assemblies of God leaders had expressed concern for providing biblical training for potential workers since the beginning of the movement in 1914. However, the need for solid, Bible-based training was tempered somewhat by the fear of "intellectualism", which had infiltrated the great denominations of the nineteenth century. Seminaries in the traditional denominations had become seedbeds of doubt, and some early Assemblies of God leaders feared education would provide carnal pride and that ministers would be less likely to depend upon the operation of the Holy Spirit.[1]

It was 1922 before the General Council could successfully create a Bible school for Assemblies of God college students (although Glad Tidings Temple in San Francisco had established Glad Tidings Bible Institute before that). Oklahomans J.W. Welch, the former general chairman, and S.A. Jamieson, a well-known Bible school educator and a former pastor in Tulsa, promoted the founding of Central Bible Institute (now

Central Bible College) in Springfield, Missouri. Welch later became president of CBI in 1932.[2]

In 1925 the Oklahoma District Council met at the Full Gospel Tabernacle in Tulsa and authorized the opening of a Bible school in Oklahoma. District Superintendent Oscar Jones led a committee of Glenn Millard, C.E. Shields, Dexter Collins, Guy Bewer, William Kitchen and Jonathan Perkins. Perkins was elected president of the school and Glenn Millard was elected secretary.

The District Council suggested that the school be opened by the following September and that it be called the Bell Bible Institute in honor of the first Assemblies of God general chairman, E.N. Bell. J.W. Welch, who had just left the office of general chairman, was asked to be dean of the school.[3]

The idea for a Bible school that would offer high school and college courses came from leaders who feared the influence of secular schools on their children:

"We certainly need a good school where the young people of our ranks can be given a literary training under favorable influence that will save them from the ruinous atmosphere of the modern High School where our young men and women are being taught under the leadership of instructors who do not believe in the Blood or Bible. Surely it is unwise to let the devil have our young people for four years before we put them into Bible School to train them for missionaries and Christian workers."[4]

For various reasons, the Bell Bible Institute never got off the ground; but Oklahoma would have an Assemblies of God Bible school by 1927, through the efforts of a former Baptist preacher named P.C. Nelson.

Peter Christopher Nelson was born in Ellitshoi, Denmark, on January 28, 1868. His father was one of the first Baptists in Denmark. He was jailed and put on a ration of bread and water for his beliefs. The family came to America in 1872 and settled in Avoca, Iowa. Tragedy struck the family often. One of the children drowned. The cave where they lived caught fire and their meager belongings vanished in the smoke. The elder Nelson was injured on the job and died. The early tragedies helped form unusual strength in young P.C. Nelson:

"Early in life the cup of sorrow was pressed to my lips, and that had the effect of sobering me down and making me more sympathetic with those whose life is filled with grief and disappointment and trouble."[5]

God had dealt for the soul of P.C. Nelson even before his father had died:

"Many a night I cried myself to sleep, seeking for salvation, but not knowing how to find it. When I was alone herding cows in the woods...my mind was occupied with thoughts of God and heaven and hell, and how to escape the latter and gain the former."[6]

In the summer after his father's death, Nelson was converted at the home of a nearby farmer where he was staying and working. He ran two miles to tell his mother of his conversion. His family sat at his feet in the living room as he told what the Lord had done for him. It was Nelson's first sermon, "I spoke til I broke down and cried and then fell on my knees and prayed. Then Mother's heart was touched...and how she prayed and cried to God for mercy. It was the first Holy Ghost service I was ever in."[7]

Nelson backslid for nine years but was reclaimed in 1888 and called to preach. However, his first efforts were less than successful. Some of his best friends predicted utter failure if he did not get the preaching bee out of his bonnet.[8]

171

Nelson realized his need for Bible school training and went to college and seminary. (He later would be named one of the seven most educated men in America by Literary Digest. He spoke at least seven languages fluently and could read another 15.)

Upon graduation, he pastored a little country Baptist church in Lucas County, Iowa. By 1900 Nelson was a well-known Baptist evangelist across the Midwest. In 1919 he settled in Detroit, Michigan, as pastor of the Conley Memorial Baptist Church. It was there that divine providence changed his life and his ministry forever.

In October, 1920, while waiting for a street car in Detroit, Nelson was run over by an automobile. His left knee was badly injured and infection set in. He had been in the ministry for 31 years and had seen many people healed, but he lacked faith for his own healing. After Nelson endured five days of severe pain, the Lord told him that He would heal him instantly if he only had the faith:

"The friends prayed and anointed me... While I was praying, the words of Peter to Aeneas (Acts 9:34) were given to me as direct from God, 'Jesus Christ maketh thee whole: arise.' I had not been off my bed for one moment for over five days, but I called for my clothes, dressed myself, and walked downstairs... I walked up and down the stairs frequently, and like the lame man at the Beautiful Gate of the Temple, I felt like 'walking, and leaping, and praising God.'"[9]

Nelson's healing prompted him to seek a deeper walk with God. Within a few weeks he was gloriously baptized in the Holy Spirit and spoke in tongues. His healing testimony appeared in newspapers across the Midwest. He was invited to hold large healing campaigns from Pennsylvania to Texas. He now carried the label as a "Pentecostal":

"With a clearer vision than ever before, I saw the real meaning of the gospel and its power to minister to man in

172

all of his needs... The conviction that I had preached only a partial gospel for 31 years was brought upon my soul, and I resolved to make amends...by preaching a fuller and richer message... I saw now why multitudes came to Jesus and clung to Him... I saw why the multitudes had forsaken the churches, leaving their seats empty while learned men, backed up by great financial resources, robed choirs, pipe organs, and powerful equipment are preaching eloquent sermons to small groups of people in cathedral-like buildings... I realized I had been chasing after people to come to the services instead of offering them a gospel so rich and full that they could not be kept away."[10]

With his new vision, P.C. Nelson preached to major crowds in tents, tabernacles, and open fields. The nation's major newspapers contained full-page stories of thousands saved and healed during his crusades.

In Enid, Oklahoma, in 1925, a thousand conversions were recorded during a tent revival. In early 1926, Nelson returned to Enid, and God moved even more mightily than the year before. More than 2,500 came forward for salvation in a 14-week revival. After two months in the Convention Hall and a skating rink, Nelson built a tabernacle on East Broadway and preached for another six weeks. He left D.A. Griffith in charge of the new church, which was called Enid Gospel Tabernacle (the name was changed to First Assembly of God in 1953). Nelson then preached six weeks in Alva and held a revival at Full Gospel Tabernacle at Fifth and Peoria in Tulsa.[11]

After preaching a series of meetings in California, Nelson felt a need to settle down and establish a Bible school. His friends had been urging him to settle in Enid—a growing city of 30,000—and to use the strategic location to train ministers and missionaries in the Southwest. He arrived in Enid on April 8, 1927:

173

"We received a royal welcome and immediately began special revival meetings in our tabernacle... We were in constant prayer and consultation in regard to the wisdom of establishing a permanent work, and how it could be accomplished... On May 6, our people met and formed this assembly, and voted to affiliate with the General Council."[12]

That same evening, the church voted to buy the Roosevelt Central School on East Cherokee. The $6,000 deal for the property was closed the next day. Nelson had found a permanent location for a new tabernacle and had acquired an old school building for a Bible college.[13]

Nelson's founding of the new school, Southwestern Bible School, was heartily endorsed by Assemblies of God leaders. Central Bible Institute in Springfield, Missouri, was already overcrowded and too far away for many students in the Southwest. Nelson wrote in *The Pentecostal Evangel*:

"We hope to draw students from all over Oklahoma and nearby states... A drive by automobile will impress one with the opportunities and the need for this gospel in this great section. Our people are inspired with the hope of helping to evangelize this great region."[14]

Southwestern Bible School opened on October 23, 1927, with 44 students. Most came from Oklahoma, several from Kansas, two from Arkansas, one from Texas, and one from Michigan. The first faculty was headed by "Daddy Nelson," as P.C. was known. He was both president and teacher. The entire Nelson family had responsibilities in the new school. Nelson's son Merrill taught some subjects, his younger brother Paul worked in the office, and Sister Nelson helped wherever she could.

John E. Jeter was the first principal. Jeter, a Presbyterian minister, had been baptized in the Holy Spirit under Nelson's ministry. After founding and directing a Presbyterian mission school for 10 years, Jeter and his wife Callie left the Presbyterian church and joined the Assemblies of God. Both Brother and Sister Jeter taught at Southwestern, and two of their children, Hugh and Ernestine, enrolled in the first class.

Annie "Mother" Bamford, an Englishwoman and accomplished musician who had traveled with the Nelsons in revivals, was dean of women. D.A. Griffith and Ruth H. Campbell were teachers.[15]

The students and members of the Enid Gospel Tabernacle worked hard to get the old school building in shape. $3,200 was raised to complete the remodeling and purchase a proper heating unit.[16]

Southwestern Bible School offered a three-year course designed to give training in areas of church service. A diploma was presented to students who successfully completed the course.[17] The school was officially dedicated February 6, 1928. General Superintendent W.T. Gaston and Oklahoma District Superintendent James Hutsell presided over the ceremony, which had to be held in the adjacent church because "the crowd was too large for the chapel."[18]

The school grew and prospered. Then the Great Depression hit. The student body had grown to 164 in 1929, but money was tight. Hugh Jeter, later a distinguished missionary and author, was only 15, but remembers how the school operated on a shoestring:

"We went through a lot of financial duress... Every time a new student would come and pay his tuition, we would go down to the dime store to buy another plate, knife, fork, and spoon. The budget was that lean."[19]

Nelson spent much of his time on the road raising money for the school. Students like Hugh Jeter, Klaude Kendrick, T.C. Burkett, and Carl Holleman drove Nelson to campmeetings and churches in the region. Nelson had been prohibited from driving because of several accidents that resulted from him falling asleep at the wheel. Jeter recalls some of the trips:

"He would love to go down the road singing choruses. When we passed a salvage yard, he would say, 'Now Chevy, see where you're going someday?' When we arrived at a fellowship meeting or revival, he would explain the purpose of the Bible school and take an offering. If there was a used bookstore in town, Brother Nelson would buy as many books as he could afford and set up a table at the back of the church to sell the books. He usually made enough money to buy our gasoline and take a few books back to the school library, which he built up tremendously over the years. Brother Nelson cleared a lot of money from his book sales to help run the school."[20]

Many churches during the Depression could not give cash to SBS but contributed in other ways. Often Nelson returned to Enid with a frozen beef and sacks of vegetables and canned goods in the trunk or in a trailer pulled behind his car.[21] Fund-raising efforts allowed the school to keep tuition and room and board costs low. For the first few years, tuition was $25 per year and room and board was $4.50 per week.[22]

In 1932 the Oklahoma District Council formally took over SBS (at Nelson's suggestion) and assumed a $7,500 debt on the Enid property. In 1933 financial problems fueled attempts to merge SBS with other Assemblies of God colleges. However, leaders decided to keep SBS in Enid. The District Board oversaw the operation of the school until it was returned to Nelson in 1940.

By the late Thirties, Southwestern was one of the major Pentecostal Bible colleges in the nation. An alumni brochure in 1938 boasted that the school had eight faculty members, offered commercial courses such as typing and shorthand, and operated the school's own laundry, print shop (Southwestern Press had been established in 1933), and book bindery. It had served more than 3,000 students and had 17,000 volumes in the library, including "one of the rarest collections of Bibles in America." A student could attend the college for just $125 per year.[23]

Students at SBS were expected to be active in many phases of ministerial training. The slogan of the school was "The whole gospel for the whole world." Students visited jails and hospitals. Street services were held in Enid every Saturday night. Students fanned out on weekends to preach and pastor many small assemblies in nearby towns. Some of the students started new Assemblies of God churches in surrounding communities.

The "outstation" assignments provided valuable training for young preachers. Charles Blair, later the highly successful pastor of 6,000-member Calvary Temple in Denver, remembers his "outstation" work:

"One of the group would play the guitar while the rest of us sang four-part harmony gospel songs, then someone would give a short sermon. It didn't matter that our team often outnumbered the congregation. I might be speaking to a couple of farm wives with babies on their laps and one old man whose own snores kept waking him. I knew that to preach was what I wanted to do the rest of my life."[24]

The 1934 yearbook has photos of students at their "outstations": Jimmie Mayo at Garber-Covington, Allen Hurt at Fairview, Hubert Robinson at Eagle Grove schoolhouse near Nash, Ralph Lotridge at Okeene, Mr. and Mrs. Elmer Pickel at Vining, Robert Sellers at Isabella, and Alfred Jensen at Willow Glen, 50 miles north of Enid. Singing groups from the college ministered in surrounding states.

A typical day for students began when the big bell near the boys' dormitory, built in 1929, pealed forth at 5:45 a.m. Another bell at 6:30 signaled a short devotional period. Every student read his or her Bible and bowed in prayer. The 7 o'clock bell announced breakfast. The girls—all with long hair and dressed in clean, white blouses and dark blue skirts (which had to be no more than 11 inches from the floor) marched from their building to the dining room two by two. The boys—dressed in their Sunday best—followed the girls to the tables. Before they were seated, they sang a spirited chorus, a scripture portion was read, and grace was offered.

After breakfast, students spent a half-hour cleaning their living spaces. The last bed was made and the last dish was dried as the chapel bell rang. Again the students marched two by two. In the chapel, the orchestra played a good marching song like "Onward Christian Soldiers." Chapel service was filled with singing, preaching, and praying.

If students were sick, they were anointed and prayed for. Matt Goss, later an Assemblies of God minister, had an appendicitis attack in 1935. After Brother Nelson prayed for him, he was instantly healed.[25] Lillie Bennett of Norman had been poisoned in 1940 and was very ill. After "Daddy Nelson" prayed, she recovered immediately.[26]

Classes began at 8:45 and ended at noon, when students spent 30 minutes in prayer for missionaries. The 1934 yearbook described the rest of the day:

"Intense study during the morning makes the student body unusually hungry by dinner time... The afternoon is divided into a recreation period, study period, and house cleaning period for those in the dormitories... When the housework is finished, some evidences of musical talent come forth. It is not unusual for one to hear a piano, cornet, trombone, or violin all at the same time... After the evening meal, a season of prayer precedes the night study period. A spirit of intercession often prevails over those in the buildings, and strangers passing by can easily tell when they reach the hill where stands Southwestern Bible School."[27]

The Spirit of God hovered over the Enid campus. Even mealtime was not without a move of God. Louise Unruh worked in the dining room:

"I have seen the power of God manifested so many times in that room. Students would come in singing. I have seen them slain in the Spirit and dance in the Spirit. They would forget to eat. There were whole days that students would just pray."[28]

Not all students were fortunate enough to stay in the dormitories. Many young women had to stay with families in the Enid area to work for room and board. They were called "outside girls." Connie Walker was a typical "outside girl" who stayed with a family two miles from town but always made it to school in time for 8:00 chapel.

Winters in Enid could be difficult, but the "outside girls" braved snow-covered roads to get to school. On the coldest days of winter several girls would chip in for a nickel cab ride to school. The "outside girls" were faithful to attend Sunday morning service, stay with friends all Sunday afternoon, attend a long Sunday night service, and walk home in the dark, arriving just in time to get a few hours sleep and start all over again.[29]

SBS was blessed with outstanding faculty members. In addition to the first faculty mentioned above, F.R. Davidson, Cecil Lowry, Celia Swank (Lotridge), Robert L. McCutchen, William Burton McCafferty, Delila Ann Howard (Ahlf), Martha Thompson, M.J. McClellan, Klaude Kendrick (later a famous Pentecostal author and the first president of Evangel College in Springfield, Missouri), Inez Milam, Earl Ayers, Winne Fontenot, J.P. Ireland, Lottie Flowers, Francis Berkihiser, Harold Miles, Austin Unruh, Ethel Kappen, Peter Migliori, and Mr. and Mrs. Finis Jennings Dake taught at various times. The

179

November 23, 1929, edition of *The Pentecostal Evangel* announced that Dake would teach "prophecy, epistles, and other subjects, and Mrs. Dake will take over the department of English and music."[30] Dake taught at SBS until 1931 and authored many books. He is best known for *Dake's Annotated Reference Bible*, published in 1963.

A SCHOOL OF MISSIONS

Southwestern Bible School had a lasting impact on the world by training missionaries. The 1940 yearbook listed 25 graduates who were serving on mission fields. William Edward and Helen Harding Davis, Ted and Estelle Barnett Vassar, Martha McLean, Norman and Helen Armentrout Moffat, and Carl and Margaret Holleman were all in India. Katie Wise and Elizabeth Galley were in China. Hugh, Ernestine, and Louise Jeter, Agnes Sloan, and Jane Collins were in South America. Berta Vaughn and Charles Hirschy were in Alaska. Murray and Marjorie Ball Brown and J.W. Tucker were in Africa; Edith Sumrall Edwards was in Panama; and Joseph Goss was in Canada. Jennie and Annie Kulka were missionaries to Czechoslovakia.

Missions was a major emphasis at SBS. Every student belonged to one of six different prayer groups that met on Friday afternoons to intercede for their particular area of the world. The 1931 yearbook described "missionary day" at Southwestern:

"Eternity alone can ever reveal all the good that has been done by the floods of tears that have been shed, the agonizing prayers that have battered their way through the resisting powers of the Evil One to Heaven's gate, and to the throne of God. How many have heard that still small voice of God that speaks so distinctly saying, 'Go and tell them. I suffered for them too.'"[31]

Louise Jeter Walker (class of '33) wrote a poem in the 1936 yearbook:

The Heathen Cry

How long, O Lord? How long? How long?
The cry is still the same:
How long in darkness must we wait?
How long without Thy name?

How long, O Lord? We've waited now
For nineteen hundred years,
All crushed with sorrow, bowed with grief,
And blinded with our tears.

How long, O Lord? The night is dark,
No ray of hope have we;
Blind lead the blind, we stumble, fall,
Because we cannot see.

How long, O Lord? We perish now;
Thy heralds, where are they?
Then must we die—no God—no hope?
Is there no other way?

How long, O Lord? How long? How long?
The cry is still the same:
How long in darkness must we wait?
How long without Thy name?[32]

Students kept coming to SBS during the Thirties. Attendance reached a high of 297 in 1935.[33] But the high cost of running a small Bible school finally caught up with P.C. Nelson in 1941. Financial problems forced Southwestern to merge with Shield of Faith, a Bible school at Amarillo, Texas, and Southern Bible College in Houston, Texas, to form what is now Southwestern Assemblies of God College in Waxahachie, Texas.[34]

ENID GOSPEL TABERNACLE

Southwestern Bible School was closely connected with Enid Gospel Tabernacle. The school used the church for chapel services and for special missionary services. The church orchestra was made up primarily of SBS students. In the beginning, P.C. Nelson pastored the church while serving as president of the college. Nelson was one of the best-known Assemblies of God ministers of his day. He traveled from coast to coast. No one knew when he ever slept or rested from his travels. He often took a nap on the platform during a service. Legend has it that he once was asleep when called upon to pray just *before* the featured speaker was introduced; Brother Nelson went to the microphone and *dismissed* the service![35]

Enid Gospel Tabernacle became known nationally for its healing ministry. Crutches and braces hung from the walls. Nelson preached powerful sermons based upon simple ideas. His audience would sit spellbound by his anointed presentation. No one dared leave a service early for fear of missing a miracle healing or a supernatural altar service.

P.C. Nelson's influence as pastor of Enid Gospel Tabernacle continued long after his death in 1942. Ron McCaslin, who pastored the church in the early 1980's, says:

"A half-century later, I lived in the shadow of P.C. Nelson as pastor of the great church he started. Having myself been trained at Southwestern Assemblies of God College, I now sensed what a truly great work for God Nelson did in founding both the Enid Gospel Tabernacle and Southwestern."[36]

P.C. Nelson's legacy lives on in the 1990's. Assemblies of God colleges still use his book, *Bible Doctrines*, as a textbook on the fundamental truths of the Assemblies of God. Assemblies of God ministers in America must pass a test on the contents of *Bible Doctrines* before receiving credentials. Until his death, "Daddy Nelson" was considered the most prestigious theologian in the Assemblies of God movement. He played an important role in the exciting story of the Oklahoma Assemblies of God.

HEAR STANLEY COMSTOCK
Nationally Known Evangelist
Speaking Nightly 7:30 at
Enid Gospel Tabernacle
312 E. Cherokee Ave.

Sunday,— "Hell, What and Where is It?"

Monday,— "Signs of a Coming World War"

Tuesday,— "EVOLUTION, From Whence came Man, God or Gorilla?" Rev. Comstock will present six witnesses, three will testify that man is the creation of God and three will declare he is the product of Evolution.

Wednesday,— "Cultism, or Roads to Hell"

Thursday,—"The Carnival of Death"

Friday,—"Divine Healing, Is it for Us Today?" __

Capacity crowds have filled Churches and Auditoriums in many sections of the United States and Canada to hear his soul-stirring sermons.

ALL WELCOME   **FREE FREE**   P. C. Nelson, Pastor

▲ *Revival poster for Stanley Comstock at Enid Gospel Tabernacle.*

▲ *The R.H. Hoyer family. Hoyer pastored Enid Gospel Tabernacle in the 1930's and served as District Secretary-Treasurer from 1932 to 1939.*

▲ *Enid Gospel Tabernacle, 1940.*

*Bynum and Irene ▶
Green, pastors of Enid
Gospel Tabernacle, 1940.*

Chapter 17

War Brings More Hard Times

World War II brought the Assemblies of God a tidal wave of seemingly insurmountable difficulties due to shrinking congregations and financial problems in local churches.

On December 7, 1941, U.S. Grant was the 31-year-old pastor of First Assembly of God in Bartlesville. War was raging overseas. The Grant family gathered around the Sunday dinner table and listened to the radio. Grant remembers:

"The news was disturbing to us... As we ate, the program was interrupted with a bulletin stating that the Japanese had made a surprise attack on our installations at Pearl Harbor."[1]

America was at war, and Assemblies of God families had to make a decision: fight for their country or refuse to serve on religious grounds. During World War I, the Assemblies of God had taken an official pacifist stand. The church was opposed to war and the killing associated with war. Many

Assemblies of God laymen took advantage of the "conscientious objector" status and served in special camps in non-combat roles in World War I. However, the reaction of Assemblies of God believers to World War II was totally different.[2]

The 1939 General Council had authorized the general superintendent to send a telegram to President Franklin D. Roosevelt supporting America's efforts to stay neutral. The attack on Pearl Harbor drastically changed the minds of Assemblies of God people across the country. By 1942 *The Pentecostal Evangel* featured stories on chaplains in the war. Letters to the editor were overwhelmingly in favor of America's attempt to stop the ravages of Hitler, Mussolini, and the Japanese. Only a few Assemblies of God laymen asked for "conscientious objector" status in World War II. By 1944 more than 50,000 Assemblies of God men and women were serving in the armed services.[3] The General Council never officially endorsed the war, but completely supported the service of its members. Thousands of Oklahoma Assemblies of God men and women served courageously and honorably in both combat and non-combat roles.

In Oklahoma, district officials were concerned about the effects of war. District Superintendent G.W. Hardcastle told the 1943 District Council in Tulsa: "The present war... certainly is not an asset to Christianity and especially the youth of our churches. As the War Department steps in to call for the best of our young manhood and at times our womanhood, there is created a condition most serious."[4] At the 1944 District Council, Superintendent F.C. Cornell called the war "a great tragedy" to the youth of Oklahoma. However, Cornell reported that Oklahoma soldiers were finding many opportunities to witness:

"From our ranks many of the finest Christian characters in the world have been called into the service, and from these we are hearing that Christ's name is being highly exalted and they are proving the Lord every day, that He is able to keep from the world and the devil. Many who have left very timid, have turned into brave Christian warriors and have become soul winners."[5]

The Oklahoma District responded to the call from the Assemblies of God headquarters in Springfield in 1944 for financial support of the Servicemen's Department. At the October District Council, delegates passed a resolution recommending that Oklahoma churches send regular offerings to headquarters to "meet the urgent need of caring for the spiritual life of our own men and the tremendous opportunity of reaching others."[6]

HARRY MYERS

Muskogee native Harry Myers played a significant role in the Assemblies of God program to minister to American servicemen during the war. In 1944 Myers left his job as song leader and youth leader at Faith Tabernacle in Tulsa to promote Christian Service Centers. The centers were established in major cities in the nation to provide a place of fellowship and worship for Christian soldiers. Myers directed the effort from his post in the Home Missions Department in Springfield.

A DECLINE IN CHURCHES

World War II squelched the growth of Assemblies of God churches in Oklahoma. There had been an increase in the number of churches every year since 1914. Two months before Pearl Harbor there were 444 officially recognized congregations in the state.[7] Thirty-three new churches had been added just the year before. But within one year, the total number of churches had shrunk to 359, a loss of 85 congregations.[8] The war had taken many men and women, and their financial support, from local congregations. Not only were soldiers off to war but thousands left the state to work in defense plants from Kansas to California. Dozens of churches were struggling just to keep their doors open.

The Oklahoma Home Missions Committee deplored the war and its effects in its report to the 1943 District Council:

"The Committee suggests that members of our congregations who have relocated should kindly and faithfully return a portion of tithes to their home churches... In view of the exodus of many people from small towns and rural communities, due to present war conditions, resulting in many of our pastors in such areas being left with insufficient income and depleted congregations: we recommend that such pastors...be granted additional financial support from the Home Missions Fund."[9]

The 1943 District Council authorized the Executive Board and the sectional presbyters to grant financial assistance to struggling congregations unable to pay for minor repairs to existing church buildings.[10]

The war often dominated the pages of the *Assemblies of God News*, the monthly Oklahoma District newsletter. In June, 1945, Superintendent F.C. Cornell sadly reported the death of Carbondale Assembly's C.A. leader, Russell Ford, in Italy; the death of the son of Pastor Henry Porter; and the report of J.B. McDonough's son "missing in action" in the South Pacific. Cornell called Oklahomans to "pray for these men and their families."[11] The war even caused cancellation of the annual Christ's Ambassadors convention in Ponca City in 1945.[12]

Rationing and shortages during World War II were hard on laymen and pastors alike. Gasoline was in short supply for several days each month. Pastors who drove long distances had to borrow gasoline from neighbors to get to church. Cecil and Verena Pearcy were trying to farm and pastor the church at Cherokee—21 miles from their farm. When the gas tank was about empty, they simply prayed. God blessed their faithfulness and somehow kept the old car running. Gasoline, however, was not their only problem. When the Pearcys moved to pastor a country church six miles from Mulhall, they found a church and parsonage with no electricity and no running water. Church services were held using gas lanterns and kerosene lamps. Water had to be hauled from a neighbor's house.[13]

J. Floyd Schaeffer, longtime pastor at Duncan, looks back at 1941 as "not our best year by any means." Schaeffer didn't even own a suit when he "tried out" for his first pastorate, and had to borrow his parents' car to get to the church:

"Our parents thought we would starve in this pastorate. We did without a lot of things we needed, but God saw us through. We prayed in food time and again. We know what it is to try to live on $2 to $4 a week... I worked for $1 a day to help support my family. We lived in two small Sunday School rooms while pastoring."[14]

Building materials were hard to buy during the war. Rufus Strange completed a new building for First Assembly in Norman by "much prayer and hard work." Work on the building was often delayed for weeks while waiting for God to send money or materials or during squabbles over the price of materials with the Office of Price Administration, a federal government agency set up to control prices during the war.[15]

In Edmond, H.L. Walker built the first permanent home for First Assembly (now Cathedral of the Hills) in 1943. He remembers how tough the times were:

"When the church ran out of money, we held a prayer meeting and God answered. Materials were so short that our men were forced to pull nails from used lumber and straighten them out for reuse. The ladies of the church—including my sister Connie—baked and delivered pies to raise funds. The men went directly from their jobs to the property to work on the building."[16]

Pioneer pastors in the 1940's lived in absolute poverty at many churches. Leslie Moore and his family moved to the Riverside Church on the corner of a cornfield seven miles north of Seminole. They stuffed rags around the windows and doors of the back room of the dilapidated old church building to keep from freezing to death. God told Brother Moore to build a new church and consolidate three struggling Assemblies of God congregations in the area. Members balked, but Brother Moore began digging the footing for the new church by himself. His willingness to "do it himself" softened the hearts of his opponents. Soon the people showed up with their tools and their offerings, and the Lord turned the three churches into one.[17]

The Moores found another sagging church building when God called them to Ardmore in 1949. It looked like a "sway-back old horse." God provided money and materials and a new church was constructed. The Moores led Lighthouse Assembly in Ardmore from 59 to 500 in attendance.[18]

Local churches normally had no facilities to house evangelists. Often the parsonage was so small that it strained to hold just the pastor's family—much less an evangelist. Viaretta Myers Johnson, called to preach at the age of 16, held her first revival at the Tabernacle church east of Chickasha in the 1940's. She slept on the floor in a Sunday School room with only a screen door separating her "quarters" and the sanctuary.[19]

NEW CHURCHES

Despite the war and hard times, many new Assemblies of God churches were set in order in the 1940's, replacing the small town and community churches that had closed. The decade began with 411 churches and ended with 414, a net gain of three.

First Assembly in Vinita was the first church set in order in the decade—January 1, 1940. It resulted from a tent revival held on a lot next to the jail three years earlier. After meeting in the tent and believers' homes, the people, under the leadership of Pastor J. Raymond Harris, hauled sandstone from coal pits in nearby Lightning Creek and built a permanent structure with "slat-type benches and a sawdust floor."[20]

E.B. Wells purchased two lots on South Miami Street in Okmulgee for $25 in 1940. He bought an old grocery store building and had it moved to the property. People from all over Okmulgee helped Wells remodel the building, and East Side Assembly was born. Thirteen persons attended the first service on September 13, 1940. In less than three months, attendance jumped to more than 150. By 1943 the church outgrew the old store building and built a new sanctuary. Other pastors of East Side Assembly include C.R. Franklin, R.C. Coffey, George Patterson, and Fay R. French.[21]

Charles Decker pioneered the Assembly of God at Meeker. Home prayer meetings began in 1941 and a store building was rented for services the next year. In 1943 a one-room church building from a nearby town was purchased. It served as an adequate facility until it was destroyed by a tornado in May, 1949. The church members moved quickly to build a new building by the fall of 1949.[22]

The Mingo Assembly of God began in a meeting with George B. Cason in a brush arbor in the spring of 1944. While Robert Goggin was pastor of the church, the old Springdale Assembly building was purchased, torn down, moved to Mingo, and rebuilt.[23]

Reed George held a revival in an old saloon in Coyle in April, 1946. The revival resulted in a new church that met in the old Goble schoolhouse east of Coyle. Orville Mills was the first pastor. By 1947 the church had bought an old Lutheran church building and moved it to a new location on North Broad Street in Coyle. The Coyle Assembly of God was set in order October 30, 1947. Pastors of the church include Bob French, Cleo Johnson, W.C. Vernon, Ray Cook, R.L. Stuart, and Jimmy Capps.

In 1947 a devastating tornado hit Woodward. It killed 112 people and reduced much of the city to rubble—including the First Assembly of God church and parsonage. Ernest A. Willeford was the pastor when the tornado hit during a revival service on the night of April 9:

"Due to the stormy weather, the crowd for the D.L. Brankel meeting was small. Brankel had just taken charge of the service when the 'twister' came. First it extinguished all the lights; then it swept the building away, leaving the little group of believers huddled in prayer on the spot where the altar had been. Everyone in the building was injured to some extent but all miraculously escaped death. One of the deacons who had been present in the service left the church by the side door and was never seen alive again. Several other church members who were absent died in the storm, but those assembled in the church were preserved by the power of God."[24]

In 1949 Elloween Penuel and Evie Anthony founded what became Northwest Assembly of God in Ardmore. They called the new church Pleasant Hill Assembly of God. Sister Penuel was the first pastor. Under the leadership of Neal Sims, the church was moved into Ardmore and renamed in 1965.[25]

First Assembly in Prague officially became an Assemblies of God church in October, 1949, even though a C.A. group and Women's Missionary Council had been formed three years earlier by Pastor Neal Sims. The Oklahoma District bought four lots and provided a tent for services until a permanent structure could be built. District C.A. President L.B. Keener held the first revival for the church.[26]

A complete list of churches set in order in the 1940's appears in the appendix.

Chapter 18

Progress in the Forties

The most exciting event at a District Council in the 1940's was the miraculous healing of a young U.S. Army private. It occurred at the District Council in Seminole in 1942.

James P. Sturgeon, of Eagle City, Oklahoma, had cracked his skull in a fall in the Army. After he suffered several strokes, his entire right side was paralyzed. His eyesight was deteriorating daily. He walked with a crutch.

Two thousand people jammed the city auditorium in Seminole on October 7, 1942, as Private Sturgeon was carried to the platform for prayer. Two preachers laid their hands on him:

"As they prayed, the young man's right hand, which had been badly drawn, straightened out; then he raised his whole right arm, which had been paralyzed. Like a flash he jumped up from his chair and began leaping for joy and dancing all over the platform. He was completely healed. He needed a crutch no longer."[1]

People stood to their feet and shouted and praised the Lord for 20 minutes. Gordon Speed was a young pastor attending the District Council. He recalls the "Hallelujah" time:

"I was late arriving at the service and had to sit in the balcony. After Sturgeon was healed, I looked out over the audience and saw what looked like a haze or cloud or mist. It must have been the glory of God settling down over the people. It was the first and last time in my life I ever saw anything like that. The miracle was headlined in the local paper the next day. The whole town was stirred."[2]

The Sturgeon healing received nationwide attention when the story was printed in the *C.A. Herald* in February, 1943. Sturgeon graduated from Southwestern Assemblies of God College in 1950. He and his wife Violet later ministered in Cuba and Germany.

The Forties were a decade of harvest. Oklahoma Assemblies of God churches reported 6,734 conversions in the 12 months ending September 1, 1940. During the same period 1,688 were filled with the Holy Spirit and 1,065 were baptized in water. 631 new church members were reported that year.

More than 6,000 conversions were reported in 1941 and another 2,257 were filled with the Holy Spirit.[3] Those numbers compare with 8,000 conversions and 3,000 filled with the Holy Spirit in 1946.[4]

The number of Assemblies of God ministers and licensed Christian workers in Oklahoma grew by 250 in the 1940's. On September 1, 1940, the District reported 273 ordained ministers, 354 licensed ministers, 45 exhorters (a special classification for applicants not meeting the criteria to be licensed or ordained), and 45 persons on the "extra" list, for a total of 714. By September 1, 1949, there were 408 ordained ministers, 431 licensed ministers, 77 exhorters, and 28 on the "extra" list, for a total of 964.[5]

Revival fires continued to burn across Oklahoma. Each month the *Assemblies of God News* carried "field reports" from all corners of the state. The June, 1945, edition reported:

"U.S. Grant reports from Bartlesville that five were saved. Eight saved in a meeting with S.B. Douglass at North Utica in Tulsa. Estelle Moore, in a meeting at Quapaw, saw three saved and two filled. Ten saved in a Broken Bow meeting with F.E. Dollar of Edmond. Pastor Charles Taylor reported seven saved and two filled in services with Jimmie Justus. Pastor R.C. Clay in Pickens had five saved and one filled in a revival with Lillie Gorden. Wesley Goodwin saw ten saved and two filled in a Wellston revival. Pastor Olen Craig at Oil Field Assembly at Garber-Covington reported ten saved in a meeting with A.K. Davis. Evangelist L.B. Keener had three saved in Frederick."[6]

District C.A. (Christ's Ambassadors) President Clifford Burkett described one revival in 1946:

"The local people had maintained a 24-hour prayer chain for a week before the meeting... They were in the temple continually praying and blessing the Lord, when suddenly there came a sound from heaven...and fell on all of them. Brother, it fell on us. Pentecostal fire fell round us and on us. Several times the power of God fell in such waves that I did not preach."[7]

Homer Boyd began an annual section-wide campmeeting in Poteau in the late 1940's. A tent was erected in the Poteau city park for ten days each summer. Churches from the area manned the hamburger stand that served the hundreds that attended the services. In 1993 the annual Poteau campmeeting continued, making it the longest continuous annual event of its kind in the state.[8]

There are thousands of stories of conversions in the Forties. One Sunday night a young football player caught a ride into town to attend First Assembly in Spiro. Armon Newburn, now the Oklahoma District superintendent and national executive presbyter, had been invited to church by a friend:

"I walked in and for some reason did not sit down on the back row. I sat near the front, and the preacher preached about the soon coming of the Lord. The Spirit really got hold of me. I knew that I wasn't ready to go. I was scared to death. But someone came back and realized that God was dealing with me and led me to the altar. They stayed with me until the burden of sin rolled away."[9]

Not all revivals started in a grand fashion. S.J. and Leenetta Scott went to Coalgate to plant a new church. They found a vacant building and cleaned it up. Everything was set for opening on Sunday night—but no one came. Undaunted, they printed handbills and Sister Scott drew chalk drawings and played her accordion on street corners, and Brother Scott preached. Three people showed up the next night, and within a week the building was full—proof again that God is faithful.[10]

CHANGES IN LEADERSHIP

The twentieth century Pentecostal movement was now 40 years old. Many of the original leaders were dead or retired. The next generation of Oklahoma Assemblies of God churches was led by men like F.C. Cornell of Tulsa who was elected district superintendent in 1943. Cornell replaced G.W. Hardcastle who did not seek reelection because of his desire to pastor Full Gospel Tabernacle in Tulsa.[11]

Cornell, who would serve until 1947, was a powerful preacher who emphasized the commandment for believers to be filled with the Holy Spirit:

"We cannot ignore it, and we must obey it to be in the will of the Lord. The Church of the last days is to be a Holy Ghost baptized church. If she is not, then she is dead and cold and formal. It is up to the ministers to preach the Holy Ghost baptism... If we are to survive this age, we must have the Holy Ghost in our lives. If our folks are to survive this age, they must have it, too."[12]

One of the problems of a district superintendent in a spacious state like Oklahoma is the amount of time consumed by travel. In January, 1947, Cornell described a typical week:

"Monday I stopped and visited with Brother Rumbaugh at Henryetta...Tuesday night I conducted two business meetings after spending the day in the office. The next two days were spent in the office with the exception of a short trip to Purcell to try to find a location for the new church planned by the Central Section Christ's Ambassadors group... Most of Friday was spent in the office and then another business meeting at Anadarko with Brother Moore and his fine people. On Saturday I drove to Miami and secured a room in the Main Hotel, out of which I worked the following week. On Sunday morning I ministered for Brother Alexander at Commerce, and at Welch in the evening service where Brother Austin Wilkerson is the pastor. This church was set in order with 16 charter members."[13]

Cornell was greatly respected by the preachers in the Oklahoma District. A.K. and Vadie Davis were young pastors—completely dependent upon God and the leadership of Cornell. Brother Davis remembers how strong Cornell's influence was:

"He would come to our house week after week to tell us what was going on in the District. If he hadn't taken us under his wing, I don't know where we would have been. When he got through with us, we knew exactly what he wanted us to do, and that was to put all things in the hand of God. When things upset us, he said, 'Go on your knees and tell it to God, and God will tell you what to do.' That meant more to me than anything else. After his counsel, a peace was always present in our hearts."[14]

Brother and Sister Davis later founded First Assembly in Bethany and pastored the church for 21 years.

Cornell was succeeded by V.H. Ray as district superintendent in 1947. Berl Dodd served as assistant district superintendent from 1939 to 1943, followed by G.W. Hardcastle, 1943-1946, and Roy L. Steger, 1946-1953. Wallace S. Bragg was replaced as district secretary-treasurer in 1942 by V.H. Ray. When Ray was elected district superintendent in 1947, Robert E. Goggin was elected secretary-treasurer.

William C. Shackelford, Harvey Mitchell, S.J. Scott, Clifford Burkett, L.B. Keener, and Carl McCoy all served stints as district C.A. president in the 1940's.

The office of district Sunday School superintendent was combined with that of the district C.A. president from 1936 to 1944. After the division of the two jobs, J.E. Wilson served in the Sunday School post in 1944-1945. In 1945 Paul Copeland, the pastor at First Assembly in Okmulgee, was elected district Sunday School superintendent. He served until he resigned in 1948 to become the national Sunday School director for the entire movement. W.M. Rumbaugh was elected district Sunday School superintendent in his place.

W.L. Miles was elected to a newly created position of home missions secretary in 1945. He served until June, 1946, when he resigned, saying, "Someone else might be able to get more accomplished than I have." The position was never again filled.[15]

Organizationally, the Oklahoma District changed its alignment of sections in 1940. The state previously had been divided into six sections: Northeast, Southeast, North Central, South Central, Northwest, and Southwest. At the 1940 District Council the number of sections was expanded to nine, adding East Central, Central, and Panhandle Sections. In 1948 the number of sections rose to its present 12 and were numbered one through 12.[16]

On the national level, Oklahomans continued to play major roles. Harry Myers, who was serving as assistant pastor under Thomas Zimmerman at Central Assembly in Springfield, was named national C.A. secretary in 1947. Bert Webb, saved in the great Wellston revival of 1922-24, began 20 years of service as assistant general superintendent in 1949. He had served from 1939-1943 as pastor of the "mother church," Central Assembly in Springfield. From 1943-1949, Webb had been superintendent of the Southern Missouri District. During his term as assistant general superintendent, Webb was executive director, at various times, of the Sunday School, Christ's Ambassadors, Evangelism, Radio, Personnel, and Publications Departments at the Assemblies of God headquarters. Bert Webb clearly exerted tremendous influence and direction on the entire Pentecostal movement in the 1950's and 1960's. He was active in the National Association of Evangelicals and headed the National Sunday School Association, whose members came from 40 denominations.[17]

COUNCIL BUSINESS

My pastor once said that God is a God of "amazing variety." Likewise, Oklahoma District Councils have had amazing variety. A review of the minutes from the District Councils in the 1940's brings this out.

In 1940 Oklahomans were being asked to repeal the state law prohibiting the manufacture and sale of liquor in the state. Delegates to the District Council unanimously approved a resolution "voicing strong opposition" to the proposed repeal bill. The resolution read, in part:

"Since the Assemblies of God stand for righteousness and holiness, in state and nation as well as in the individual; and since we believe that the Word of God is plain in its teaching against intemperance, drunkenness, and defilement of the body which is the 'temple of the Holy Ghost', and that it is wrong to put temptation in another's way...we just say no."[18]

Also in 1940 some 800 persons present at the Wednesday night service during District Council witnessed a dedication ceremony for nine infants and children. It would be interesting to know how those nine turned out since they were dedicated by larger-than-life Assemblies of God leaders P.C. Nelson, Berl Dodd, David Burris (district superintendent in Arkansas), and "Uncle Jake" Miller.[19]

The chief problem discussed at the 1941 Council was the transfer of lay members from one congregation to another. The Oklahoma Assemblies of God Constitution and By-Laws contained provisions allowing members to receive a letter of transfer if they were in good standing. The minutes from the meeting read:

"We do recognize that lay members have individual rights that no church or pastor can deny them. And if some lay members cannot work in one church, we must endeavor, if possible, to save their souls, that they might find a workable condition and be valuable in some other church. Therefore, no pastor shall have the right to count it a breach of ministerial fellowship if a neighboring pastor shall receive into his congregation a lay member who has not found a happy condition existing in another church, unless such member is found unworthy of membership in any Assembly of God."[20]

In 1946, offices for district officials were added to the front of the tabernacle at the district campgrounds on North Kelley in Oklahoma City. That same year, a kids' tabernacle was constructed for children's services during campmeetings and councils.[21] However, the 1947 Council voted to sell the campground if "we can get back what we put into it." A price of $75,000 was never met by prospective buyers. Records indicate that no more than $25,000 was ever offered for the property, so officials decided to improve the buildings.[22]

In 1948 the Shawnee Chamber of Commerce proposed that the district headquarters be moved to Shawnee. At the October District Council in Shawnee, delegates thanked Shawnee but rejected the idea and voted to enlarge office space and develop the present campgrounds site in Oklahoma City.[23] The 1948 District Council was the last to be held outside Oklahoma City. Delegates in 1949 voted to permanently hold all future District Councils at the tabernacle on the Oklahoma City campgrounds.[24]

The 1946 Council suggested to the state school board that a Bible course, providing for 45 minutes of daily Bible teaching, be instituted in the public schools. No one at headquarters ever heard back from the state school board regarding that suggestion.[25]

The 1947 minutes reported "another fine camp meeting" with 50 filled with the Holy Ghost. Superintendent Cornell also announced a new caretaker at the campgrounds. "Cleo Johnson is doing a fine job. He will be happy to show you around any time... Some new cabins have been built and other improvements have been made."[26]

The outward appearance of women, specifically "long hair," was the subject of discussion at Councils in 1947 and 1949. Brother Cornell told the 1947 meeting:

"The spiritual tide of the District is fairly good although there is a tendency toward compromise with some. Bobbed hair, rouge, and lipstick are still the victors over some of the lady folk, until they look so cheap that no one cares to lift them up as spiritual examples. Many of our men are also selling their ministry for idleness and worldly pleasures in excess, and then wonder why they are not anointed and their churches are cold."[27]

The first resolution taken up at the 1949 Council concerned "bobbed hair":

"Whereas, we have on our application blanks for license a question concerning bobbed hair, and ladies on their word of honor say they will let their hair grow and, Whereas, we have a recommendation on worldliness in our Minutes and both of these requirements are Biblical and should be honored as God's Word and, Whereas, many of our Ministers' wives have short hair and capped sleeves, Therefore, be it resolved that these rules be enforced."[28]

"After considerable discussion" the delegates voted to table the motion. It was never voted on.[29]

USING THE MEDIA

In the 1940's, Assemblies of God churches began heavily using radio and newspapers to carry their message to the masses. In January, 1946, "Sermons in Song" with General Superintendent E.S. Williams as speaker, aired on stations across the country. Oklahoman Harry Myers was the first soloist on the program. By 1950 the format changed, and the weekly program from Springfield became known as "Revivaltime."[30]

In Oklahoma, First Assembly in Okmulgee had climbed past the 1,300 mark of broadcasts over the local radio station by November, 1945. The program was called the "Sunshine Hour."[31] In 1946 Pastor James C. Dodd of Broken Arrow Assembly began a daily program, "Tidings of Peace", on KAKC in Tulsa. The program originated from Dodd's living room on weekdays and from the church auditorium on Sundays. Brother Dodd was preacher, producer, and engineer. Sister Dodd was the featured gospel singer.[32] And in Ponca City, Kenneth and Nadine Roork had a radio program on WBBZ as early as 1941. The program was simply called, "Kenneth and Nadine."[33]

Many of our Oklahoma churches began publishing newspapers or bulletins. In 1943 First Assembly of Okmulgee launched a monthly paper called the *Assembly of God Review*. Broken Arrow Assembly called its monthly publication *Assembly Gleanings*.[34]

District Superintendent G.W. Hardcastle set the tone for a renewed emphasis on Sunday School in his annual report to the District Council in October, 1940:

"Sunday School is the base and foundation for a permanent church structure in the human hearts, and from our Sunday School come the ones who are to take the lead in developing and maintaining the church of tomorrow should Jesus tarry... We are happy to report that in many of our churches greater interest is being shown in the preparations for bigger and better Sunday Schools."[35]

Longtime Pastor Harold Baker, who began preaching in 1946, believes that Sunday School was—and is—as important for adults as it is for children. Baker says if you build a strong Sunday School, you build a strong church. Baker served more than 25 years as a sectional Sunday School representative.

The official 1940 Sunday School report showed 573 Sunday Schools with an enrollment of 51,000 served by 2,865 teachers. (There were more Sunday Schools than officially recognized churches. Often a local group would call itself an Assemblies of God Sunday School and use denominational literature even though an Assemblies of God church had not been set in order.)[36]

Oklahoma actually led the nation in opening new Sunday Schools in the first quarter of 1940 with 47 new schools.[37]

By District Council time in October, 1941, the District Sunday School Department reported an enrollment of 53,500 in 641 Sunday Schools with 3,060 teachers. Teacher training courses were introduced, and churches were encouraged to begin vacation Bible schools in the summers.[38]

The first statewide Sunday School convention was held in January, 1946, at Faith Tabernacle in Oklahoma City. Nearly 500 attended to hear national Sunday School Director William E. Kirschke speak. District Sunday School Superintendent Paul Copeland reported that Sunday School attendance had decreased during the war but "with the war coming to a close, our schools generally have begun to build numerically, and there has been spiritual and organizational development due to the increased vision in Sunday School work by our pastors, evangelists, and other Christian workers."[39] By 1946, there were 45,888 believers enrolled in 380 affiliated Sunday Schools. The average enrollment was 95.6 and the average weekly offering was $5.20.[40]

In 1946-47, the top 10 Sunday Schools in Oklahoma were:

1. Full Gospel Tabernacle (Fifth and Peoria), Tulsa—565
2. North Utica Assembly, Tulsa—363
3. Bartlesville Assembly—295
4. Southside Faith Tabernacle, Oklahoma City—282
5. Sand Springs Assembly—280
6. Faith Tabernacle, Oklahoma City—275
7. First Assembly, Shawnee—261
8. Faith Tabernacle, Tulsa—238

9. Miami Assembly—237
10. First Assembly, Okmulgee—230[41]

Even though Sunday Schools were in hundreds of communities, District Superintendent F.C. Cornell noted in 1947 that Assemblies of God Sunday Schools were in only 60 percent of the towns and that there were no Assemblies of God churches in 13 county seats.[42]

C.A.'S ON THE MOVE

In 1941 the General Council of the Assemblies of God authorized the formation of a national Christ's Ambassadors Department in Springfield. Oklahoma had been among the most active districts in C.A.'s, having begun an official youth program in 1925. The importance of local C.A. groups was expressed in the 1940 District Council report of District Superintendent G.W. Hardcastle:

"I am convinced more than ever of the need for a vital connection between our young people and adults, that spiritual life might be a mutual affair between them... There have been some marked changes in world conditions since we last met,...and we are now at a greater loss to determine the future of our young people than ever before in the history of our churches; therefore, I again appeal to you for prayerful consideration in behalf of our C.A. work."[43]

Forty new C.A. groups were formed in Oklahoma in 1940 and 130 C.A. rallies were held. Oklahoma City Mayor Robert Hefner addressed the state C.A. Convention in June of that year at Faith Tabernacle. 287 cars, trucks, and floats took part in a parade through downtown Oklahoma City during the convention.[44]

District officials were sensitive to the effects of war on the youth of the movement. Superintendent Hardcastle said in 1941:

"We have nothing to fear about the future developments in our district regarding our youth. Some of the most spiritual services I have had the privilege of attending have been conducted by and in the interest of our young people... With us, our young people face the hour of crisis... Let us deal tenderly and wisely with our policies concerning the welfare of our youth."[45]

District C.A. President S.J. Scott called the 1943 C.A. Convention "the greatest ever held." More than 2,000 C.A.'s came from all over the state "in spite of gasoline rationing." Oklahoma Governor Robert S. Kerr gave the welcoming address. Governor Kerr told the C.A.'s: "You honor the nation with your Christian patriotism, courage, devotion, and faith."[46] Nearly a hundred C.A.'s greeted national C.A. Secretary Ralph Harris, and *C.A. Herald* Editor Robert Cunningham, singing "We are Christ's Ambassadors" as they stepped from the train. The opening night service was broadcast on 50,000 watt KOMA radio, whose signal covered much of the western United States. There was such a powerful move of the Holy Spirit during the opening service that one young girl received the baptism while the offering was being taken.[47]

The 1949 state C.A. Convention was designated "Homecoming" to honor former district C.A. presidents. Bert Webb, the state's first C.A. president, was joined by W.C. Shackelford, Glenn Millard, S.J. Scott, Harvey O. Mitchell, and Clifford Burkett as featured speakers during the convention. The minutes of the meeting indicate that former presidents Wallace Bragg, Earl Davis, and Albert Ogle were unable to attend.[48]

First Assembly, Chandler, 1940. Pastor Leonard Belknap is at left.

James and ▶
Francine Dodd,
1939.

▲ *Rev. and Mrs. U.S. Grant.*

226

◀ *Robert, Marie, and Bobby Goggin, 1947, the year that Robert Goggin began a 34-year career as an Oklahoma District official.*

▲ *A.K. Davis plays the steel guitar during radio broadcast in El Reno, 1948.*

Waynoka First Assembly Sunday School, c. 1948.

~~~~∞~~~~

Chapter 19

Facing Doctrinal Differences

The face of America drastically changed in the decade following World War II. The blemishes of war gave way to a new complexion of peace and prosperity. The very social fabric of the nation was stretched in conflicting directions. The population shifted from farms and small towns to the cities. Family and neighborhood ties were weakened. New roles for women and minorities weakened long-established cultural patterns. Technological advancements and the booming wartime economy contributed to prosperity after years of depression. The post-war Pentecostal movement faced tremendous challenges as a result of this massive social change and as a result of doctrinal differences from within.[1]

THE LATTER RAIN PROBLEM

The Assemblies of God had enjoyed almost 30 years of tranquility on doctrinal issues when the "New Order of the Latter Rain" problem arose in the late 1940's. There was a genuine move of God after many Pentecostals began reemphasizing fasting and prayer and the gifts of the Spirit. In Oklahoma and across the land, Assemblies of God churches were caught up in what they thought was a new outpouring of the Spirit.

Something went wrong, however, when leaders of the "New Order" began teaching that gifts could be obtained only by the "laying on of hands," that certain men were prophets and apostles, and that all organized religion was bad. Much of the denunciation of organization came from former Assemblies of God ministers who had been disciplined by the movement.[2]

The Assemblies of God and other Pentecostal groups fought back at what they thought was an attempt to divide and break up organized works. The 1949 General Council voted to disapprove of the "New Order" because its teachings strayed from Scripture.[3] In 1952, in his first year as Oklahoma district superintendent, Robert E. Goggin warned pastors about the "New Order":

"There is a susceptibility on the part of many of our folk to be deceived by false, erroneous teachings and doctrines whose main appeal is a pseudo spirituality without any real consecration. It would be well if all our ministers, and especially our pastors, would give more time to teaching the people the Word of God so that they might avoid being led astray."[4]

The "Latter Rain" problem probably had a lot to do with the election of Goggin as district superintendent in 1951 over incumbent V.H. Ray. Several churches in Tulsa and Oklahoma City were infected with the "New Order" virus. Delegates at the 1951 District Council elevated Goggin from the secretary-treasurer position to the top position in the district because "many felt he would be stronger in dealing with the churches caught up in the 'New Order.'"[5]

Much of the "Latter Rain" message was spread across America from Oklahoma City in a publication known as *The Latter Rain Messenger*. The magazine shook the Assemblies of God leadership in January, 1951, when it carried an article by former *Pentecostal Evangel* Editor Stanley Frodsham. The article was favorable to the "New Order" and resulted in Frodsham's resignation from the Assemblies of God. Fortunately, Frodsham later discovered the extremes of the movement and abandoned his support for it.[6]

In the end, only a few Oklahoma churches left the fellowship over the "New Order" problem. It faded away almost as quickly as it appeared.

SALVATION-HEALING CAMPAIGNS

Another dispute arose in the Assemblies of God over methods used by some prominent "faith healers." The "New Order" and the Salvation-Healing campaigns of the 1940's and 50's were strikingly similar. Both began at about the same time. Both had scriptural truth as a foundation. Both found an enthusiastic response in the Assemblies of God movement. And, unfortunately, both were exploited in many cases by men with selfish aims.[7]

Any preacher with a strong divine healing message caught the ear of Assemblies of God congregations, for healing was an integral part of the services in most churches in the 1950's. Our churches always believed strongly in divine healing. From the very beginning, *The Pentecostal Evangel* carried healing testimonies. Earl Oliver's story of his mother being healed of a broken thumb as she was prayed for on the front steps of the church in McCurtain is typical of the era.[8]

Lawrence Langley, a longtime Oklahoma pastor, was saved because of a healing in Broken Bow during an Orville Manning revival in 1948:

"Sonny Rodgers was a 14-year-old neighbor boy whom doctors had sent home from Childrens' Hospital in Oklahoma City to die. He had only four to six months to live. We asked his parents if we could keep him at our house for a few days. We took him camping and to a rodeo. He said he wanted to go to a church. We took him on a Sunday morning to First Assembly where my wife had been going. I had never been in a church with an altar. When Rev. Manning asked if anyone needed prayer, I volunteered Sonny. I pushed his wheelchair down to the front of the church. He was anointed with oil and was instantly healed. He simply got up from the wheelchair and walked and laughed and cried. I was under such strong conviction that I knelt at the altar and begged God to forgive me. My wife got saved at the same time at the other altar. The church didn't waste any time and bap-

251

tized my wife, Sonny, and me in nearby Yashua Creek that same afternoon."[9]

Eugene Burke (the author's father) gave his heart to Jesus while the author, at age 17 months, lay dying in the Burke house on North Broadway in Broken Bow in January, 1950. Lois Burke (the author's mother) remembers that afternoon:

"Bobby had no pulse and had quit breathing. His body was limp from five days of severe dehydration, a result of complications from an epidemic virus. About 2:00 p.m. we knew he was dying. That was when my unsaved husband Eugene went out to the washroom behind the house and promised God that he would live the rest of his life for Him if He would heal his little boy. Eugene came back into the house and said, 'He'll be all right.' Within 30 minutes, Bobby was completely well, drank a large glass of buttermilk, and played around the house until bedtime."[10]

Miracles of divine healing impressed Christians and non-Christians alike. Seventeen-year-old Kenneth Stafford was called to preach after an awesome healing:

"We were riding home from a service in the back of a pickup. A girl by the name of Faye Young was in tremendous pain because of a large knot in her side. We stopped on the side of the road, got out of the pickup, and gathered around her in prayer. Immediately, the knot went away and God healed her completely. Someone started singing. That night I went home and knelt down beside my bed and answered God's call to the ministry."[11]

Cleo Johnson's mother was taking large daily doses of insulin when she was prayed for. Brother Johnson remembers the day:

"God literally filled that room with His divine presence. You could almost reach up and touch heaven. God healed Mother instantly and she stopped taking her insulin, even though the doctor warned her she would die without it. We stood on God's Word and His promises and she never took another shot of insulin. She lived a healthy life for a number of years."[12]

252

Oklahoma was at the center of the salvation-healing movement. Oral Roberts, son of a Pentecostal Holiness minister, was born near Ada, Oklahoma, in 1918. He was called to preach, and God healed him of tuberculosis and stuttering. Roberts held his first city-wide healing campaign while pastoring the Pentecostal Holiness church in Enid in 1947. The next year he began criss-crossing America with the largest portable tent ever used.

Crowds of more than 10,000 at a single service were common. From his headquarters in Tulsa, Roberts took the healing message to the country with books, through his monthly magazine *Healing Waters* (later renamed *Abundant Life*), and by radio. In 1955 Roberts initiated a national weekly television program, which took his crusades into millions of homes never previously exposed to Pentecost.[13]

Over a span of 20 years Roberts held more than 300 major crusades. By the mid-1950's he was heard on 500 radio stations each week, and his television program remained the top-rated religious telecast for almost 30 years. Assemblies of God members in Oklahoma and elsewhere regularly attended Roberts' crusades and received his magazine and books.

Wayne Warner, Assemblies of God Archives director, describes a typical Oral Roberts service:

"Oral Roberts—during his tent meeting heyday—would remain behind the platform during the song service, prayer, announcements, special numbers, and book promotions. At a given moment, Roberts' manager introduced him, the drapes parted, the organist boomed out the unmistakable 'Where the Healing Waters Flow,' and Roberts bounced to the big floor microphone ready to lead the congregation in his theme song."[14]

Roberts shocked many Pentecostals in 1969 by leaving the Pentecostal Holiness church to join the Methodist denomination. He later became independent and built Oral Roberts University in Tulsa, considered by many to be the nation's premier charismatic university. In the 1990's Roberts is considered America's foremost healing evangelist. Even though he is sometimes controversial, God used him in this century to take the healing and salvation message to millions of Americans.[15]

Another prominent faith healer with Oklahoma ties was A.A. Allen, an Arkansas boy who had been delivered from alcoholism and called to preach. In 1951 Allen bought a tent and established headquarters in Dallas, often holding tent meetings and revivals in Oklahoma. (His son-in-law Danny Smith later pastored an independent Pentecostal church in Broken Bow.) Allen began broadcasting "The Allen Revival Hour," a radio program in 1953. Soon many Oklahoma Assemblies of God believers were on the mailing list of his *Miracle Magazine*. He ran afoul of Assemblies of God leaders in the 1950's, however, due to so-called miracles that many considered questionable or at least exaggerated. After he was arrested and charged with drunken driving in 1955, he maintained his innocence but surrendered his Assemblies of God credentials.[16]

Allen built "Miracle Valley," a complete community in the Arizona desert in the late 1950's. He continued to be a successful fund-raiser until his divorce in 1967. He died of sclerosis of the liver in 1970.[17]

Kenneth Hagin preached a powerful healing message in many Oklahoma Assemblies of God churches in the 1950's. Hagin had been born with a deformed heart and was an invalid when God healed him in 1934. After pastoring for a few years, he began an itinerant ministry as a Bible teacher and evangelist in 1949. E.W. Swift, who served for three decades as a deacon, remembers a Kenneth Hagin revival at First Assembly in Broken Bow:

"The revival lasted for eight weeks. Brother Hagin would call people out of their chairs, describe their condition, and pray for them. Almost every time, the Lord would touch them and heal them. I personally saw many of my neighbors and fellow believers healed during that early revival. There was a powerful presence of God in the services. The church was packed every night. No one wanted to miss a single service. Sinners were saved just because of the awesome power of God demonstrated during the healing services."[18]

Oklahoma City native Jack Coe was also a major personality in healing crusades in the 1940's and 1950's. He was ordained by the Assemblies of God and quickly won the hearts of thousands with his dynamic preaching and his *Herald of Healing* magazine. Coe's first healing campaign was in 1947 in the high school gymnasium in Broken Bow. He opened a giant church, the Dallas Revival Center, in 1952 and was expelled from the Assemblies of God the next year when "church leaders became increasingly frustrated and embarrassed by some of his methods and teachings." Leaders questioned both the quantity and nature of healings claimed by Coe. They felt his lack of credibility was demeaning to other preachers with a strong healing message.[19] Coe died of polio in 1956.

Incidents such as those involving A.A. Allen and Jack Coe irritated Assemblies of God leaders. The General Presbytery appointed a committee in 1956 to study the alleged "unscriptural, unethical, and extravagant practices of some of the evangelists in the movement."[20] That same year, General Superintendent Ralph Riggs wrote an open letter in *The Pentecostal Evangel* entitled "The Doctrine of Divine Healing Is Being Wounded in the House of Its Friends."[21] The problems of the salvation-healing movement eventually resulted in the adoption of ethical and spiritual standards for independent corporations or evangelistic associations affiliated in any way with the Assemblies of God. The standards emphasized honest and open accounting procedures and cautioned against wild and unsubstantiated claims of miracles.[22]

The controversy that surrounded some faith healers in the 1950's did not diminish the strong belief of the Assemblies of God in God's power to heal the sick. Despite the personal failure of some major proponents of divine healing, local churches continued to emphasize healing as a major benefit of living a Spirit-filled life.

Chapter 20

Strong District Leadership

The Oklahoma District has always been blessed with strong, able leaders. Among them was Robert E. Goggin, whose term of office as district superintendent set a record for longevity.

No one who met Goggin ever doubted his authority in leading the Oklahoma District. His tall, imposing figure and straight-laced voice brought authority to any meeting. Goggin was elected district secretary-treasurer in 1947 and ascended to the superintendent's post in 1951, a position he would hold for 29 years.

The District made tremendous financial strides under Goggin's leadership. In his first five years, he pumped new life into the old plan of financing the district office (ministers were asked to give one-half of their tithes to the district) and almost completely retired the indebtedness against the district campgrounds and tabernacle. In his first year in office, tithes from ministers increased 16 percent.[1] By 1959 the annual receipts of the Storehouse Fund (made up primarily of tithes from ministers) topped $75,000, compared with $53,000 in 1951. And the assets of the district grew to almost $700,000 by 1959.[2]

Superintendent Goggin led a major development of the campgrounds and district office property in the 1950's. A new tabernacle was built for children's services. New seats and air conditioning were added to the main tabernacle in 1953.

The old tabernacle could not handle the growing crowds at campmeetings and district councils. The district offices were still in the front section of the tabernacle, and officials were squeezed together in the limited space. To alleviate the problem, the 1955 District Council authorized the purchase of 10 acres adjacent to the campgrounds for the purpose of building a district office and bookstore.[3]

By the summer of 1956 the office building was completed at a cost of approximately $45,000. When district officials moved in, the building was already half paid for because of donations given in response to appeals by Goggin and other district officials. Goggin reported that 269 ministers and 120 churches had sent in offerings to pay for the new building. With the offices moved out, the seating capacity of the tabernacle was increased by 300.[4]

Probably the most significant financial move made by the Oklahoma District in the Goggin era was the creation of a "revolving fund" to assist local churches who were having difficulty borrowing money for construction and repairs. At the 1952 District Council, Goggin introduced a resolution calling for the creation of the fund to provide low interest loans:

"...Loans shall be made to local assemblies to buy, build, repair, or redecorate church buildings or parsonages or to purchase equipment...Loans shall only be made to Assembly of God churches of the Oklahoma District...Loans shall only be made to churches who show an ability and willingness to repay and are recommended by their Sectional Presbyter...No loan shall be made without adequate security...All other details shall be worked out by the Executive Board."[5]

The District Revolving Fund began making small loans of up to $500 at five percent interest in May, 1953. The District Executive Board also solicited investment in the Revolving Fund by advertising in the May, 1953, *Assemblies of God News* that it would pay up to three percent interest.[6] By October, 1954, 21 loans totaling $7,000 had been made.[7]

258

HE LOVED HIS PREACHERS

Robert Goggin cared deeply about the welfare of the 1,028 ordained and licensed ministers and exhorters in Oklahoma who were on the rolls when he became superintendent. He helped local pastors protect their churches by backing resolutions in 1955 that prohibited a new Assemblies of God church from locating within 12 blocks of an existing church, and recommended one church for each 5,000 in population.[8]

He stressed attendance of ministers and their wives at annual sectional councils. The District Board traveled to the sections to field questions from ministers in small groups and to meet potential candidates for licensing or ordination. Under Goggin's leadership, the first annual Ministers Institute was held in May, 1953, at Robbers Cave State Park near Wilburton. The event drew more than 100 ministers and proved to be so positive that it remains an annual event 40 years later.[9]

Goggin emphasized "spirituality" among the pastors and evangelists over whom he was shepherd:

"Without the Spirit of God, no man, no matter what his physical strength or his intellectual ability, can successfully lift up Jesus Christ. Many of us forget this important truth and consequently find our ministry insipid and uninteresting... It is not uncommon to hear ministers analyzing their ministry and wondering why it is not what it ought to be. Usually we come up with every answer but the right one—a definite lack of spirituality... Spirituality makes any minister sincere, and without sincerity we are as sounding brass or a tinkling cymbal... When we are completely filled with the power of God's Spirit we can shout and sing and preach the Word with victory."[10]

THE INTEGRITY OF PREACHERS

The integrity of Assemblies of God ministers was a great concern of Superintendent Goggin. In May, 1955, he wrote:

"The pastor's success in any church depends upon his ability to conduct himself in such a way that he can win the respect, confidence, and cooperation of his congregation. We can make ourselves common to the congregations we pastor by an unkempt appearance and carelessness of speech that can rob any minister of his influence... A congregation will overlook many things in a minister's life if they know he is honest... I know of some towns where the churches have suffered irreparable damage because of some minister failing to meet his financial obligations... I know of one town where the church or pastor cannot obtain credit because of the unsavory record established by a man several years ago. These things have a way of getting around and to say they hinder the ministry would be the understatement of the year."[11]

Longtime Pastor Virgil Claxton recognized that he and other Assemblies of God pastors could not be successful without supernatural help:

"The Assemblies of God doctrine is too heavy for a man to carry without the anointing and that is why many desert it for an easy way. You cannot carry the weight of it without the power of the Holy Ghost. With the power of God it ceases to be a burden and becomes a joy to our hearts."[12]

Goggin, like all district superintendents, spent most of his waking hours either in the office or on the road. His 1957 District Council report showed he drove 40,000 miles, preached 189 times, conducted 52 business meetings, attended dozens of special meetings, and spent 170 days in his office during the year.[13] In a ten-day period in March and April, 1953, Goggin joined E.F. Pierce in dedicating the new addition to the front of First Assembly in Edmond; was with Paul Riggs and the congregation of South Side Faith Tabernacle in Oklahoma City for the dedication of a new 750-seat auditorium; dedicated a new church pastored by George McGee at Hartshorne; and preached the funeral of pioneer minister R.L. Lister, pastor of Sentinel Assembly.[14]

However, Goggin's administration of the Oklahoma District was not entirely unblemished. He wrote in the November,

1953, *Assemblies of God News* that he had lost his diary with all his engagements and dates. He said, "If I promised to be with your church, write me and tell the time and occasion." Undoubtedly, he was greatly embarrassed. Churches readily cooperated and some may have been tempted to use the occasion to try to fit themselves into Goggin's busy schedule.[15]

Oklahoma was blessed with other strong district leaders in the 1950's. R.L. "Pa" Steger served as assistant district superintendent until 1953. V.H. Ray served as secretary-treasurer from 1951 to 1953. Floyd L. Poag, pastor at First Assembly in Ada, was elected to that position in 1953 and served until 1958 when he resigned to pastor Evangel Assembly in Oklahoma City. L.H. Arnold, the 22-year veteran pastor of First Assembly in McAlester, was appointed secretary-treasurer and served until he retired in 1972.[16]

Carl McCoy continued as district C.A. president until 1953. T.A. McDonough served in that capacity the remainder of the decade. L.B. Keener was district Sunday School director in 1950-53, and W.M. Rumbaugh held the position during 1953-60.

TOO POOR TO GET THERE

Delegates to the annual Oklahoma District Council often faced problems of distance and lack of money in making the trip. Pastor T.C. Burkett, Jake Gilbert, and Eugene Burke were elected to represent First Assembly in Broken Bow at the 1951 District Council. The church raised an $11 offering to finance the trip. None of the three delegates owned a car and they were forced to "hitch" a ride on the back of a flat-bed truck. Burke describes the trip to Oklahoma City:

"We put our clothing in a grocery sack and rode in the back of the truck for six hours. We stayed on the district campgrounds in a cabin with only one bed—which we gave to the preacher. Within a day or so we had exhausted the $11 expense money and had to leave the meeting early so we could catch the same truck headed back home to Broken Bow. Our backs were sore from sleeping on the floor, but our hearts were pumped up because of seeing so many fellow Pentecostals from around the state."[17]

One of the most interesting elections in Oklahoma District Council history was in 1953. Delegates saw the need for a full-time district official to coordinate home and foreign missions. The position of district missions director was created with a salary of $90 per week. When the votes were counted on the sixth ballot, James C. Dodd, pastor of Broken Arrow Assembly, was elected missions director. Dodd told the delegates he would need 30 days to seek God's will about taking the job.

On November 9, Dodd announced to the District Board that he did not feel he should leave his church, and resigned as missions director. J.R. Keith was appointed to the post but declined the offer two days later. John Grace, pastor at Wewoka, who earlier had been elected assistant district superintendent, was then named missions director. Grace would serve for almost two decades and become a legend. Dodd in turn was appointed assistant district superintendent and would serve more than a quarter century until his elevation to the top post upon Brother Goggin's retirement in 1980.[18]

There was continuing Oklahoma influence at General Council Headquarters in Springfield in the 1950's. Bert Webb was assistant general superintendent, Paul Copeland was national Sunday School director, and L.B. Keener was a national Sunday School representative. Harry Myers headed up the first public relations department, created in 1954. G.W. Hardcastle was elected as a non-resident executive presbyter representing the Gulf region in 1953.

Virgil Claxton became chairman of the Board of Directors of Southwestern Bible Institute in Waxahachie, Texas. During his term of office, the P.C. Nelson Memorial Library was built. On September 11, 1959, the building was dedicated. During the dedication ceremony, Claxton reminded the audience of the sweat, toil, and suffering of P.C. Nelson and others in building Southwestern. He concluded that "everyone has a moral and religious obligation to leave something good behind for others who will follow."[19]

The national fellowship chose the Municipal Auditorium in Oklahoma City as the site for its General Council in 1955. General Superintendent Ralph Riggs; Assistant General Superintendents G.F. Lewis, Bert Webb, J.O. Savell, and Thomas Zimmerman; Secretary J. Roswell Flower; Treasurer W.A. Brown; and Foreign Missions Secretary Noel Perkin were all returned to office.[20]

Chapter 21

Special Ministries

Children were a special target of Assemblies of God ministries in the 1950's. John McPherson, a native of Drumright, Oklahoma, got involved with children's ministries while at Bible school. He was half Cherokee, so it was natural for him to put on a headdress and tell exciting stories to kids.

His talent as an artist and a storyteller led "Chief" to many churches in Oklahoma and 43 other states for four decades. Most Assemblies of God children growing up in the '50's and '60's attended "Chief" services either in their local church or at special rallies and camps. "Chief" has heard from thousands of those children down through the years. One lady wrote to "Chief":

"I was very poor as a child and never had any money to give in the offering when you came to my church. It is now 20 years later and I am sending you $20 to help in your work. I want you to continue to take the message of Jesus to kids everywhere."[1]

Another unique ministry was begun in Oklahoma prisons by W.W. Hays in April, 1959. Hays had previously served prison time for crimes committed to support his morphine and alcohol addiction. At age 31 when his life was no longer worth living, God gloriously saved him:

"Jesus took me by the hand and lifted me up out of the pit of sin. I was free at last from drugs and alcohol and death and all the things that had me bound... A few days later I was filled with the Holy Spirit and called to preach the gospel. Twenty-one days later I started giving my testimony, reaching into prisons and jails. From the outset God blessed and we saw souls come to Calvary."[2]

Edith Hays had prayed for her husband earlier the same day that he was saved: "God save him, deliver him or take him out of my life. I cannot live with the pain."[3] Save and deliver him He did.

"Chaplain" Hays loaded up his family in a 1953 Plymouth station wagon and began a two million-mile journey to minister to inmates. In the early days his family ate bologna and old doughnuts and they slept in the car when there was no money for motels. In 1960, when he appeared before the District Executive Board to obtain credentials, his sordid past was brought out. Later, Superintendent Goggin told Hays that when he appeared before the Board he had looked like a skid row bum, but that God had given him a peace about approving Hays for a license. After 10,000 sermons, "Chaplain" Hays has no regrets. He and Edith are still going strong. In 1993 Hays borrowed a tent for a revival inside prison walls at the Jess Dunn Correctional Center. In one Sunday night service 45 inmates responded to Chaplain Hays' altar call.[4]

The Men's Fellowship Department had been added to the General Council programs in 1947, and Oklahoma churches immediately began officially forming their men into groups. In the 1950's the men began the tradition of spending their Saturday mornings helping the less fortunate members in their church on projects ranging from oil changes to home repairs. Oklahoman Don Mallough was the first national director of the Men's Fellowship Department.

The use of radio by local churches in Oklahoma increased in the 1950's. A survey of *The Assemblies of God News* shows a number of local programs: "Musical Meditations" by Altus First on KWHW, "Hour of Grace" by Cushing First on KWHP, Muskogee First on KMUS, Oklahoma City Faith Tabernacle on both KLPR in Oklahoma City and KNOR in Norman, and "Tidings of Peace" by

Broken Arrow Assembly on KAKC in Tulsa.[5] Nationally, the General Council signed a contract with ABC in 1953 to broadcast "Revivaltime" every Sunday night coast to coast. Ratings showed tens of thousands listened during the Sunday night prime-time broadcast.[6]

LET'S ALL GO TO SUNDAY SCHOOL

Thomas F. Zimmerman of Cleveland, Ohio, who later became an outstanding general superintendent, was the featured speaker at the Oklahoma District Sunday School Convention in December, 1951. With Oklahoman Paul Copeland at the helm of the national Sunday School effort, the Assemblies of God saw large growth in Sunday Schools in the 1950's. The Gold Crown program provided awards for Sunday Schools that grew substantially and met strict requirements such as good record-keeping and active promotion. In 1951 District Sunday School Director L.B. Keener reported that Bartlesville First and Comanche Assembly were two of only 12 churches in the nation that had won a Gold Crown award five years in a row. (Both churches made it six in a row the next year.) Broken Arrow, Enid Gospel Tabernacle, Guthrie, and Mannford received the award for four consecutive years. Thirty Oklahoma churches received the Gold Crown in 1950.[7]

In 1953, 435 Sunday Schools with a combined attendance of over 41,000 were reported in Oklahoma.[8] In April, 1954, the top 10 Sunday Schools in the District were:

1. Broken Arrow—567
2. Lewis Avenue, Tulsa—503
3. South Side Faith Tabernacle, Oklahoma City—500
4. Full Gospel, Tulsa—444
5. Bartlesville First—433
6. Faith Tabernacle, Oklahoma City—386
7. Capitol Hill, Tulsa—318
8. Capitol Hill, Oklahoma City—312
9. Evangel Tabernacle, Oklahoma City—282
10. Home Gardens Assembly, Tulsa—272[9]

Broken Arrow Assembly won a national Sunday School attendance contest sponsored by *Christian Life* magazine in 1952. An all-time record attendance of 937 was reached on November 8, 1952, the day before the church was destroyed by fire. Broken Arrow's Sunday School success—of moving from 100 to almost 1,000 in attendance—inspired many church leaders to value the importance of Sunday School.

YOUTH DISCIPLESHIP: CHRIST'S AMBASSADORS

Of the 439 churches in the state, 320 had organized C.A. groups by 1950.[10] Sectional C.A. rallies were increasingly popular with teens who got together monthly with other teens from surrounding communities. Many happy marriages today began with a C.A. rally courtship.

In November, 1950, the District C.A. Department began publishing a monthly bulletin, *The Oklahoma C.A. Messenger*. It included reports of local groups and monthly office support records.[11]

The first annual Oklahoma Youth Day was organized in 1952. Special services were held in many churches to honor the youth of the community and to raise support for the district youth program.[12]

The 1956 District Council authorized Superintendent Goggin to appoint a five-man committee to arrange for an annual youth camp. The idea originated in a resolution presented by J.B. Oaks as chairman of the Oklahoma City area ministers group.[13]

District C.A. President T.A. McDonough conducted the first youth camp in Oklahoma in August, 1957, at Robbers Cave State Park near Wilburton. Otis Keener, the assistant camp director, described the occasion:

"They came by car, station wagon, and bus. By noon Monday the camp was buzzing with the merriment of young people who had come to enjoy spiritual blessings and a week of Christian fellowship. The busiest place that first day was the office where Rev. and Mrs. Newburn found themselves swamped with campers anxious to be assigned their cabin. Upon being assigned a place, they would be seen headed through the shady grounds, suitcase and blankets in hand, to make up their bunk and meet their roommates... Everyone seemed eager to get into the first night service... Before seven, the campers were dressed up and winding their way to the tabernacle... The sounds of gospel hymns began to echo across the grounds... History was being made. A camp for which many had planned and prayed was about to begin, and the presence of the Lord was sensed from the opening song."[14]

G.W. Hardcastle, Jr., was the speaker for that first youth camp, which was attended by more than 300 campers, counselors, and ministers.[15]

At the second youth camp held in 1958 at the Church of God campgrounds near Bristow, 175 showed up. That same year Paul Lowenburg of Kansas was the special speaker at the C.A. Convention attended by more than 3,000.[16]

In the 1958 District Council, C.A. President T.A. McDonough cited alarming statistics. He reported that the Assemblies of God was losing 65 percent of its girls and 75 percent of its boys between the ages of 13 and 16. McDonough pleaded with pastors to strongly support the local C.A. group and stop the exodus of young people.[17]

Chapter 22

Challenged by Social Change

The great changes in American society in the 1950's had a profound effect on how Assemblies of God believers lived and worshiped. Church services began to have a more "professional" quality and less spontaneity.

Participation had been the rule in Pentecostal worship since the beginning of the century. The lack of a formalized service allowed maximum participation in testimonies, singing, and manifestations of the Spirit. Most congregations were small, and the worship was enthusiastic.

Variations from the old-style Pentecostal worship began to appear—especially in larger churches in cities where the members tended to be more educated and more affluent. However, Oklahoma may have been affected less than some other parts of the country in changes in the style of worship in the 1950's.

Since an overwhelming majority of Assemblies of God churches in Oklahoma were located in rural areas, old-fashioned Pentecostal worship continued to be the norm. If you passed by an Assemblies of God church in Oklahoma during the 1950's you probably heard the congregation singing some of the "new" songs of the day: "I Want to Know More About My Lord," by

Lee Roy Abernathy; "In the Sweet Forever," by Luther Presley; "Where Could I Go?," by J.B. Coats; "Keep on the Firing Line," by J.R. Baxter Jr.; "What A Savior," by Marvin Dalton; and "Mansion Over the Hilltop" and "Room at the Cross for You," by Ira Stanphil.

The prosperity of the 1950's allowed families to have more leisure time—and, unfortunately, less church time. Activities in the local church that once consumed almost every night for believers now were limited to two or three nights a week. Revivals that once ran for weeks began to last only one week or just Sunday through Wednesday.

Time limits put on services by the changing culture resulted in a more "organized" or formal service. The jury is still out on the trend toward formalism. Assemblies of God historian William Menzies comments:

"Some view with anxiety the apparent loss of fervor; others are relieved to see reverence and content displace noise and unintelligibility. Still others see values in both the 'old-time Pentecost' and in the increased refinement in expression of corporate worship, preferring a 'middle-of-the-road' journey."[1]

The popularity of television brought substantial social changes. Viewers saw how other people lived, what they drove, and how bright their teeth were. Even the most liberal theologians admit that television had a negative influence on the Assemblies of God. Even when the programs were not blatantly sinful, they took away from family and prayer time.

The 1952 Oklahoma District Council saw the growing problem and expressed official disapproval. However, a resolution signed by Matt Goss, J.D. Keen, and C. Livingston that would have prohibited a minister of the Oklahoma District from owning a television set was tabled and never voted on by the delegates.[2]

Assistant District Superintendent James Dodd deplored the breakdown in the moral fiber of America. In 1958 he wrote:

"We have crossed the threshold of a new era. Our Western civilization is at the crossroads... Ideologies are crashing about us... There is an increasing tendency to gloss over the awfulness of sin, to condone and to compromise. There is disregard for the worth of the individual... Our nation has a rendezvous with destiny. It is a question of world revival or world catastrophe... The Holy Ghost has been grieved out of many churches. People file into the pews with broken hearts, burdened souls, tormented lives, doubts, fears, hestitations. The only message that will help them is the message of the Lamb of God... We cannot fulfill our mission by criticizing the modernist, finding fault with our fellows, blaming juvenile delinquency, saying our churches are worldly. I believe in separation, but separation is not enough. We must demonstrate to a lost world what it means to be indwelt by the Spirit."[3]

One positive aspect of social change in America was the move from isolationism to cooperation by the Assemblies of God in the late 1940's and 1950's. Before World War II, the Assemblies of God was isolated not only from the old-line church denominations but also from other Holiness and Pentecostal groups. That changed with the forming of the Pentecostal Fellowship of North America in 1948. The Assemblies of God decision to cooperate with other denominations encouraged local pastors to join ministerial alliances and civic clubs to become part of the communities they served.[4]

The Assemblies of God and its people had to face dynamic social changes in post-war America. The new lifestyle of Americans presented a serious challenge for its leaders: how would old-time Pentecost fare in an ultra-modern society?

273

Chapter 23

Going On with God

Even though America was more prosperous after World War II, Assemblies of God preachers often continued to sacrifice greatly. Paul and Dreta Hutsell were holding a revival for Pastor Walter Gore at Leedey Assembly in 1951. They had no groceries and no milk for their six-week-old daughter Diana. Paul Hutsell tells the miraculous story:

"Dreta and I knelt to ask the Lord to provide milk for our baby. While we were praying, there was a knock on the door. When I opened it, there stood a woman who was dressed provocatively with an excessive amount of perfume and jewelry. She said she was driving by our apartment when a voice told her there was a baby that needed milk. With tears streaming down my cheeks, I told her we had been on our knees asking God for milk. She told us that she would make arrangements for us to get milk and groceries at a nearby grocery store within a few minutes. When we arrived at the store, we found plenty of milk and a large box of groceries... And, the lady was saved before the end of the revival."[1]

In the 1950's, pockets of poverty still existed in many rural areas of Oklahoma. Not all congregations had the money for new buildings and padded pews. Cecil Pearcy drove 150 miles each Sunday for four months to start a new church at Oakdale near Wann. As many as 48 people crammed into a 16 x 20-foot building with no electricity and no water. The pastor sat on a nail keg and the people sat on planks. God blessed the congregation and soon a larger building was built.[2]

There was a need for new churches in many towns in the state. Assistant District Superintendent R.L. Steger was pleased with the great reports of many saved in revivals in the summer of 1951, but called for even greater efforts:

"Yet there are millions without Christ waiting for someone to bring the message of salvation to them and it should constrain us to want to do everything we can to redeem what time we have left to get the gospel to everyone that we possibly can. I do believe that the time is short and we must put forth every effort we can."[3]

The decade of the 1950's began with 414 Assemblies of God churches in Oklahoma and ended with 490, a gain of 76.[4]

In February, 1950, Skyview Assembly in Sand Springs had its official opening. Pastor Lawrence M. Reed had founded the church on a bluff overlooking the Arkansas River the year before in an area that had no full-gospel work.[5]

First Assembly in Moore had a humble beginning as a mission in the Community Building in 1950. H.A. Smith led the church into a permanent brick structure in 1953.[6]

Sectional Presbyter Homer Boyd reported in 1950 that the church at Arkoma purchased an old building that once had been the largest night club and gambling center in eastern Oklahoma and converted it into a lovely church.[7] New church buildings were built that year in Sallisaw, Heavener, Leflore, at Tuxedo Assembly in Bartlesville, Sand Springs, Dustin, Yale, Marietta, Wapanucka, Elmore City, Waynoka, Garber-Covington Oilfield, Newkirk, Hollis, and Stecker.[8]

Major building projects were reported in Miami, Disney, Moffitt, Fanshawe, Muldrow, Broken Bow, Ogelsby, Oak Grove (near Beggs), Stroud, Pruitt City, Durant, Ada, Midwest City, Oklahoma City Southside Faith Tabernacle, Duncan First Assembly, Woodward, Texhoma, and Semplar in 1951.[9]

The year 1952 saw another dozen churches added in Oklahoma. New church buildings were reported at Inola, Pocola, Eagletown, Hartshorne, Sheridan Road Assembly in Tulsa, Prue, Glad Tidings Tabernacle in Oklahoma City, and Lawton First Assembly (where Pastor J.L. McQueen reported spending $100,000—a giant building project in the 1950's). At Wetumka, Pastor C.A. Rich dedicated a new church with a large auditorium and a Sunday school annex.[10]

Guymon was the first Assemblies of God church in the Oklahoma panhandle. It had begun in the early 1950's when a group of believers met in a private home. The congregation soon moved into a store front which became known as "The Revival Center." J.B. McDonough was pastor when the group decided to affiliate with the Assemblies of God. The Guymon church is still 100 miles from the nearest Assemblies of God church.[11]

Forty-three persons attended the first Sunday service in 1952 in a tent at Fifteenth and Pecan in Duncan to hear Alvin Stewart preach. The congregation formed Bethel Assembly of God.[12]

Putnam Assembly of God was set in order in 1952. The church began in June, 1947, in Bethany. Kenneth and Pearle Wray pioneered the new work which later changed its name to Parkview Assembly. It is now Cornerstone Church, pastored by David and Linda Brooks. An early member of Putnam Assembly was Col. Robinson Risner, the highest ranking American to be held as a prisoner in the Vietnam war.

Robert Rider pioneered the Assembly of God in Tecumseh in a 1949 tent revival. The church was set in order in 1953. Rider, who has pastored the church for 44 years, may hold the record for Oklahoma—or the world—for spending the most continuous years in one pastorate. Rider was saved at age 16. When Arthur Arnold baptized him, he prayed, "Make this boy a preacher." Rider was called to preach in 1937 in a cottage prayer meeting. While he was slain in the Spirit, he saw a vision of hell and knew he would spend his life trying to save people from that terrible place.[13]

Central Assembly in Muskogee began holding services in March, 1953, in an old laundry across the street from Central High School. Neal Burns was the first pastor. The church would eventually see as many as 500 in attendance. Conrad Barrett pastored the church for 26 years.[14]

The Oklahoma District continued its active role in planting and assisting new churches in the 1950's. A new church was built in Crowder in May, 1953, with Thelma Reynolds as pastor. A new work at Wagoner began in December, 1953, with a $130 offering to be applied on the purchase of property.[15]

South Heights Assembly in Sapulpa had 18 in Sunday School on its first Sunday in March, 1954. E.R. Roberts was the first pastor of the congregation that rented an old furniture store as its first meeting place.[16]

In February, 1955, a group of believers began meeting in the Soldier Creek Elementary School in Midwest City. J.C. Girkin became the pastor the next month and Soldier Creek Assembly of God was founded.[17]

Franklin Blair started the Lawton Heights church in an old store building in Lawton in 1955, with only his wife and daughter present for the first service. Within a year the church was averaging 60 in attendance. Blair pastored the church, which changed its name to Calvary Assembly in 1956, for 29 years.[18]

H.A. Brummett held his first services in the Redfork area of Tulsa County in an Army squad tent in November, 1956. What became Redfork Assembly of God met in the tent that was warmed by an open-flame heater for the entire winter until a building could be built in the spring of 1957.[19]

The official records of the Oklahoma District show a continuing decrease of rural churches in the 1950's. Many rural churches closed while others consolidated because of rising expenses and better transportation that allowed believers to drive farther to larger churches. An example is the 1959 consolidation of the churches at Girard and Buffalo.[20]

Photos of several Oklahoma Assemblies of God churches graced the cover of *The Pentecostal Evangel*. In 1950 the new building of First Assembly in Okmulgee was featured. In 1953 the cover photo was of the new building occupied by First Assembly of Ada. Three Oklahoma churches—First Assembly of Enid, Sayre Assembly, and First Assembly in Lawton—were so honored in 1954. In 1958 the *Evangel* featured Central Assembly in Tulsa on the cover and in a full-page article on the dedication of the new 800-seat sanctuary built after fire had destroyed the original building.[21]

For a year-by-year list of the new churches established in the 1950's, see the Appendix.

▲ *Oklahoma students at Southwestern Assemblies of God College in Waxahachie, Texas, early 1950's.*

▲ *Sunday School at Airport Assembly, Oklahoma City, early 1950's. Kenneth Stafford was the pastor.*

▲ *Oklahoma sectional Sunday School representatives, December, 1950.*

▲ *L.L. Ammons was a popular evangelist in Oklahoma in the 1950's.*

282

▲ *A.B. Cox, General Superintendent Ralph Riggs, and W.T. Gaston, 1954.*

▲ *Bert Webb and Paul Copeland, 1954.*

▲ *District headquarters and tabernacle, 1955.*

▲ *First Assembly, Wetumka, c. 1955.*

▼ *Laura, George, and Jean McCoy, 1954.*

▲ *Jones Assembly of God, 1950. Pastor George McCoy is at left.*

▲ *S.J. and Leenetta Scott were "flying" preachers.*

▲ *Fire destroyed Full Gospel Tabernacle (Fifth and Peoria) in Tulsa in 1956.*

▲ *(l to r) Oscar Bolin, John Grace, Otis Keener, unidentified, G.W. Hardcastle Jr., 1957.*

▲ *Youth group at Wellston First Assembly, 1957.*

▲ *First Assembly of God, Norman, 1957.*

▲ *The girls of cabin 6, youth camp, 1957.*

◀ *District youth camp, 1957.*

301

Floyd Poag was District ▶ Secretary-Treasurer from 1953 to 1958.

▲ *District Superintendent Robert Goggin at his desk, 1958.*

302

▲ *The Junior Boys class at Broken Bow First Assembly, 1958. The author, with his hands in his pockets, stands next to teacher P.A. Potts at right. H.A. Austin is the teacher at left.*

▲ *Sister Potillo's Bible class at Capitol Hill Assembly in Tulsa, Mother's Day, 1958.*

Chapter 24

Not Conformed to This World

Paul's warning to the church at Rome presented a perplexing problem in the 1960's and 1970's. "Be not conformed to this world," the apostle wrote in Romans 12:2. The question burned in the hearts of Assemblies of God leaders: "Have we conformed to the world so much that we have lost our distinctive Pentecostal identity?"

The prosperity of the 1960's brought new church buildings, nice cars, fine clothing, full-time ministerial staffs, great sound systems, taped music, air conditioning, and padded pews—none of which is inherently bad. Architecturally, the local Assemblies of God church looked like other churches in town. The cars parked outside of the Assemblies of God church on Sunday morning looked like the cars at any other church. But the most dramatic change from previous decades was the change in the outward appearance of the members of the congregation. The Assemblies of God had modified its official stand on holiness standards on long hair, the use of makeup, and modern dress. The reality that the Assemblies of God congregation looked like most other congregations in town caused Assemblies of God pastors and leaders to ask, "Are we still a separated people?"

Assemblies of God leaders knew that outward appearance was not the only thing that had changed. Influences of society made lying, cheating, and infidelity less shocking than in the previous generation. Many blamed television for desensitizing Americans—including Assemblies of God believers—to violence, family breakups, and abuse of alcohol.

In 1960 more people were attending Assemblies of God churches in Oklahoma than ever before. However, with some notable exceptions, most Assemblies of God churches saw fewer people saved, fewer filled with the Holy Spirit, and fewer healed than in previous years. Sunday School attendance was down. Leaders searched for answers.

There was no change in the doctrinal stance. Officially, the Assemblies of God still stood firmly on the 16 points of the Statement of Fundamental Truths of the fellowship that had basically remained unchanged for a half century. And the same God that had wrought supernatural miracles in Pentecostal services since the beginning of the movement was being served. Did the more comfortable atmosphere in Assemblies of God churches make a difference in believers' relationship with God? Had prosperity tempered believers' need for God? What was different?

Some characterized the differences over standards of dress and behavior as simply "cultural." Many breathed a sigh of relief to see the erosion of "clothesline" standards that had been preached by so many of our early leaders who had come from the Holiness tradition. On the other hand, some saw the change as a warning signal. They felt Pentecostal blessings earlier enjoyed had been sacrificed for "worldliness." Assemblies of God theologian Stanley Horton pointed to an economic factor:

"With more money for fashionable clothing and participation in leisure-time recreation in the years after World War II, Assemblies of God people tended to lose their image of separateness from the prevailing norms of society."[1]

In the late 1950's the district superintendents met in Springfield and issued a "Call to Holiness":

"It has been our sad part to take note of a trend to worldliness and a declension from early spiritual principles in some quarters. We have been shocked and grieved by cases of immorality and sin in the lives of some. There is an ever-increasing problem of discipline in the churches and districts, and a rising tide of indifference to any standard of Christian living which may depart from the personal opinion or desire of the individual."[2]

Leaders were not just talking about the way Assemblies of God men and women dressed; they were concerned about how they lived. Leaders defined a "separated people" as a people who loved righteousness and hated evil. As a symbolic action to establish a national example, employees of the General Council at Headquarters were ordered to pay their debts, stay away from questionable places of entertainment, avoid careless living, refrain from gossiping, and dress modestly.[3]

Issues such as going to the movies and sporting events were dealt with differently in the cities than in rural areas of Oklahoma. Most Assemblies of God pastors in rural areas vigorously preached against going to sporting events or movie theaters as recently as the early 1960's, while many churches in Oklahoma City and Tulsa relaxed their prohibitions of such activities. The same city/rural difference applied to women wearing pants and shorts, and to the length of men's and women's hair.

In 1961 Oklahoma District Superintendent Robert Goggin expressed concern that many of our Assemblies of God believers in Oklahoma had never seen the real manifestation of God's power. He blamed the sins of the human spirit: self-righteousness, self-pity, self-confidence, self-sufficiency, self-admiration, and self-love. Goggin warned that selfishness must be eliminated if Pentecostal blessings were to continue:

"These things [sins of the human spirit] dwell so deeply in us and are so much a part of us that they do not come to our attention until the light of God is focused directly on them... This attitude of selfishness is so foreign, so contrary and so at variance with the Word of God that I am amazed sometimes at our spiritual simplicity. This veil...can only be removed by spiritual experiences and not by instruction. We might as well try to

307

instruct leukemia out of our bloodstream... Mightier revivals as well as greater victories in our own lives cannot come until the veil is removed from our hearts and we enter into...the blazing, fiery presence of God."[4]

Oklahoma pioneer Pastor Leslie Moore addressed the issue in March, 1961:

"The old principles of spiritual life have not changed with the times. There are no short cuts to spiritual power. We are where we are because we have had little time for God in our hurried schedules. The criminal neglect of private prayer and meditation with His Word in our hands accounts for the small amount of interest in the Sunday School work. Spiritual power is born in contact with God. As we live with Him and He lives out through us His soul passion, the weariness and monotony will be swallowed up in the radiance of His nearness. Beyond mere enthusiasm are the deep currents of His passion for men that will sustain and help us. Let us fix our eyes on Him."[5]

Recognizing the need to stay close to the original denominational objectives, the 1963 General Council authorized the formation of a Spiritual Life-Evangelism Committee to draft a plan to rejuvenate the revival in local churches. The committee analyzed the problems of slow growth and stagnation and soon found the answer: there was not enough emphasis on the Holy Spirit and His manifestation, and...believers were not praying enough.[6]

William Menzies summed up the problem and the hunger for renewal in 1971:

"There seems to be evidence that following the spectacular success in gathering converts during the Great Depression, there was a tendency to displace [in our services] the spontaneity, the inner reality, that dominated the 1930's with 'techniques and gimmicks'. After a generation has passed, a period in which proliferation of special programs has replaced the earlier simplicity, there seems to be a growing quest for spiritual renewal on all levels of the fellowship... Pastors, youth leaders, individuals in various parts of the land are thirsting for the springs to flow again."[7]

PROSPERITY BRINGS SHORTER SERVICES

Prosperity and the ability to have more leisure time negatively impacted the length of Assemblies of God services in the 1960's and 1970's. At the beginning of the era, a typical Sunday night "evangelistic" service would go something like this:

1. A prayer meeting before the service;
2. Corporate prayer to begin the service;
3. A spirited song service, mostly from the hymnal or "songbook";
4. A fervent time of prayer with spoken and "unspoken" requests, and anointing with oil of the sick;
5. Three or four special songs (only southern gospel);
6. Testimony service;
7. Offering;
8. Sermon by pastor or evangelist; and
9. Altar call and altar service usually accompanied by singing (shorter than in earlier days but longer than five minutes). Every altar call made a plea for the lost and those who needed to be baptized in the Holy Spirit.

Time constraints eventually eliminated the testimony service, the pre-service prayer meeting, and, tragically, the long altar service in many congregations. The Sunday morning "opening exercise," which featured birthdays and anniversaries and the famous "penny march" (Children and adults marched by the altar to drop their pennies in the offering), also disappeared from most Assemblies of God churches.

THE CHARISMATIC RENEWAL

One factor in the changing scene in America was the Charismatic Renewal that appeared in many of the country's mainline Protestant denominations and the Roman Catholic Church. Many people with no background in traditional Pentecostal teachings were introduced to the baptism in the Holy Spirit. Many maintained their worldly standards while enjoying the Pentecostal baptism. Most stayed in their own denominations hoping to be catalysts for spiritual renewal. Others were kicked out of their local churches for speaking in tongues and exercising other gifts of the Spirit. Many of these people migrated to the

309

Assemblies of God—bringing new lifestyles and new ideas on worship and content of services.[8]

The Assemblies of God was suspicious of the Charismatic Renewal and its lack of teaching on holy living. P.D. Hocken explains why:

"Holiness of life was a much more dominant concern among Pentecostals than charismatics. This aspect reflects the Holiness background of many pioneer Pentecostals, whereas the charismatics have come from a wide variety of church backgrounds. This difference helps to explain a constant source of Pentecostal suspicion about charismatic authenticity, namely depth of conversion and moral transformation."[9]

Oklahoma played a significant national role in the growth of the Charismatic movement. Oral Roberts, T.L. Osborn, and Kenneth Hagin, all Charismatics operating from bases in Tulsa, created the "electronic church" with massive infusions of radio and television programs. These and other television ministries became multi-million dollar businesses with huge followings.

Melodyland Christian Center in Anaheim, California, became known as the international crossroads of the Charismatic movement. Melodyland was founded by Ponca City, Oklahoma, native Ralph A. Wilkerson who was licensed as an Assemblies of God minister in 1948.[10]

The Charismatic movement spawned many independent churches in Oklahoma and drew some members from Assemblies of God congregations. However, it had many good aspects as recognized by Assemblies of God leaders in 1972:

"The winds of the Spirit are blowing freely outside the normally recognized Pentecostal body... The Assemblies of God does not place approval on that which is manifestly not scriptural in doctrine or conduct. But neither do we categorically condemn everything that does not totally...conform to our standards."[11]

The Charismatic worship services were marked by enthusiasm. Leslie Moore warned in 1961:

"Enthusiasm is wonderful, but if that enthusiasm is not deeply rooted in the Spirit of God it falls flatter than an Oklahoma pancake, and leaves a heart discouraged and beat down... Enthusiasm rooted deeply in the power of God has set men's souls aflame for two thousand years... It was this power that impelled spiritual giants [like Paul] and drove them relentlessly on in their struggle with error and darkness, it was the secret of their passionate living. We have the same gospel they had—but alas, little of their spirit."[12]

One aspect of the Charismatic movement was the preaching of the "prosperity" doctrine. The "prosperity" preachers created the phrase, "Name it and claim it." Assemblies of God leaders warned the doctrine over-emphasized God's promise to provide material wealth to His followers.

A number of Assemblies of God ministers turned in their credentials in the 1960's to join Charismatic and non-denominational groups. In February, 1971, District Superintendent Robert Goggin felt compelled to explain why some were leaving:

"I have been asked the question a number of times recently why some have departed from the faith and have become associated with other groups of questionable doctrines and practices... This is not as widespread as some would have us believe and involves only a small minority... [Those who have left us] are members of one of three groups: A group who would like to appear to have great spiritual power but who do not want to make the consecration necessary to having such power...another class who are either unwilling or unable to distinguish truth from error...still another group who are chronic troublemakers and rebels."[13]

311

Chapter 25

The Great Pickens Revival

Pickens, Oklahoma, was an unlikely setting in 1963 for one of the greatest Pentecostal revivals in America in the last 50 years. Pickens was nestled in the foothills of the Kiamichi Mountains in McCurtain County in southeast Oklahoma. It was "at the end of the blacktop" about 40 miles northwest of Broken Bow.

The revival began in 1963 when several mothers in the local Assembly of God began fasting and praying for the salvation of their children. They put the names of their children in a shoebox and gathered around it on Tuesday mornings in a prayer meeting led by Pastor Odell Stuart.

The prayer meeting grew in numbers present and in strength. One by one the teenagers were saved and their names were pulled out of the shoebox. The C.A. group exploded from four to 46 in attendance within a few weeks.

Revival broke out among the youth who met in a special Saturday night service. A few weeks later the revival fire spread to the entire congregation. For the next year, an awesome move of God hovered over the community of 200. Amazingly, 300 people—more than the town's population—were saved. Thirteen present Assemblies of God pastors and missionaries were called to preach during the revival.

Walter Spradling, presently pastor of Crystal Rock Cathedral in Ardmore, was one of the names in the shoebox. He was gloriously saved as a result of the prayer meetings and subsequent revival. Spradling and others were away at college but came home every weekend just to get in on the revival services:

"Men would leave their jobs, go home and shower, and without even eating, go directly to church to the 'upper room,' a prayer room in the back of the church. The ladies were on one side and men on the other. The power of God was so strong in the room that countless men and women were slain in the Spirit. The room was small so when someone was slain in the Spirit we carried them out and laid them at the altar to make room for others. When it came time for service, we literally staggered out of the prayer room with the presence of God surrounding us. The services, which always lasted past 11:00 p.m., were out of this world. Men and women who had never been to church were strangely drawn to the revival and fell on their faces in repentance.[1]

The Pickens congregation simply wore out several evangelists during the long period of revival. After two or three weeks an evangelist would be physically unable to continue. Pastor Stuart would preach every night to as many as 300 people, many of whom drove from nearby Arkansas and Texas, until another evangelist would come for a few weeks. Don Burke, Ann Black, and Simon Peter were among the evangelists who preached at Pickens in 1963-64.

Pioneer Pentecostal preacher R.C. "Bob" Clay assisted Pastor Stuart in keeping the Pickens revival fires burning. Clay was a tall, imposing figure, whose powerful sermons and prayers brought new life into many congregations.

Don Holmes, currently pastor at First Assembly in Wetumka, was also called to preach during the Pickens revival. He remembers the marvelous services:

"As early at 5:00 p.m., men gathered in the prayer room. Many times I have seen men unable to get through the door into the church because they were 'drunk' with God's presence. They would just be piled up at the altar, trying to get up and sit in the pews so service could begin. One night an old man named Holly showed up at church. He couldn't explain why he was there. He had never been to a Pentecostal church, but told the preacher that something had made him get up from bed and come to church. He walked in, was knocked to the floor by the power of God, got saved and filled with the Holy Ghost, all in a matter of minutes. He died a few days later."[2]

Healings were a frequent occurrence during the Pickens revival. Don Holmes' grandmother had been told that both of her kidneys were ceasing to function. One Sunday night, the ladies in the prayer room laid hands on her and prayed. She was perfectly well by the next morning and lived many years after the revival.

Walter Spradling, who had been asked by Pastor Stuart to lead the youth group, was bitten by a poisonous snake and spent the night in the hospital. He told his youth group that he could not come to church because his leg was so severely swollen. Several of the young men went to Spradling's house and physically carried him to church. The men gathered around. Doyle Clay hugged Spradling's legs and started speaking in tongues. Spradling relates the rest of the story:

"Something hit me. At that time I couldn't even put my foot down because the pain was so bad. All of a sudden, something came through me. All I know is when I came to, I was on the other side of the building dancing and praising God in the Spirit. I had been completely healed."[3]

Missionary to Ireland Gary Davidson, Don Spradling, Robert Sullivan, Robert and Dennis Stuart, Melvin Baker, Jerry Cooper and the present Pickens pastor, Larry Morris, were also called to preach during the 1963-64 revival.[4]

Pickens was not the only site of revival in Oklahoma in the 1960's. *The Assemblies of God News* contained reports every month of revivals in communities around the state with hundreds saved and filled with the Spirit.

315

There was an unusual revival in 1969 at Sheridan Assembly in Tulsa with Evangelist-Author Bob Larson. Larson had written a book on the degrading influence of rock 'n' roll music. More than 700 attended the last night of the revival. Thirty were saved and nearly $2,000 worth of rock 'n' roll records were publicly destroyed.[5]

Eugene Howeth almost drowned during a baptismal service during his first pastorate at Taloga in 1965. Howeth, at 5'9", was baptizing a new 6'9" convert in deep water when he lost his balance and his breath. God honored the occasion and Howeth survived.[6]

Members of Faith Tabernacle in Tulsa set a new world record for Bible-reading in 1968. In 12 months the congregation read 106,452 chapters. Thirty-seven people read the entire Bible. Pastor Harry Myers, in a feature article in *The Pentecostal Evangel*, said, "A new realization of the importance for reading God's Word has gripped our entire Sunday School."[7]

Oologah Assembly of God had its beginning in an old Methodist church building in December, 1964, with 31 in attendance. It was set in order the following year.

Full Gospel Assembly in Cushing was born in 1971 in prayer meetings in a home. The revival moved to a store building until a permanent structure could be built.[8]

It took 40 years of praying, but an Assemblies of God church opened in Indiahoma in 1971. Many years before, Grandma Shuck had been saved and filled with the Spirit in a 1928 revival in the tiny community near Lawton. She prayed for a church in her town. Grandma Shuck never gave up on her petitions to God. In the end, her faithfulness and vision were rewarded. In 1971, when she was 77, she sat through the first service at the new Assemblies of God church in her hometown.[9]

Pastor O.F. McAlister must have set some kind of speed record for building a new church building at Meridian, south of Duncan, in 1972. In just seven weeks, he, along with many volunteer workers and neighboring pastors, completed a 36 x 70-foot building.[10]

Also in 1972, Bill Weaver became pastor of First Assembly in Sand Springs. What made the event unusual was the fact that

Weaver did not hold credentials as a minister, but only went to the church to "fill in" between pastors. District Superintendent Robert Goggin helped Weaver go through the licensing process. Weaver is still "filling in" over 21 years later.[11]

MEGA-CHURCHES

A new development in the 1970's was the rise of mega-churches. Prior to this, no Assemblies of God church in Oklahoma had consistently attracted a Sunday morning crowd of more than 600. In metropolitan areas, the tendency was to have many small churches rather than a few large ones. New Life Center, Christian Chapel, Capitol Hill, and Calvary Temple became mega-churches in Tulsa. And a small First Assembly congregation in Oklahoma City became one of the largest Assemblies of God churches in the nation.

Dan and Bonnie Sheaffer were called to Oklahoma City's First Assembly in 1969. The church had actually been measured by the loan company for repossession. The air conditioner was burned out. The Sheaffers' first paycheck was only $42. However, the poor financial condition and the small crowd did not intimidate Sheaffer. He had been told by God several years earlier that he would someday pastor a large church in Oklahoma City.

Only 15 people showed up at the first Wednesday night service. When a few dozen more appeared on Sunday morning, Sheaffer boldly told the small congregation:

"Folks, I don't know where you were Wednesday night, but we are here to build a church. If you are not going to be here on Wednesday night, then I don't want you here on Sunday mornings. I will need your seat pretty soon for a person who wants to serve God and build here what God has asked us to build. You either have to get in, get committed and pray through, or you will have to find somewhere else to go."[12]

Not one listener left the church. Sheaffer knew from that moment that his people were serious. Revival began. The church began to explode. New facilities were not large enough so services were held in the Oklahoma City Civic Center. In 1979 the church changed its name to Crossroads Cathedral and built a multi-million

317

dollar sanctuary and education complex in south Oklahoma City. The 6,000-seat auditorium was filled on many Sundays.

Sheaffer attributes the phenomenal growth of Crossroads Cathedral to strong, bold preaching and his "elder program":

"We didn't immediately hire a large staff. We developed elders to take care of the congregation. Every retired preacher I could get hold of I made an elder in my church. Elders multiplied my effectiveness. They received calls at night, they could go to the hospital on an emergency, and they could take care of so many ministry opportunities that I physically could not handle in a large congregation. The people were not neglected because there was always somebody to be by their side in times of sickness and crisis."[13]

Chapter 26

More Members, Fewer Churches

In the 1960's the number of Assemblies of God churches in Oklahoma decreased while total attendance increased. In each of the previous decades there had been a net increase in the total number of churches. But in the decade of the 1960's, the fellowship had a net loss of 41 churches in the state. In 1959 there were 490 churches compared to only 449 in 1969. Only one church was set in order in each of four different years of the decade. Only 23 churches were officially recognized for the entire ten-year period, while 64 closed their doors for good.[1]

The demise of the country church in Oklahoma was similar to the disappearance of the country schools. Most of the church closings were economically motivated. Small country churches with a small group of believers could not keep up with rising electric bills and the increasing cost of keeping even a part-time pastor.

Herbert Wharton began pastoring a small church in 1960 and was fortunate to get $4 in tithes some weeks.[2] With better cars, many members found it easy to drive to a larger town nearby where the larger church with a full-time staff provided a wider range of programs for all members of the family.

Churches that existed in 1959 but had either consolidated with other churches or disappeared completely by 1980 are: Hockerville, Lone Chapel, Long, Row, Topsy, Latham, Wolf Center, Clebit, Messer, Pleasant Hill, Bald Hill, Baum, Powell, Provence, Asphaltum, Banner, and Sugden.[3]

The Oklahoma population continued to shift from rural areas to metropolitan areas in the 1960's. However, the tremendous population increases in Oklahoma City and Tulsa did not result in a corresponding number of new churches. In the 20 years from 1960 to 1980, the number of Assemblies of God churches in Oklahoma City actually decreased from 34 to 27, while Tulsa saw an increase from 28 to 30 churches.

Medium-sized towns in Oklahoma saw growth in the number of churches. For example, Sapulpa jumped from three to five churches in the 20 years and Edmond increased from one to three churches.[4]

With special home missions effort, there was a net gain of 24 churches in the 1970's.

One of the negative impacts of the Charismatic movement was the emphasis on praise and worship and the de-emphasis on Bible-teaching in Sunday School. Sunday School attendance declined substantially, even though much larger crowds attended Sunday morning worship.

In Oklahoma, Sunday School enrollment in 1965 was 48,982, down 4,000 from the early 1940's. Total attendance on an average Sunday was down to 37,364. The average per Sunday School in Oklahoma was 80.5, under the national average of 84. The decrease came despite a nationally-recognized effort in Oklahoma to train the force of 4,000 Sunday School teachers and officers. Oklahoma led the nation in 1965 by handing out 3,311 Training Class Certificates, 1,000 more than the next highest district.[5]

The top ten Sunday Schools in Oklahoma in July, 1962, were:

1. Tulsa Central Assembly—436
2. Broken Arrow Assembly—434
3. Miami First Assembly—388
4. Oklahoma City Faith Tabernacle—384
5. Tulsa Lewis Avenue—310
6. Bartlesville First Assembly—263
7. Collinsville First Assembly—262
8. Tulsa Carbondale Assembly—252
9. Broken Bow First Assembly—235
10. Muskogee First Assembly—230[6]

In 1963 District Sunday School Director Leslie Moore expressed concern that the Sunday School was thriving in one town and dead in another town a few miles away. He drew a parable from a recent trip he had taken from one end of the state to the other. The trees were green in northwest Oklahoma where rain had been plentiful. The forests were brown in southeast Oklahoma that was suffering through a severe drought. He concluded that the difference in the foliage and in Sunday Schools was "rain, spiritual rain, rain that comes from God."[7]

Sunday School promotion was big business in the 1960's. Local churches received from Springfield a steady flow of ideas on how to promote and increase attendance. There were enlargement campaigns, cradle roll days, loyalty days, training months, counselor months, and teacher recognition days.[8]

Training of teachers and a renewed emphasis on Sunday School paid off in the 1970's. By 1979 the average attendance at an Oklahoma Sunday School was 99.1, and 46,582 Oklahomans attended Assemblies of God Sunday Schools on an average Sunday. Enrollment hit an all-time high of 62,225 one Sunday in 1979. That same year, the Sunday School Department was changed to the Christian Education Department on both the national and the district levels.[9]

CHRIST'S AMBASSADORS: ABUNDANT GROWTH

One area of ministry that experienced abundant growth in the 1960's and 1970's was the youth program. Annual attendance at monthly C.A. rallies in Oklahoma grew from 51,000 in 1963 to 65,000 ten years later.[10]

Youth camp played a vital role in the lives of Oklahoma Assemblies of God youth. The camps grew and thousands of young men and women were saved and filled with the Spirit. Many church leaders in the 1990's look back at youth camp as a turning point in their personal spiritual growth.

In 1960 the District Council called for a special committee to consider the feasibility of building or buying the District's own youth camp. It was getting too expensive to rent other camps because of the growing number of youths who signed up for camp.[11] By 1963 hundreds were being turned away from camp even though the program was expanded to three weekly sessions.[12]

Armon Newburn was Oklahoma District C.A. President in 1963. He had been involved with the very first youth camp in 1956 and actively sought a location for a district-owned youth camp. He found a 40-acre camp with several old dormitories and buildings at Turner Falls near Davis. The Methodists wanted to sell the property for $40,000. Newburn approached Super-intendent Goggin with a novel idea to raise the necessary money: let the young people sell candy supplied by the World's Finest Chocolate Candy Company. Goggin wasn't overly excited, but believed in and approved Newburn's project.[13]

After the District Council in 1963 authorized the purchase of the property, Newburn went into action. He first needed to borrow the funds until the candy sale money came in. He was apprehensive about approaching a loan officer at Local Federal Savings and Loan in Oklahoma City about borrowing $40,000 to buy a youth camp. However, God paved the way. The loan officer was a Methodist who had attended the Turner Falls camp as a youth. He approved the loan without even looking at the property.[14]

C.A.'s in every corner of the state came to their churches with boxes of rich chocolate. Hardly anyone could turn them down. A $20,000 profit was made in only a month. More choco-late was sold the next year, and another $13,000 was raised to retire the debt on Turner Falls. Churches were asked to send $2 per month to maintain the youth camp project.[15]

Armon Newburn saw the value of youth camps early in his ministry:

"We were seeing more people receive the baptism of the Holy Ghost at youth camp than at district campmeeting or at revivals. Youth camps were such a tremendous blessing to our fellowship because kids go and are not bothered by peer pressure or what adults will think or what somebody else knows. Before the week is over they have an experience with God that is real."[16]

Poteau First Assembly pastor Roger Mattox was called to preach at age 14 at youth camp at Bristow in 1963:

"The spiritual emphasis at camp was great. Even the recreation time was in a spiritual atmosphere. In our Bible classes, the Spirit would fall, we would worship God, and have an altar service. The camp allowed me to block out everything else in my life except my personal relationship with God."[17]

The annual report in 1968 showed 1,260 youth attended four camp sessions with 180 saved and 147 receiving the baptism. New dormitories, a new tabernacle and a new dining room were added. Other buildings were remodeled to increase the capacity of Turner Falls because youth were still being turned away.[18] Each year, guest speakers of the highest caliber were brought to Turner Falls to teach and preach to the youth. For example, in 1964 the special speakers were George Brazell, Jesse Moon, Dan Sheaffer, S.J. Colburn, and Paul Savage.[19]

The impact of youth camp on Oklahoma's young people was highlighted in the C.A. Committee report in 1970:

"As headlines have focused on demonstrations, drugs, and destruction on the youth scene of today, we have been privileged to witness time and again, the victories of God's grace. While some were seeking satisfaction in rock festivals, revolution and LSD, over 1,000 young people were experiencing spiritual reality in our youth camps at Turner Falls...In church after church, revival has followed as a direct result of youth camp. For countless young people, camp has meant a revolution in their lives, their commitment to Christ, and their eternal destiny."[20]

By 1979 youth camps expanded to five one-week sessions, and 332 conversions and 181 Holy Spirit baptisms were reported.[21]

Oklahoma had its own C.A. song introduced in the 1960's. It was called "Oklahoma C.A.'s":

> *We're Oklahoma C.A.'s, Oklahoma C.A.'s,*
> *Yes, we love our Savior*
> *He is all we need, for His blood we plead,*
> *And joy we find in serving Him.*
> *Oh, yes we're cleansed from every sin*
> *And Jesus dwells within,*
> *Salvation Jesus freely gives*
> *To those who trust in Him.*
> *We're Oklahoma C.A.'s, Oklahoma C.A.'s,*
> *We are Christ's Ambassadors!*[22]

In the 1970's larger churches saw the need for full-time youth pastors. Greg Whitlow and Randy Miller were among the first full-time youth leaders in local Oklahoma Assemblies of God churches. As the decade progressed, many Oklahoma churches added youth pastors to their staff as the importance of youth ministry was recognized.

Assemblies of God high school graduates were encouraged to attend Southwestern Assemblies of God College and other Assemblies of God institutions of higher learning. However, the high cost of tuition at the privately-funded schools often created problems for students. They had to work night jobs and summers to pay their way. An exception to the tuition-hardship story is Jim McNabb, pastor of Mustang First Assembly. McNabb knew God wanted him to attend Southwestern, but did not know how he could pay. He went in faith. Upon reaching Waxahachie, Texas, he went to the college business office. He was stunned to find his tuition had been paid by a man McNabb had never heard of. McNabb later met the man from south Texas who was visiting McNabb's home church the night he announced he was going to Southwestern and that he was trusting God to provide his tuition.[23]

Chapter 27

New Programs Added

The 1960's saw the creation or expansion of several special programs for Assemblies of God high school and college students. Prayer was being eliminated in public schools where students were receiving little or no moral training. The Assemblies of God stepped in with programs such as Bible Quiz and Teen Talent in 1962. Teen Talent featured vocal and instrumental music performances. Oklahomans excelled in the regional and national competitions from the very beginning.

In 1966 the national C.A. Department launched a new program called Ambassadors in Mission (AIM), a summer evangelistic ministry in which teams of carefully-screened young people between the ages of 16 and 24 conducted intensive house-to-house witnessing in the United States and abroad.[1] Oklahoma's first AIM trip was taken during Christmas vacation in 1971. Forty Oklahoma C.A.'s joined District C.A. President John Gifford and C.A.'s from several other districts on a week-long blitz of Monterrey, Mexico. The crusade resulted in over 800 decisions for Christ and the establishment of a new Assemblies of God church in Monterrey.[2]

The first annual college and career retreat was held at Turner Falls in September, 1966. That year Rita Bly of Shawnee and Paul Spinden of Eufaula were named as the first Miss and Mr. C.A. of Oklahoma. The first statewide Discipleship Camp was held in

1973.[3] And a new youth newspaper, *Oklahoma Sooner News*, began publication in 1975.[4]

Another new program was the Assemblies of God campus ministry called Chi Alpha. In Oklahoma, churches were urged to send in names of college students attending secular colleges and universities because the C.A. Department had a "deep concern for the spiritual welfare of those attending non-Assemblies of God colleges."[5] By 1979 three Oklahoma campuses, Oklahoma State University in Stillwater, Southwestern Oklahoma State University in Weatherford, and Central State University in Edmond, had Chi Alpha chapter houses where students lived. Chapters were in operation on seven other campuses also. The Campus Evangelism Committee in 1979 noted the progress, but realized more work needed to be done: "Literally thousands of youth walk our Oklahoma campuses seeking reality and hoping for something in which to believe."[6]

The C.A. program gave teenagers who felt a special call for ministry in preaching and in music an opportunity for service. Phil Taylor, pastor of Carbondale Assembly in Tulsa, is an excellent example. He preached his first sermon at age 10 to a kids group. C.A. services allowed him to "practice his preaching" during his formative teen years. Taylor, Roger Sharp, and Jeff Taylor formed a successful singing group—The Peacemakers—a direct result of interaction with other teenagers in the local C.A. group. Taylor is unique in that he now pastors the church where he grew up.[7]

Curtis Owens, pastor of Claremore First Assembly, was another C.A. who was given a chance to preach at an early age. Even though he was "scared to death," Owens' first revival as a teenager produced converts. When he saw people responding to the gospel, he knew he wanted to spend his life preaching.[8]

BRING THE LITTLE CHILDREN UNTO ME: PROGRAMS FOR KIDS

No Assemblies of God kid can ever forget the song, "This little light of mine, I'm gonna let it shine," and especially the second verse, "Hide it under a bushel? No!" Songs like "Deep and Wide," "The B-I-B-L-E," "Jesus Loves Me," "Into My Heart," and "I'm in the Lord's Army" made a lasting impression.[9] Assem-

ow critically important it was to
nile boys and girls were young.
e kids' hearts.

egan sponsoring Kids Kamps in the
rray. The kamp was later moved to
the kamps mushroomed to 1,362 in
foul   443 youngsters were saved and 363
were fil   10

ROYAL RANGERS

Royal Rangers, a camping program much like Boy Scouts, was introduced in the Assemblies of God in 1962. Over 350 men and boys attended the first Oklahoma statewide Royal Rangers Pow-Wow at Turner Falls in 1966. Eugene Meador was the first district Royal Rangers commander.[11] In 1979 the national Royal Rangers Commander and founder of the program, Johnnie Barnes, was the main speaker at the Oklahoma Pow-Wow, which was attended by 681 boys and leaders. Sectional Pow-Wows began in the 1970's. Leadership training courses began in 1977. The District leased a Royal Rangers camp—Camp Hoppes it was called—at Stroud in the 1970's.[12]

MISSIONETTES

In 1955 the General Council initiated a program for the training of young women. It was called Missionettes, and its history has been marvelous. By 1965 there were 159 Missionette clubs in Oklahoma.[13] In 1978 Oklahoma had 4,900 Junior and Senior Missionettes, more than any other district. The state also led the nation that year in the number of new Missionette groups formed (25) and in Missionette offerings.[14]

Fourteen-year-old Gloria Jean Kelly of Midwest City First Assembly answered the question, "Why am I a Missionette?", in the July, 1961 *Assemblies of God News*:

"Since I've taken Christ as my Savior, He has taught me to serve Him, and I find this possible through being a Missionette... I have learned to be a Bible reader and a prayer warrior, and these two together make me a witness for my Lord."[15]

The Stairway to the Stars achievement program was introduced in Missionettes in the 1960's. The top level for girls was Honor Star. It became a tradition at the annual campmeeting for Honor Stars to be crowned in a special service.

OTHER MINISTRIES

Oklahoma played a key role in the organization of Action Crusades in the Men's Fellowship Department in 1964. Oklahoma City Pastor Otis Keener, Jr., found great response from the men in his church to a program of planned personal witnessing for Christ. Men would travel to a nearby community or to foreign countries to witness. Keener's idea was adopted by national leaders. Oklahoma laymen participated in many Action Crusades in the 1960's and 1970's. In 1971 the name of the Men's Fellowship Department was changed to Men's Ministries.[16]

The Oklahoma District has always been a consistent supporter of the General Council Department of Benevolences, the agency that administers programs for aged ministers, child welfare, and disaster relief. In 1966 First Assembly in Muskogee was eighth and Capitol Hill Assembly in Tulsa was tenth in the nation in giving to benevolence projects, which included giving to the Hillcrest Children's Home in Hot Springs, Arkansas.[17]

In 1972 Earl Berryman, Jr., of Oklahoma City became the first full-time Assemblies of God chaplain in the Oklahoma prison system. He conducted chapel services and Bible studies at the Lexington Regional Community Treatment Center.[18]

The First Deaf Camp for the hearing impaired was sponsored by the Oklahoma District in August, 1963, at Turner Falls. Bible classes were conducted in sign language for the 30 participants. Elmo and June Pierce reported that "deaf souls left the camp with a new determination to live for Christ, knowing full well that they may not have an opportunity to attend Spirit-filled services until another year brings another camp."[19]

Teen Challenge, a successful effort to help delinquent youth and teen gangs in urban areas, was born in the ministry of Assemblies of God Evangelist David Wilkerson, author of *The Cross and the Switchblade*. In 1970 Oklahoma's first Teen Challenge program was launched in an old church building on S.W. 25th in Oklahoma City. Bill Rigsby, the program's first director, credited

W.W. Hays, founder of the Union Rescue Mission in Oklahoma City, with starting him in street evangelism. Witnessing in the inner city was tough. One of Rigsby's first converts was a 19-year-old gang leader who had just been released from jail. When Rigsby first tried to witness to him, the young man sneered. He shouted obscenities and said, "Nobody cares about me!" A dozen Teen Challenge workers surrounded him and told him Jesus cared. The young rebel accepted Jesus on the spot.[20]

Chapter 28

Raised from His Deathbed

One of the greatest miracles of healing in Oklahoma in the 1970's involved District Sunday School Director W.G. Baker.

Oklahoma Assemblies of God pastors gave weekly reports to their congregations in 1977 and 1978 on Baker's condition. The doctors said he was near death. He had developed severe, bleeding ulcers in his stomach.

He spent five months in intensive care, underwent five major surgeries in a two-month period, and was given as many as 20 pints of blood in a 24-hour period. For months, Baker lingered while doctors said he could not live more than another hour because he was losing blood faster than it could be replenished. Baker's stomach had to be completely removed.

The night before a critical, life-saving surgery at Veterans Hospital in Oklahoma City, Baker's wife Doris was attending a service at Lakeside Assembly of God. Sister Baker relates how God spoke to her:

"The Lord told me to request prayer that Gene would be given a new stomach. I thought it was impossible and that people would make fun of me. Just as Pastor Greg Whitlow began dismissing the congregation, I raised my hand and made the bold request. We all joined hands and heaven came down. When I went home that night, I sang the little chorus, 'Trust and Obey.' I believed God would honor the prayers of His people."

The first sign that God had honored the prayers of literally thousands of Oklahoma believers occurred the next day. Tests run at the V.A. Hospital perplexed doctors. There was something different about his X-rays. The Bakers knew God had supernaturally intervened when an X-ray technician took them to a viewing room and pointed out "a new little stomach" that had mysteriously formed.

Baker completely recovered and served another decade as Sunday School or Christian education director. The story of Baker's brush with death and God's miraculous intervention has been told hundreds of times and thousands have been blessed by his testimony.[1]

STABLE LEADERSHIP

Oklahoma didn't spend a lot of money on nameplates for district officials in the 1960's and 1970's, because changes were rare. It was a remarkably stable period for leadership in all district positions.

District Superintendent Robert Goggin, Assistant Superintendent James Dodd, and Women's Missionary Council President Marie Goggin served the entire period. Three longtime district officials retired in 1972. John Grace was succeeded by James C. Girkin as missions director, Elmer T. Watkins replaced L.H. Arnold as secretary-treasurer, and W.G. Baker was elected Sunday School director to succeed Leslie Moore. T.A. McDonough, Armon Newburn, Eugene Meador, John Gifford, and Frank Cargill served as district C.A. presidents. In 1968 former District Superintendent F.C. Cornell retired as executive presbyter—after 30 years as a district official. He was replaced by Armon Newburn.[2]

Improvements were made to the Oklahoma City campgrounds and office complex. A bookstore was opened in 1962 and a new auditorium was constructed in 1964.[3] The auditorium was chosen in 1968 as the site for the "anchor" service of a world prayer meeting following a four-day crusade by C.M. Ward. The weekly ABC radio presentation of Revivaltime was broadcast from the district auditorium on the last night of the crusade.[4]

The financial picture of the Oklahoma District in the 1960's and 1970's was bright. The Revolving Fund, set up to help build new churches and repair older ones, had net assets of just under $3.5 million by 1979. The fund was administered by a three-man committee headed by Conrad Barrett.[5] In 1980 the Oklahoma District had total receipts of $1.8 million and a net worth of $7 million.[6]

The number of ordained and licensed ministers and Christian workers showed only a slight increase in the District from 1960 to 1980—from 1,160 to 1,198.[7]

Oklahoma was blessed with the cream of nationally-recognized preachers at campmeetings and district councils. The Who's Who list included Robert Ashcroft, Willard Cantelon, Philip Crouch, Owen Carr, Hardy Steinberg, C.C. Burnett, John G. Hall, James Hamill, and every General Council leader during the period.

Okmulgee native Owen Carr led the Oklahoma contingent at national headquarters in Springfield. Carr served as national youth secretary. Oklahoma pastor and missionary John Garlock replaced a fellow Oklahoman, Raymond T. Brock, as editor of foreign missions publications in 1963.[8] Bert Webb continued to serve as assistant general superintendent. In 1977 L.B. Keener of Bartlesville became a field representative for the Gospel Publishing House after serving more than 20 years as a national Sunday school representative. H.A. Brummett became president of Southwestern Assemblies of God College in Waxahachie, Texas, in 1978. Brummett characterized as absolutely essential a Bible school education for potential workers in the Assemblies of God fellowship:

"Those who will pastor our churches should at least have their undergraduate degree from one of our Bible schools. Students are greatly influenced by their professors. If the precious doctrines that we hold fully essential to our faith are not taught, or if they are treated negatively, in the secular college classroom, there is an adverse effect upon the student."[9]

335

Thomas F. Zimmerman was elected general superintendent in 1959, a position he held until 1985. By 1979 the Assemblies of God counted 1.6 million adherents in the United States and eight million overseas.[10]

▼ Robert Goggin and Armon Newburn, 1963.

▲ Robert Goggin, Randall Ball, Harold Stockton, Earl Taylor, 1960.

▲ Lawrence Langley (l) receives award from DCAP Armon Newburn, 1964.

▲ *1961 Youth camp committee, (l to r) Harold Powell, Russell Herndon, Charles Shipman, J.D. Keen, DCAP T.A. McDonough.*

▲ *Youth camp, an exciting spiritual experience.*

◀ *"chow time" at youth camp, 1961.*

▲ *1962 Youth camp trophy winners.*

The Dan ▶
Sheaffer family,
1963.

▲ *Oklahoma's first Deaf Camp at Turner Falls, 1964.*

▲ *1965 Bible quiz champions, Broken Arrow Assembly. Pastor James Dodd is at left. Coach Jimmy Bowles is at right.*

▲ *Broken Arrow Assembly of God.*

▲ *The Tri-tones trio of Oklahoma City Faith Tabernacle, Teen Talent vocal ensemble winners, 1965.*

▲ *Baby days at Velma Assembly of God, 1966.*

342

▲ *First Assembly, Ponca City, 1967.*

▲ *The Joe Calabrese family, 1967.*

▲ *Missionettes Honor Star crowning service.*

▼ *Teen Talent. (l to r) Ric Freeman, Dana Brooks, Kari Goins, Tom Kidwell, Kelly Goins.*

▼ *Rev. and Mrs. Elmer T. Watkins. Watkins served as District Secretary-Treasurer from 1972 to 1986.*

▲ *Woodlake Assembly of God, Tulsa, 1975.*

▼ *H.A. Brummett became president of Southwestern Assemblies of God College in 1978.*

▲ *Ron Brannan, District Royal Ranger Commander, 1975 to 1985.*

George Brazell, the ▶ perennial offering-taker at campmeetings and district councils.

Chapter 29

Oklahoma Leads the Way

In 1980 Oklahoma was third nationally with an average Sunday School attendance of 46,982 and second in the number of established Sunday Schools. District Christian Education Director W.G. Baker worked hard to try to reverse the trend of decreased Sunday School growth. For the first 50 years most Assemblies of God churches had more people in Sunday School than in the morning worship service. That situation had reversed by 1980 when statistics showed 51,984 as an average attendance for morning worship and only 46,982 for Sunday School.[1]

By 1984 there were 474 Sunday Schools in Oklahoma with an average attendance of 48,792, compared with average morning worship attendance of 56,573. And yet thirteen thousand more people were attending Oklahoma Assemblies of God Sunday Schools in 1984 than in 1954.[2]

In 1988 Oklahoma rose to second in the nation in Sunday School attendance. Four Oklahoma churches, Faith Tabernacle in Oklahoma City, Tulsa Woodlake, Crystal Rock Cathedral in Ardmore, and Sand Springs First Assembly, placed in the top 100 churches in the nation in Sunday School attendance.[3]

In 1992 the Sunday Schools of Oklahoma could say, "We're Number One." That year they led the nation in attendance with 485 Sunday Schools reporting a total enrollment of 65,880 and average attendance of 46,516. Sunday School attendance in 1992 was at about the same level as 1980, underscoring the trend of more people skipping Sunday School to attend only the Sunday morning worship service.[4]

The top ten Sunday Schools in Oklahoma in September, 1993, were:

1. Sand Springs First Assembly—743
2. Tulsa Woodlake Assembly—614
3. Tulsa Eastland Assembly—527
4. Oklahoma City Lakeside Assembly—514
5. Oklahoma City Faith Tabernacle—491
6. Mustang Assembly—459
7. Lawton First Assembly—452
8. Broken Arrow Assembly—395
9. Tulsa Carbondale Assembly—325
10. Oklahoma City-The Rock—323[5]

YOUTH PROGRAMS

Oklahoma's strong youth programs became even stronger between 1980 and 1994. Youth camps burst at the seams as more and more weeks of camp were added to the schedule. More than 2,400 youth attended five different sessions of youth camp at Turner Falls in 1993. Youth camp continued to have a major spiritual impact upon hundreds of Oklahoma young people each year.

Participation in Teen Talent competition (the name was changed to Fine Arts Festival in 1986) also increased. Tecumseh First Assembly became the first Oklahoma church to win the national Bible Quiz competition in 1982 and Ken Henderson of Tecumseh was the top quizzer in the nation that year.[6] In 1986 Holly Breese of Owasso Assembly and David Kim of Broken Arrow Assembly were crowned national champions in instrumental music divisions and Nicole Brandon of Tulsa Woodlake Assembly was named the country's top individual Bible quizzer.[7] First Assembly of Bartlesville put together impressive Bible Quiz teams.

At the 1993 Fine Arts Festival, Bartlesville First finished second nationally for the second year in a row. Lisa Wootton finished number one in the national individual competition and her brother Bryan finished number six. In 1993 Oklahoma ranked second in the nation in number of Bible Quiz teams.[8]

The District Youth Convention continued to be a highlight of youth activities in the 1980's and 1990's. More than 4,000 attended the 1993 convention. Excellent speakers and great musical guests like Ray Boltz kept youth interested in the annual event.

In 1986 District Youth Director Tom Greene praised Oklahoma Assemblies of God youth:

"As delinquents dominate the headlines, the story of the good kid remains untold. More than ten thousand Oklahoma Assemblies of God young people are endeavoring to conduct themselves in a manner pleasing to Christ. A mighty army of dedicated teens are stepping forward in their communities, schools, and neighborhoods, proclaiming victory in Jesus."[9]

The District Youth Department sponsored its first ski trip in 1985. Discipleship Camp continued to provide excellent intensive spiritual training. Youth pastors Randy Morgan and Damon Isaacs began "A Night Like This," an alternative to the high school prom, for district teens in 1991. Christian Fun Day is an annual event at Frontier City in Oklahoma City. Praisong, directed by Dennis and Debbie Sprouse of Sallisaw, began its annual summer tour in 1989. Praisong features skilled high school singers and actors in a dramatic and musical tour of state churches.[10]

Youth Alive Bible club chapters, led by coordinator David Mewbourne, have been formed on many public school campuses in the state. And, hundreds of Oklahoma teens and college students took AIM trips for short-term missions service to Russia in 1992 and 1993. Almost 40,000 Oklahoma youth attended youth rallies in 1993.[11]

The Chi Alpha program has expanded to 16 Oklahoma campuses. In 1985 a College Ministry Division was added to the District Youth Department with Bill and Wendy Snyder as coordinators. They pastored the Chi Alpha effort on the O.S.U.

campus in Stillwater. Greg and Susan Tiffany ministered to the students at O.U. in Norman and became district coordinators when the Snyders moved to an inner-city ministry in Kansas City in 1991. Rodney and Shannon Fouts replaced the Snyders on the O.S.U. campus. In 1993 Ron Boshela became the Chi Alpha pastor for college and university campuses in metropolitan areas of the state.[12]

CHILDREN'S MINISTRIES

Numbers were strong for Kids Kamp as the 1980's began. 2,045 kids and staff attended the kamps in 1981 where 531 were saved and 616 filled with the Spirit.[13] The 1993 Kids Kamps attendance was 1,684. In 1992 the first Intermediate Camp for over 400 boys and girls from the ages of 11 to 13 was held at Turner Falls. Faye Salkil, wife of District Christian Education Director Jack Salkil, introduced a new District Children's Ministry team in 1992 to hold Kids Krusades in Oklahoma churches. The team ministered to more than 2,200 persons in 1993.[14]

A special kids program was begun in 1990 by Mustang Assembly using a mobile ministry trailer. Neighborhoods were blitzed by volunteers with fliers announcing a "kids' roundup" the next day. The trailer was taken to a nearby park where children came to hear Bible stories and enjoy puppet shows.[15]

Royal Rangers and Missionettes continue to be vital parts of children's ministries in Assemblies of God churches in Oklahoma. In 1993 there were 234 Royal Ranger outposts (tops in the nation) with 4,740 boys enrolled. Ronald Brannan served as district Royal Ranger commander from 1975 to 1985. He was followed by Altus First Assembly Pastor Richard Ventonis in 1986 and Pawnee First Assembly Pastor James Eubanks in 1987.[16] More than 1,000 boys and staff jammed into Camp Hoppes at Stroud for the 1987 Pow-Wow.[17]

As of August, 1993, there were 6,607 girls involved in Missionettes in Oklahoma. The Oklahoma District has crowned 1,758 Honor Stars, more than any other district in the fellowship. Oklahoma has many special young ladies in Missionettes. One is Heather Lockler of Verdigris Assembly. Heather was awarded the Miriam Award from the national Women's Ministries Department in 1988 after saving the life of another girl riding on the church van. The other girl was choked on a piece of hard candy. Heather calmly leaned the girl forward in the seat and hit her with her hand between the shoulder blades, dislodging the candy.[18]

SPECIAL MINISTRIES

According to statistics, 51 percent of the adults attending the average Assemblies of God church are single by choice, divorced, or widowed. In order to meet the special needs of these believers, the Singles Ministry program was placed under the district Christian education director in 1991. That same year, the first annual Singles Conference sponsored by the district was held in Oklahoma City. Workshops like "Passion, Purity, and Being Single" were offered. The conference report stressed the urgency of ministry to singles: "The next ten years will produce more single adults than in the history of mankind."[19]

Men's Ministries in Oklahoma has accepted the challenge from the national office to build at least one new church in the state each year during the Decade of Harvest. Men's Ministries was placed under the district missions director in 1986. The 1988 District Council heard a call to action for men in Oklahoma:

"This is the age of the layman... Men's Ministries offers something for virtually everyone in the life and service of the church. There is Royal Rangers for boys and men, Light for the Lost for missions involvement, Lifestyle Evangelism and Kingsmen for soul winning, and work projects for hands-on help."[20]

The first statewide Men's Retreat was held at Turner Falls in 1988. It was a rousing success, and the retreats are growing in popularity each year. Attendance mushroomed from 185 in 1988 to more than 400 in 1993.[21]

The first Decade of Harvest project in 1990 for Men's Ministries was at the North Rock Creek Indian church north of Shawnee. More than 100 men gathered to build a new church in just two Saturdays. Materials for the building were purchased with $8,000 raised in a special offering at the District Men's Retreat.[22]

Oklahomans have been active in the MAPS R.V. program. Recreational vehicle owners gather to complete special projects for churches. In November, 1992, Billy Moore led a team of ten couples that painted and roofed the church at Fallis in just four days.

Each year in the 1980's, Oklahoma was near the top in benevolence giving to Hillcrest Children's Home, Highlands Child Placement Services, Aged Ministers Assistance, Disaster Relief, and Refugee Resettlement. Valliant Assembly of God was the top church in benevolence giving in the nation in 1981 and Tulsa Woodlake Assembly was third. The Valliant church, in a community of only 1,000 people, gave over $21,000.[23] In 1991, Oklahoma gave $216,548 to benevolences—second only to Arkansas. Forty-three Oklahoma churches gave more than $1,000 each. Tulsa Woodlake topped the list.[24]

The New Lifehouse, a juvenile training center for teenage girls, opened in August, 1984, at Disney, Oklahoma. The center was a vision of Disney Pastor Bill Goldner that grew out of an unusual encounter with a teenage girl whom he realized was "lost, confused, and tossed about by the circumstances of life."[25]

Trucker's Chaplain Fred Wright in 1992 oversaw the conversion of a 40-foot trailer into a "Chapel of Peace." Many churches and individuals pitched in to finance the project, which provides ministry to truckers at a truck stop on I-44 in east Tulsa 24 hours a day.[26]

Sonrise Ranch in the Wichita Mountains near Cache in southwest Oklahoma was dedicated in 1992. It is a Teen Challenge project to house young men who need long-term discipling. Bill Everitt is in charge of this Teen Challenge effort, which is called New Life Challenge of the Wichitas.[27]

THE DISTRICT OFFICE

Oklahoma is among the most financially stable districts in the Assemblies of God. The Revolving Fund has continued to grow with 1993 assets of more than $4.2 million. As of August 31, 1993, the District had a net worth of $7.3 million. Total receipts in all departments during the preceding 12 months exceeded $4.2 million.[28]

In 1985 the District Council authorized the appointment of a special committee to look at long-range plans for district-owned property. The question of whether or not to sell the campgrounds on North Kelley in Oklahoma City had never been fully answered since it first arose in 1947.[29]

After several years of review, the Executive Board made a final decision:

"We searched long and diligently and discovered it would cost in the neighborhood of $4-5 million to relocate and replace our present facilities. The Board felt this would be too much of a financial burden to place on us, our kids, and our grandkids. Thus the decision was made to remodel our present facilities."[30]

Improvements were made to the District Auditorium, and a beautiful, spacious new office complex was completed in 1991. Should the Lord tarry, the Oklahoma District is ready for growth well into the twenty-first century.

THE ASSEMBLIES OF GOD IN THE NEWS

The 1980's was a decade of highs and lows for Assemblies of God believers. President Jimmy Carter in the late 1970's had made it fashionable to be called "born again." Ronald Reagan was elected President in 1980, and the church-world applauded. James Watt, an Assemblies of God layman, was appointed Secretary of the Interior in the Reagan cabinet. John Ashcroft, the son of a pioneer Assemblies of God preacher, was elected Governor of Missouri. Jim and Tammy Bakker and their PTL (Praise the Lord) television program became an institution in millions of American households.

Assemblies of God churches were no longer located on the wrong side of the tracks. Through hard work and prayer, the movement had blossomed spiritually and in numbers. Ministers had gained respect of their entire communities and were often elected to lead civic clubs. The Assemblies of God had arrived! Then the fellowship's public image was dealt a crushing blow by two scandals.[31]

In 1987 a long-simmering feud erupted between Jim Bakker and Jimmy Swaggart—both of whom held credentials with the Assemblies of God. Bakker was accused, and later convicted of, bilking hundreds of thousands of dollars from supporters while building a Christian theme park and resort in North Carolina.

When Bakker was accused of both sexual and financial wrong-doing, Swaggart told a national television audience on ABC's Nightline that Bakker was "a cancer that should be excised from the body of Christ."[32] The PTL scandal was front-page material for the nation's newspapers and a prime-time subject for the liberal television producers of national nightly newscasts. The media labeled the scandal "Pearlygate." Christians, and especially Pentecostals, were crushed.

Television ministers had sought and reaped a great harvest among Pentecostals in America. Historian Edith Blumhofer reasons:

"Many Pentecostals enjoyed seeing their own become stars. Having gone unnoticed for many years, they took pride in and lavished funds on those who gave them visibility. Like Bakker and Swaggart, many of them recalled years of deprivation. Some seemed inclined to revel in possessions which they rationalized, indicated God's blessings... When Jim and Tammy Bakker decided to open a lavish Christian amusement park and offer their devoted supporters the opportunity of participating in a setting that featured the stars of Christian pop culture, the faithful responded enthusiastically. The setting, after all, brought them about as close to the country club milieu as they were likely to get."[33]

Jim Bakker was dismissed by the Assemblies of God in 1987 for conduct unbecoming a minister, including allegations of sexual misconduct. Oklahoma, unfortunately, had a part to play in the scandal. Oklahoma City Evangelist John Wesley Fletcher admitted introducing church secretary Jessica Hahn to Jim Bakker for immoral purposes. And former Illinois District Superintendent Richard Dortch, a frequent speaker at Oklahoma campmeetings, supplied hush money to Hahn.

Jim and Tammy Bakker had appealed mainly to Pentecostals who favored doing away with all "legalism" and "separation" thinking. In contrast to the Bakkers, Swaggart focused on holiness, separation, and evangelism. Blumhofer says, "His warm style and honky-tonk sound attracted handclapping crowds who regarded him as the ablest exponent of the true Pentecostal message."[34] In 1988 Swaggart admitted to moral failure. New Orleans

Pastor Marvin Gorman, also a frequent campmeeting speaker in Oklahoma, told the world that he had hired a detective to follow Swaggart and a prostitute to a motel room. Pentecostals watched in disbelief as Swaggart's confession before his church in Louisiana was the lead story on the national news. Assemblies of God leaders required that Swaggart enter a two-year rehabilitation program for ministers who had suffered moral failure. When Swaggart refused to complete the program, the Executive Presbytery voted to strip him of his credentials as an Assemblies of God minister.[35]

God again turned negatives into positives. The public humiliation of two of the most visible Assemblies of God ministers caused ministers and laymen alike to reevaluate personal motives and priorities. Oklahoma District Superintendent Armon Newburn said God was "calling us back to the trenches where we had begun, where the number one priority was reaching lost souls." He told an Edmond congregation to "repent and live a holy and righteous life before God."[36]

The Bakker and Swaggart scandals showed Assemblies of God believers the importance of attending and supporting a local church. The fellowship emerged from the moral failures stronger and more united than ever before.

Chapter 30

Okies in Print

A number of Oklahoma Assemblies of God authors have made an impact in recent years. Tulsa Pastor Richard Exley became a prominent anti-abortion spokesman and wrote a best-selling book, *Abortion: Pro-Life by Conviction, Pro-Choice by Default*. The book is a call for Christians to become activists in the fight against legalized abortion. Exley writes:

"Abortion is the most critical issue now facing the American church... Every day, in abortion clinics and hospitals across our nation, four to five thousand pre-born babies are systematically put to death. The total number of casualties, in this war on the pre-born, has now reached more than 25 million and our great land is stained with their innocent blood."[1]

Many Assemblies of God believers in Oklahoma have taken a strong, activist stand against abortion and have become involved in political campaigns on the side of pro-life candidates.

Louise Jeter Walker has written 19 books, most of them textbooks in Spanish for Bible schools, local churches, and correspondence study courses. Currently, she is working on the third volume of a history of the Assemblies of God in Latin America. Her *Peruvian Gold* in 1985 was the exciting story of the pioneer missionaries in Peru.

Sister Walker's missionary and professor brother, Hugh Jeter, wrote one of the best expositions of divine healing in his book, *By His Stripes.*

Oklahoman Raymond T. Brock wrote the first of his seven books in 1961. It was called *Into the Highways and Hedges.* Brock was called to preach at age 13 in the middle of the night while visiting friends in Asher. At daybreak he told his pastor-host about the experience. The pastor allowed Brock to preach his first sermon at a C.A. service that same night. He held his first revival at age 14 in a brush arbor at Okesa.

When Brock first applied for a minister's license, District Superintendent F.C. Cornell told him he was too young to be licensed. He applied again when he was older and was accepted. For many years Brock directed various Assemblies of God publication efforts in Springfield and answered questions in a "Dear Ray" column in the *C.A. Herald.* Today, he is a licensed psychologist and has become well known in recent years as a Christian counselor. At present his question-and-answer column, "Ask Ray", appears weekly in *The Pentecostal Evangel.*[2]

John G. Hall of Newscastle is one of the nation's best known authors and teachers on Bible prophecy. He has taken his famous "big chart" to all 50 states. Cordas C. Burnett, an Assemblies of God giant in education, said audiences at Hall's lectures were "challenged and inspired—if not awed—by his grasp and presentation of the Word of God."[3]

Veteran Oklahoma pastor Grady Adcock is a published poet. Here is an example of his wit:

BABBLE OR BUBBLE

Have you heard a preacher who resembles
Sounding brass and tinkling cymbals?
The church should hold the preacher liable
Who doesn't pray and read his Bible.

With many things a man may dabble
Yet retain his pulpit babble.
Anointed sermons are added trouble
But it gives that spiritual bubble.

If God's spokesman seems to choke
Then His anointing will break the yoke.
First break up your fallow ground
And sow His good seed all around.[4]

Oklahoma missionary Don Stamps made a tremendous contribution by producing *The Full Life Study Bible*. In 1981 he felt God's call to write Pentecostal study notes on the Bible to help the untrained pastors of the hundreds of Assemblies of God churches being opened each year in Brazil.

For a decade, both in Brazil and the United States, Don wrote the notes, and his wife Linda typed and edited them. He was backed up by Wesley Adams and an editorial committee headed by Assemblies of God theologians Stanley Horton and William Menzies. Loren Triplett, now the executive director of the Division of Foreign Missions of the General Council, expanded the scope of the study notes from a Brazilian project into a world-wide project.[5]

The English version of the New Testament of *The Full Life Study Bible* was published in 1990. Meanwhile Don Stamps' health was failing. Suffering greatly from cancer and weakness, he worked on until he completed the notes on the Old Testament just four weeks before his death in 1991.

The complete English study Bible was released by Zondervan in September, 1992, as a co-publishing arrangement with Gospel Publishing House. As the first widely accepted Pentecostal study Bible in the world, *The Full Life Study Bible* has become a major best-seller among Pentecostal and charismatic believers. It is being translated into 16 other languages. Loren Triplett hailed it as "one of the finest and most powerful tools ever created for preaching and studying the Word of God as well as discipling in foreign lands." Paul Yonggi Cho, pastor of the world's largest church in Seoul, South Korea, says, "The Bible repeatedly emphasizes the absolute priority of New Testament truth, devotion to Christ, a righteous life, and the manifested power of the Holy Spirit." David Wilkerson says *The Full Life Study Bible* "comes at just the right time to strengthen the roots of evangelical Christianity."[6]

While some Okies were making an impact in the publication field, others were gaining national prominence in other fields. In

1985, Minco, Oklahoma, native Everett Stenhouse was elected assistant general superintendent of the Assemblies of God and served in the fellowship's second highest position until 1993.

George Flattery, a native of Three Sands, Oklahoma, was the major driving force in the 1960's behind the creation of the International Correspondence Institute (ICI). He continues to serve as president of this very successful worldwide effort of the Assemblies of God in theological training by correspondence. ICI, now known as ICI University, has spread the gospel to millions around the world.

Cary Tidwell from Red Oak Oklahoma, became personnel/family life secretary of the Division of Foreign Missions of the General Council in 1990.

In 1984 Lynette Jernigan of Oklahoma City was appointed as music editor of the national Music Department. Jernigan had served as music director for several Oklahoma churches.[7]

Linda Robbins of Oklahoma City presently directs music programs at Southwestern Assemblies of God College in Waxahachie.

Dwain Jones served as national Men's Ministries director and national secretary of Light-for-the-Lost before becoming pastor at First Assembly in Chickasha. In 1991 he left that church to become a spokesman for Mark Buntain's Mission of Mercy in Calcutta, India. Jones is nationally known as a missions convention, campmeeting, and retreat speaker—as well as for his funny stories.[8]

Chuck Freeman has held about every possible position in Light-for-the-Lost.

David Satterfield serves as a Christian Education/Curriculum consultant for the national Christian Education Department.

We have named a number of notable persons but none is more worthy than the pastor's wife in a local Assemblies of God church. Wives of some pastors have chosen to take an active part in the local church. Others are content to stay on the sideline and support their husbands in the prayer closet. JoAnn Newburn, the wife of District Superintendent Armon Newburn, was a pastor's wife for many years. As the current first lady of the District, Sister Newburn has timely advice for pastors' wives:

"First and foremost, wives must not be jealous of their husband's time. It can be frustrating. One night when we were pastoring, I called the church and asked Armon when he might have a free night. It was 18 nights later when our schedules gave us time alone. Wives must be willing to share their husbands. They must be careful with their comments, be good listeners, and be totally supportive. If he preaches a 'bummer', don't tell him for a few days. Fight for family time. It is imperative that a pastor and his family spend quality time each week as an example to the church. However, wives must first be a wife, then a mother, then a pastor's wife. The church will suffer if the first two responsibilities are not taken care of."[9]

———— ∞ ————

Chapter 31

Looking Back— Looking Ahead

Looking back, we see God's blessing on the Assemblies of God in Oklahoma—not only in the distant years but also in the recent past. The number of people attending the services lately has increased much more than the number of churches. In 1980 there were 473 Assemblies of God churches in the state. In 1994 there are 487, served by 1,349 credentialed ministers.[1]

In the last 15 years there has been a trend toward larger churches. Many small churches in metropolitan areas of Oklahoma saw very little or no growth in the 1980's—while medium and large churches became even larger. Crossroads Cathedral, Faith Tabernacle, and Lakeside Assembly in Oklahoma City; Crystal Rock Assembly in Ardmore; and Tulsa Woodlake Assembly regularly exceed 1,000 in Sunday morning worship services. A half-dozen other churches exceed 500 in attendance on Sunday morning. Another 10 churches average more than 400.[2]

Here are the latest statistics on Assemblies of God churches in Oklahoma:

ATTENDANCE	NUMBER OF CHURCHES	PERCENTAGE OF TOTAL
Over 700	10	2%
400-699	10	2%
200-399	51	10.5%
100-199	111	22.4%
50-99	158	32.2%
1-49	140	28.5%[3]

Churches in smaller towns have used creativity to make up for the lack of a large budget and a large staff. First Assembly in Perkins is an excellent example of what can be done. Pastors David and Bertha Raines do a little bit of everything in assuring the success of various church programs. A Wednesday night service in Perkins in the summer of 1993 found Sister Raines playing the piano and teaching the Bible lesson, and Brother Raines dressing up as "Theo" the clown to create a professional and effective children's service.[4]

Large churches also sprang up in some smaller communities in the 1980's. Evangel Assembly in Muskogee grew from 27 to more than 400 in 14 months. Crystal Rock Cathedral in Ardmore increased from 250 to 1,700 in just six years.[5] Grandview Assembly in Elk City grew from 17 to 260 in seven years.[6] In Comanche, a town of 1,900, Praise Assembly averaged 240 on Sunday mornings.[7] In four years, Calvary Assembly in Stillwater doubled in attendance to more than 300. In a decade when many churches found it difficult to find volunteer labor to build new facilities, Calvary Pastor W. Stan Formby reported in *The Pentecostal Evangel* that "God's people couldn't be stopped." Shifts of volunteers saved the church up to $100,000 in the building program.[8]

Million-dollar church buildings are not unique to Oklahoma City and Tulsa. Paul Sharpe and his congregation dedicated a new million-dollar complex in 1988 in Woodward.[9]

In recent years, there has been a beautiful cooperation among neighboring churches in Oklahoma. When natural disasters hit, surrounding churches pitched in and helped. In April and May, 1984, tornadoes totally destroyed the churches in Prue and Morris and heavily damaged Mannford Assembly. Floodwaters did extensive damage to Calvary Temple in Tulsa. Prue Assembly was rebuilt debt-free as the result of the "generosity of many people and churches."

The tornado in Mannford came during the Sunday morning service. One person was killed and several others were injured. Pastor Don Couch, a year later, looked back at the catastrophe:

"A year ago as we stood in the rubble, we really did not know what the future held. However, God showed us once again that 'all things work together for good to them that love God, to them who are the called according to His purpose'."[10]

Another shining example of multi-church cooperation was the completion in 1991 of First Assembly in Glenpool. Woodlake Assembly in Tulsa gave more than $100,000 to the project. Tulsa Carbondale Assembly contributed pews for the building. Major financial support and volunteer labor came from Bixby First Assembly, Owasso First Assembly, Ponca City First Assembly, and Vinita First Assembly.[11]

In 1993 District Superintendent Newburn preached a campmeeting in Okmulgee County, celebrating 70 years of Assemblies of God ministry in the county. Edgar McElhannon served as chairman of the campmeeting that was a cooperative effort of Okmulgee First, Okmulgee Northside, Okmulgee Eastside, Henryetta First, Dewar Faith, Beggs Assembly, Morris Assembly, and Haydenville Assembly.[12]

A CHOICE FOR BELIEVERS

In metropolitan areas believers often have a choice as to which Assemblies of God church they attend. Music plays an important part in their selection. Dan Sheaffer, pastor of Crossroads Cathedral in Oklahoma City, says a pastor cannot overemphasize the importance of music in the service:

"Music is an eternal language and an expression of praise to God. God himself sings, there is one scripture that indicates that. It's part of God's being. Music ushers you into His presence. I think the most important thing in a service is the anointed sermon, but music is a close second."[13]

371

H.A. Brummett, pastor of Woodlake Assembly in Tulsa, says music gives everybody a chance to participate in worship:

"Whether you sing beautifully or not, singing allows you to express yourself to God. Music gets you into the frame of mind so you are more receptive to the teaching of the Word."[14]

By the 1990's the old Pentecostal songbook has disappeared in many congregations as "song service" became a convergence of old choruses and new scripture choruses. Even in churches that still use a hymnal, its use is greatly limited, compared with 25 years ago. The September 5, 1993, *Pentecostal Evangel* called for a balance in music in Assemblies of God churches:

"To reach a diverse population, we need flexible methods... Let's not diminish our effectiveness by limiting the musical selections we offer... There is a time and place for everything. Hymns may minister to the left side of the brain. Choruses may minister to the right side. Together...we are built up in the faith as we sing hymns and choruses openly and gracefully."[15]

There can be no doubt that the stability of the growth and development of the Assemblies of God in Oklahoma can be attributed in large part to the godliness and wisdom of our leaders. A shining example is Robert E. Goggin. When he retired as district superintendent in January, 1981, he had led the Oklahoma Assemblies of God for almost half the years of its existence. He had served as secretary-treasurer from 1947 to 1951 and served 29 years as district superintendent. How things had changed for Goggin since he had left Arkansas on foot in 1936—with a Bible under his arm and his wife and son beside him—to hold revivals in Oklahoma!

Under Goggin's leadership, Oklahoma continued to be one of the leading districts of the Assemblies of God. The district was always near the top in church and Sunday School attendance and in every category of giving.

When Robert E. Goggin died in March, 1992, Armon Newburn wrote:

"For more than 30 years, Brother Goggin traveled the highways and byways of Oklahoma, overextending himself in his

372

efforts to establish churches, in his efforts to encourage some broken-hearted pastor and wife, in his efforts to make some load lighter and some way brighter."[16]

Brother Goggin always cared deeply about the more than 1,000 preachers under his wing. In one of his last articles written for *The Assemblies of God News*, he reiterated his burning desire that every sermon preached in an Assemblies of God church in Oklahoma be effective:

"The purity, holiness, and consecration of a community never goes higher than that of its religious leaders... It is part of the work of a minister to speak for the Lord... We are truth tellers; therefore first of all we must be truth seekers. We must dig for truth as we would for hidden treasure and having found it we must put it into circulation... This art of preaching is not obsolete. Speaking for God is the greatest and highest privilege bestowed upon mortal man...

In too many places it is being said that sermons have had their day... A hindrance has been the insatiable desire of people for the spectacular and unusual in the ministry... God did not call us to be clowns or showmen. We are first, last, and always preachers of the gospel. An ignorant pulpit is the worst of all scourges. An ineffective pulpit is a catastrophe to be decried to the high heavens... To speak for 45 minutes to a group of intelligent and hungry-hearted Christians and make no impression or lift no soul nearer heaven is something to be ashamed of and something for which we would repent."[17]

Robert Goggin was 71 and in failing health when he retired. James C. Dodd, who was elevated to the top position to lead the Oklahoma fellowship, was well qualified because of his service as assistant district superintendent for 27 years.

PREACHING WAS IN HIS BLOOD

James Dodd was a third generation preacher. His grandfather was a Methodist circuit rider in the Ozarks in Arkansas. His father Berl Dodd was a pioneer Oklahoma Assemblies of God minister and former assistant district superintendent. The three combined for more than 160 years of ministry.

After graduating from high school, Dodd and his wife Francine ran a grocery store while they led the youth group in his father's church in Seminole. After four years, they sold the store to begin full-time ministry. They pastored in Shawnee for two years at Glad Tidings Assembly. In 1942 the Dodds were called to Broken Arrow Assembly, a major church they pastored for three decades. When Dodd was elected sectional presbyter, he was the youngest preacher in District history to ever serve in that position.[18] Since he had been raised in a pastor's home, James Dodd had a special compassion for older ministers. He delighted in the Oklahoma District's program to assist needy, retired ministers. He called the effort "refreshing to see people involved in a shared concern...to assist our preachers who blazed the gospel trail before us."[19] His District Superintendent's column in *The Assemblies of God News* in January, 1983, was a glowing tribute to pioneer preachers:

"I stand in awe at their dedication. They went anywhere a door opened—brush arbors, country school houses, street corners. They established churches in homes, in empty store fronts, anywhere. They lived on meager incomes. They endured persecutions that most of us know nothing about... And now, some of these valiant old warriors are almost forgotten. They sit at home alone with their memories. No doubt they close their eyes and remember the crowds, the altars filled with sinners coming to God, the Sunday dinners with some of the saints, the recognition as a man of God... Let us not be guilty of delegating, by our neglect, our worthy forebearers to a bare existence while we fare sumptuously."[20]

Dodd encouraged pastors to use older ministers in their congregations. He declared, "They are not and will never be a threat to you or to your position of leadership."[21] Dodd also continued the tradition started by Superintendent Goggin to award 50-year pins to veteran ministers during the Pioneer Ministers Banquet each year at District Council.

Present Oklahoma City Lakeside Assembly pastor Greg Whitlow knows the value of older ministers in the local church. As a young pastor, he was blessed with three giants—John Grace, Leslie Moore, and Rufus Strange—in his congregation. He drew from their experience and their wisdom daily: "I knew they were praying for me. They called every day and told me so." Whitlow relates one experience:

"When we were building our present church, I was exhausted from the builder skipping out and almost daily rain holding up the completion of the church. I went to Leslie Moore's house and confessed, 'Brother Moore, I am so discouraged. I don't know how I am going to get a roof on the building. I know that the board is getting upset. I just feel the weight of the church government on me right now and I don't know what to do.' Brother Moore looked at me and calmly said, 'Brother Greg, I thought that the Word said that the government shall be on His shoulders.' I sat back in my chair and began to speak in tongues. I never doubted myself for the rest of the building program."[22]

James Dodd served as district superintendent until 1983 when Armon Newburn, pastor of Woodlake Assembly in Tulsa, was elected. Newburn had served as assistant district superintendent since 1980. He was replaced by Frank Cargill. Marie Goggin retired as district Women's Ministries director in 1981 and was succeeded by Rosie Yandell. James C. Girkin replaced E.T. Watkins as secretary-treasurer in 1986. Girkin resigned as missions director and was replaced by Lindell Warren. Tom Greene followed Frank Cargill as district youth director in 1983.

And in 1990, W.G. Baker retired after 18 years as Christian education director. Gene and Doris Baker lived and breathed Sunday school and Kids Kamps. He served longer than any other person in state history in the Sunday school/Christian education post. Baker was replaced by Jack Salkil.

THE DECADE OF HARVEST

In 1989 the Assemblies of God launched one of the most aggressive evangelism programs in the history of the fellowship. It was called the Decade of Harvest. The plan was unveiled at General Council in Oklahoma City in 1987.

General Superintendent G. Raymond Carlson felt the decision was so momentous that he took time from his keynote address to have the 20-minute report read to the audience at the Myriad Convention Center in downtown Oklahoma City. California Pastor Charles Crabtree was selected to head the decade-long evangelism effort which has specific goals:

1 million prayer partners;
5 million persons won to Christ;
5,000 new Assemblies of God churches;
20,000 new workers commissioned during the decade.[23]

In Oklahoma, Mustang Pastor and Sectional Presbyter Jim McNabb was appointed as district Decade of Harvest director. Later District Missions Director Lindell Warren assumed the post. The 1988 District Council set Decade of Harvest goals for Oklahoma:

To enlist 30,000 prayer partners;
To reach, win, and disciple 250,000 to Christ;
To train and equip 1,000 persons for ministry;
To establish 100 new churches.[24]

By 1993 substantial progress had been reported toward meeting the goals. Thirty-two new churches had been established and 8,000 prayer partners had been enlisted in Oklahoma. In 1993 a black church and an East Indian church were among five new churches. Inner-city ministries had begun in Tulsa and Oklahoma City. Both works featured a "Super Saturday" program where workers ran bus routes to take the gospel to inner-city children.[25]

New Life Assembly in Hitchcock, Oklahoma, is a Decade of Harvest church. Ron Kirk started the church in his living room in 1989. It was set in order in 1990. A new church building was raised from the remains of an old barn after a man offered the pastor the wood from the barn if the church members would tear it down.[26]

▲ *Doris Baker (l) and Diana Hoffman and their puppets, 1980.*

▲ *Cleo Johnson (l) was honored for his years as caretaker of the camp grounds in Oklahoma City with the dedication of a plaque in 1980. At right are Marie Goggin and "Ma" Steger.*

▼ *Dwain Jones.*

▲ *W.G. and Doris Baker walked and talked Sunday School and Kids Kamp from 1972 to 1990.*

▲ *District office staff, 1982. (l to r front) Rick Burrell, Bruce Girkin. Renae Elmore, Nancy Starr, Beverly Robinson, Donna Howard, Donna Faye.*

▲ *Mannford Assembly of God was heavily damaged by a tornado in 1984.*

▲ *Tom and Pam Greene accept a Speed-the-Light award from Brenton Osgood, 1984.*

379

▼ *Bill and Wendy Snyder became coordinators of the Chi Alpha ministry in 1985.*

▲ *Everett Stenhouse, a native of Minco, Oklahoma, was elected Assistant General Superintendent of the national fellowship in 1985.*

▲ *1987 Royal Rangers powwow.*

▲ *Trinity Assembly, Lawton, 1988.*

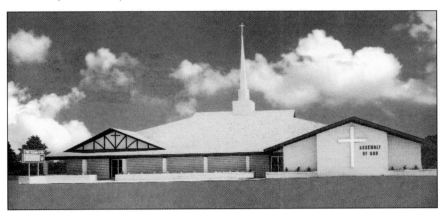

▲ *First Assembly of God, Prague.*

▲ *The new District office was completed in 1991.*

381

▼ *District Men's Ministries building project at Maud, 1988.*

▲ *Walter Spradling (r), pastor of Crystal Rock Assembly in Ardmore, receives an award form Neil Eskelin, president of Evangel College.*

▼ *Perkins Assembly pastor David Raines as "Theo" the clown.*

▲ *1990 Kids Kamp. W.G. Baker is at microphone. Chad McCaslin looks on.*

▲ *Youth camp, 1990. Adults on back row (l to r) are Marsha McCaslin, LaRoi Woods, Jean Woods, Paul Abner.*

1988 Men's Retreat at Turner Falls.

1991 P-K (Preachers' kids) Retreat at Turner Falls.

▲ *Praisong, 1991.*

▲ *1991 Royal Rangers powwow.*

▲ *Oklahoma District officials and staff, December, 1991.*

▲ *"Heirborn", the youth group at Bethany Cornerstone Assembly, 1991.*

▲ *District Royal Ranger Commander James Eubanks (right front) leads a construction crew at RangerLand near Chandler, 1992.*

Chaplain ▶ W.W. Hays on death row at the Oklahoma State Penitentiary.

388

▲ *More than 1,000 accepted Christ in this service conducted by Oklahoma youth pastors in Siberia in April, 1992.*

▲ *Adult choir of Cathedral of the Hills in Edmond performing at Quail Springs Mall in Oklahoma City, December, 1993.*

389

▲ *Lakeside Assembly of God, Oklahoma City.*

▲ *The interior of First Assembly, Okmulgee, 1993.*

▲ *This mobile chapel was provided by the District Women's Ministries Department to serve as temporary quarters for churches.*

▲ *District Secretary-Treasurer James Girkin (third from left) presides over the groundbreaking of a new building for Noble Assembly.*

▲ *Fred Wright and his "Chapel of Peace", 1993.*

▲ *First Assembly of God, Lawton, 1993.*

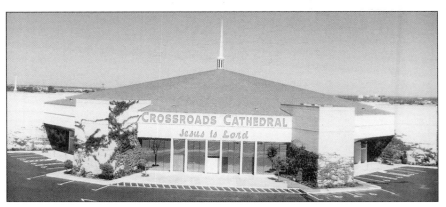

▲ *Crossroads Cathedral in Oklahoma City.*

▲ *Lakeside Assembly, Crowder, 1993.*

Chapter 32

Home Missions

Oklahoma emphasized home missions more than foreign missions for many years. Minutes from early District Councils show the concern expressed by leaders for the plight of rural churches. In the 1920's and 1930's, many small Oklahoma churches were hurting financially and the district office came to their rescue. That need began a call for larger churches to contribute to a home missions fund each year.

Since before statehood, Oklahoma has had within its borders a large Native American population. The Assemblies of God saw the Native Americans as a major mission field early in the history of the fellowship. Billy Boyles, a Cherokee Indian, was an early Pentecostal evangelist to his tribe in northeast Oklahoma. As many as 500 attended tent revival services led by Boyles near Tahlequah in 1915.[1]

Pioneer Assemblies of God evangelist R.C. Nicholson preached among the Cherokees around 1920 and took the gospel to the Apache and Kiowa tribes while pastoring at Stecker in Caddo County in 1926:

"We had to have two interpreters. The squaws sat on the floor all wrapped in their many garments... The Indians sat with their eyes closed throughout the meeting... An altar call was always given after the preaching, but many more came forward when we invited those who wanted prayer for healing. It seemed the laying on of hands for their sickness was closer to their cultural understanding than the call for spiritual healing through salvation."[2]

Gordon Speed was the first pastor of an American Indian work at Carnegie in 1941. A small building was financed by the Oklahoma District after Speed held services from one house to another for several months.[3]

For many years the Otoe Indian Assembly at Red Rock, Oklahoma was the only Indian Assemblies of God church in the state. Home missionaries Marguerite Shaw and Phyllis Hammerbacker were thrilled to receive a Maytag washer as a gift from the district WMC Department in 1959.[4] Rev. and Mrs. D.E. Suit pastored the church at Red Rock in 1963. They reported 84 at Bible school that summer:

"We all brought our blankets and cooking pans and camped out at the church. The Pow-Wow drums at night gave one a funny feeling, but truly we all enjoyed the Bible school. The second day our car had engine trouble. All it would do was back up and had a terrible smell to it. But after prayer, God healed our car and it ran fine for the rest of Bible school."[5]

The Marion F. Clarks took over the Red Rock mission in 1967.[6]

In 1969 an Indian Assemblies of God church was founded in Wright City in southeast Oklahoma. Dean and Lucille Jackson began the church called *Chihowa i Chuka* (which means "God's House") for the Choctaw Indians, in an old schoolhouse. Later a new church building was built near Wright City. Lula Morton pastored the church for several years. Its present pastor is David Impson.[7]

Thelma Cox drove 50 miles every Sunday to pastor the Indian church at Longdale after it was established in 1972. Both the Wright City and Longdale churches were built with the help of both the Oklahoma and national home missions departments.[8]

Faith Indian Assembly was established in Seiling by Grace Hopper and Flossie Hartzel in 1986. Several churches in northwest Oklahoma, including Mooreland Assembly, Woodward

First, Elm Grove Assembly-Chester, and Seiling Assembly, contributed money and labor toward the new work among the Cheyenne-Arapaho tribe.[9]

In the 1950's, Oklahoma began sending missionaries to Indians in other states. Roy and Mary Lou Nelson ministered to Apache Indians in Arizona in 1958. They later pastored Indians in Nevada and Navajos in Arizona.[10] The Caleb Smiths were appointed as home missionaries to the Indians in Gallup, New Mexico.[11] Lula Morton spent several years as a home missionary in Tuba City, Arizona. She reported in 1961:

"God has helped us greatly... We have been holding hogan [primitive Indian structure] services... We have been offered a piece of ground to build a place of worship where we can reach many that have never been touched... I have given part of my grocery supply to feed the Indians for two camps... We just closed a wonderful camp here in Tuba. God gave us many souls."[12]

Other Oklahoma home missionaries listed in 1966 were the Edgar McElhannons and the Wayne Hunters, missionaries to Alaska; the Virgil Heddlestons in Arizona; Elmo and June Pierce, missionaries to the deaf in Oklahoma City; Shirley Kenslow, missionary to the deaf in Tulsa; James and Ramona Banks, missionaries to the deaf (Banks served 13 years in the national office as representative of Deaf, Blind, and Handicapped Ministries in the Division of Home Missions from 1976 to 1989); and Gertrude Clonce, missionary to the Jews in Brooklyn, New York.[13] Mrs. Clonce had earlier established a Hebrew mission in Chicago.[14]

Don and Virginia Ramsey went to northern Arizona as missionaries to the Navajos in 1958. They began knocking on doors, looking for converts. There was no response. The Indians did not trust the Ramseys. Undaunted, they went to another camp. Don knocked on a door and a teenage girl answered. The Holy Spirit led Don to ask a simple question, "Is there someone here who needs prayer?" A moment later he was informed that the mother of the house had given permission to pray for her husband. Ramsey recalls what happened next:

"He wouldn't even look at me. I knelt down and told him the basics about Jesus and that God loved him. I laid my hands on

395

him and he didn't even flinch. I prayed and asked if we could come back in a few days to check on him. I left the house and felt a surge of the Holy Ghost. When I came back, there were 19 people in the house, all relatives who wanted to know about Jesus. That was the beginning of our church in that area."[15]

Ramsey was later highly instrumental in the building of the American Indian Bible College in Phoenix and served as president of the institution.[16]

Chapter 33

To the Ends of the Earth

The work of the Oklahoma District Council extends far beyond the borders of the state. The Lord's command is, "Go ye into all the world, and preach the gospel to every creature" (Mark 16:15). Assemblies of God people in Oklahoma have been obeying the Great Commission from the beginning of the fellowship.

Former Tahlequah pastor and General Chairman J.W. Welch was chairman of the first Foreign Missions Committee established in 1917.[1] There is no doubt that Welch was a vigorous supporter of foreign missions. Welch called the Assemblies of God "first and foremost a missionary body":

"Anyone who is filled with the Holy Spirit must be a missionary not only in theory but in reality, with a purpose of heart to take or send the light to those who sit in darkness and the shadow of death. This fellowship is and must remain an agent to spread the gospel to the ends of the earth."[2]

"Daddy" Welch, as early as 1916, recognized that it took both prayer and money to get missionaries to the field:

"There are two means of reaching the world's fields even though we may be unable to make a journey away from our own homes... Every need in the whole world is brought within our reach when we pray. We can labor in every mission field without leaving our prayer room. The other way is by supporting others who go... Many should loosen their hold upon the money God has permitted them to hold for Him and allow it to accomplish what it can to build up the kingdom of God."[3]

By 1919 the number of Assemblies of God missionaries had risen to 195. A foreign missions department was established by the General Council and J. Roswell Flower was elected missionary secretary.[4] It was Flower who began to grapple with the realities of missions finance by developing budgets. Faith was the principal ingredient of missionary work. Each missionary was responsible for raising his or her budget. The General Council only promised to send the money on to the missionary once it was received in Springfield. That concept remains viable in the 1990's. William Menzies says, "One important result of this concept has been a sense of missionary responsibility at the grass roots level of the denomination."[5]

Many early Assemblies of God missionaries left America without knowing when, or if, they would ever return. Some felt Christ would return at any moment and thought they would be raptured before their furlough. Others felt their call from God was so urgent and strong that they should remain on the field indefinitely. Examples are Alice Wood, who stayed on the mission field in Argentina for 50 years without a furlough, and Lillian Thrasher who spent most of her adult life at the Assiout Orphanage in Egypt. The missionaries considered themselves called and committed for life.

There are a thousand stories of hardships endured by early missionaries. Unsanitary conditions and extreme climate and diet changes brought sickness and death. One of the first Assemblies of God missionaries to die on the field was Eric Booth-Clibborn who had spent several years in Oklahoma preaching revivals and raising money to go as a missionary to Africa. He arrived in French West Africa (now Burkina Faso) in June, 1924. He died of dysentery 19 days later.

Forrest and Ethel Barker were probably Oklahoma's first Assemblies of God foreign missionaries. They pastored a local church in Shawnee until the summer of 1915 when they left for Peru.[6]

Historian Leroy Hawkins says Oklahoma sponsored very few individual missionaries before 1930.[7] Willa B. Lowther was one early Oklahoma missionary from the Fifth and Peoria church in Tulsa. She had been saved in the 1908 Charles Parham revival in Tulsa and served in China.[8] Harry E. Bowley spent several years in South Africa as a missionary before returning to pastor the Fifth and Peoria church in 1920. Both Bowley and Lowther were guest speakers at the 1922 district campmeeting where a special day was designated to honor missionaries—a tradition that still continues today.[9]

In the early 1920's, Oklahoma was a poor state and did not have a good reputation for supporting missionaries. Roy L. Steger reported in *The Pentecostal Evangel* in 1924 that "We have been told that missionaries have been discouraged from coming our way by being told that they would hardly get railroad fare."[10] However, Steger wrote that an offering of $102.90 had been raised at his church in Cement in a Thanksgiving Day, 1923, service for Marie Juergensen, a missionary to Japan.[11]

By 1925 Almyra Aston was an Oklahoma-sponsored missionary to India. At the August, 1925, campmeeting in Guthrie she was given the $250 missionary offering raised.[12]

National Missions Secretary William Faux was present at the Oklahoma District Council in October, 1926. A missionary offering of $116 was taken.[13]

As in other denominations, women made up a substantial portion of the missionary force in the Assemblies of God from the beginning. All four Oklahoma missionaries listed in the 1930 District Council minutes were single women: Almyra Aston and Dessie Knight in India, and Pearl Pickel and Lois Shelton in Liberia.[14]

In 1927 Noel Perkin became national missions secretary. He became known as "Mr. Missions," and the missionary program expanded greatly under his administration. He served for 32 years and "lived, ate, drank, talked, dreamed, and sacrificed for missions."[15]

Also in 1927, Oklahoma's reputation of being a poor supporter of missions was laid to rest when the state made it into the top ten districts in missions giving. Almost $10,000 was given by Oklahoma churches that year.[16]

THE P.C. NELSON FACTOR

Oklahoma's foreign missions effort "took off" as the first graduating class from Southwestern Bible School in Enid graduated in 1930. School President P.C. Nelson emphasized training for missionaries.

The first missionaries sent out from Southwestern were Hugh Jeter and his wife Theola Tucker Jeter. The Jeters landed in Callao, Peru, in October, 1932. The following year, Jeter's sister Louise knew God was calling her to Peru to join her brother. There were problems, however: she was only 19, too young for official appointment, and she had no money. On March 7, 1933 someone gave her one dollar. Here's what she did with it:

"I took it to Mother Bamford [dean of women] and asked her to pray that God would multiply it. Soon I had $10, enough for a passport... The WMC at Enid supplied some clothes and quilts, and God provided all other needs. On June 7, three months from the day we prayed over that lone dollar, I boarded a Japanese steamer in San Pedro, California, and waved goodbye to the little group of friends on the dock singing 'There's Power in the Blood' as we headed out to sea. In all the 60 years that have followed, God has supplied all my needs."[17]

Ernestine Jeter, a 1931 graduate of SBS, joined brother Hugh and sister Louise on the mission field in Peru. Malaria and tuberculosis were rampant. God healed Louise of tuberculosis but the disease took the life of Hugh's wife Theola in 1936.

Transportation was terrible in Peru as the Jeters tried to take the gospel to outlying areas. Louise remembers going to one town where the gospel had never been heard:

"The road didn't go there so we set out walking, sang, testified and preached in the town square... and saw the whole crowd kneel to ask the Lord to save them. We had services at two other places on the way, walked nine miles, and got back just in time for the Sunday evening service."[18]

In 1940 Louise married Missionary Alva Walker, whose first wife had died. Hugh Jeter married Gertrude Dudte, and Ernestine married John Doan. The Jeter family missions legacy is amazing. Hugh served in South America and Spain and was district superintendent of the Assemblies of God in Cuba from 1942-52. He was missions director at Southwestern Assemblies of God College from 1960-77.

Ernestine and her husband were long-time missionaries in Latin America.

Louise and her husband were missionaries in Peru and Cuba. Later she became coordinator of Assemblies of God Bible schools in Latin America and the West Indies; then she served as writer and editor for the International Correspondence Institute for 17 years. Louise's most lasting contribution to the missions effort is probably her writing of many Sunday School publications and textbooks for students and teachers. Some of her books have been translated into at least 25 languages. The evangelistic correspondence course—"The Great Questions of Life"—which she wrote for ICI, has been published in 90 languages and studied by 10 million persons in 124 countries.[19]

Hugh and Gertrude Jeter were part of the revival that swept Cuba in 1950 and 1951. Veteran healing evangelist Raymond T. Richey sponsored Brother Jeter on a radio program called "Marvels of Faith" that was beamed to Cuba. T.L. Osborn joined Jeter for a massive campaign in Cuba in 1950:

"Osborn was never interested in seeing the sights in Cuba. He just wanted to stay in his hotel room and pray. It paid off. We rented a stadium, but were disappointed when only 200 showed up the first night. God healed several people in the first service and news of the revival began spreading. The local newspapers began printing stories of the miraculous healings. By the end of the campaign, more than 15,000 people would jam the stadium each night. There was no way we could pray for the people individually. When they were healed, they streamed to the platform to testify of God's touch. It was not unusual for hundreds of people to come to the microphone to report their healing."[20]

The Jeter children and grandchildren are missionaries and missions teachers today. Doug and Raynan Jeter are in France. Don and Cindy Jeter ministered in Portugal and Spain. Betty (Jeter) and Robbie Jernigan are involved in home missions projects.[21]

By 1936 Southwestern Bible School was famous for producing Assemblies of God missionaries. The 1936 SBS yearbook contains pictures of graduates on the mission field. Norman Moffatt and his wife, Helen Armentrout Moffatt, were "now gathering sheaves for the Master in the whitened harvest fields of Adjmer, India." They were the first Pentecostal missionaries in the Rajputana district in north India. Jennie and Annie Kulka had sailed for Czechoslovakia. W. Edward and Helen Harding Davis had arrived at their station in South India in 1935, after spending several years in Kentucky. Agnes Sloan was with Ernestine and Louise Jeter in Peru. Katie Wise sailed in March, 1936, for her station in a rugged area of southwest China. The yearbook also mentioned Carl and Margaret Holleman and Ted and Estelle Vassar whose stories follow.[22]

Carl and Margaret Holleman arrived in Bombay, India, in December, 1934. They were joined by Ted and Estelle Vassar in 1936. The ministries of the Hollemans and Vassars in the Poona district of India were intertwined for a quarter-century. India was still ruled by the British and only a handful of Pentecostal missionaries were ministering to tens of millions in southern India. The Hollemans had no idea how they were going to raise money to get to India. Sylvia Davidson, an early Oklahoma missionary to India, cashed in an insurance policy and gave the Hollemans $500, the exact cost of fare to Bombay.

Ted Vassar came to Southwestern from Pawhuska. Estelle Barnett, (an aunt of Phoenix, Arizona, First Assembly pastor Tommy Barnett), was from Texas. When Ted graduated from SBS, he and Estelle both felt the call to take the gospel to India. Their first attempt to sail from New York failed when their tiny son, Bobby Joe, became ill and the ship's captain would not allow them to board the boat. They had to return to Oklahoma for six months to get ready to leave again. Finally, they arrived in India. A few months later, tragedy struck. Bobby Joe was now two years old. He was very ill with pneumonia and developed acute appendicitis. Carl Holleman will never forget Estelle Vassar standing over Bobby Joe's crib with her head turned toward heaven:

"Estelle prayed a simple prayer, 'Lord Jesus, we came to India for your glory, for the purpose of serving you in this country. Because you have called, we are here. But Bobby Joe is ill. If you want to take him home for yourself, we are willing to let you take him. But please do not let him suffer."[23]

A few minutes later Bobby Joe breathed his last breath. Holleman remembers the sadness that overwhelmed the two missionary couples as they carried the lifeless body of Bobby Joe out into the missions compound and buried him the same day because there was no way to preserve the body. The tombstone still stands in the compound in Poona, India. It reads, "Safe in the Arms of Jesus."[24]

By 1939 the Oklahoma District was heavily involved in foreign missions. Statewide giving had risen to $11,000 in 1938, an increase of about $4,000 over the previous year—in the middle of the Great Depression. At the 1939 District Council, delegates unanimously approved the appointment of A.J. Princic, returned missionary from the Belgian Congo, as field representative for missions to the Oklahoma District, for the purpose of "encouraging and advancing the interests of missions."[25]

During World War II, many missionaries had to return to America because of the instability of world governments and the hostilities in Europe and the Pacific. Carl and Margaret Holleman returned to Enid and pastored Enid Gospel Tabernacle from 1943 to 1948. They went back to India in 1949 where he served as general superintendent of the Assemblies of God in southern India.[26] In 1953 the government of India came out openly against foreign missionaries. Holleman notified the Oklahoma District of the seriousness of the situation:

"We may have to leave India anytime... Souls are dying and we cannot be still. Famine is sweeping the land. Millions are hungry. Above all they need the Living Bread... Doors are fast closing...we will stay on and do all we can to fight sin and Satan and win souls for Christ."[27]

In the late 1940's, Ted and Estelle Vassar felt the need to build an orphanage in Junnar, India. The Oklahoma District had been considering building an orphanage in Oklahoma but state officials decided the state had enough orphanages. God's purpose in allowing Oklahoma Assemblies of God women to raise several thousand dollars was now clear. The Vassars appealed for help with their orphanage project. The District Executive Board immediately sent $3,000 to build the orphanage, which was named the "Cornell Memorial School" after the wife of former Oklahoma District Superintendent F.C. Cornell. Mrs. Cornell had recently been killed in an auto accident in California. The Indian orphanage became a special project sponsored by the Women's Missionary Council in Oklahoma. In 1993 the Cornell Memorial School had an enrollment of about 350 children. The Vassars retired to Texas where Ted served a number of years as district missions director.[28]

Carl and Margaret Holleman served several terms in India. They helped organize the Southern Asia Bible Institute (now Southern Asia Bible College) in Bangalore and other Bible schools in India. They directed the operations of the Cornell Memorial School. They retired in 1977 after 43 years in India. Holleman left India like he came, with a broken heart for the Indian people:

"The Holy Spirit has been my constant companion for six decades. It was only the promise of Jesus that He would be with us every moment of every day that allowed us to go back to India again and again." [29]

Other Southwestern graduates to leave for the mission field in the late 1930's were George and Stella Flattery (the parents of ICI founder George Flattery) who went to primitive French West Africa. Lula Ashmore Baird pioneered churches in China and Singapore (and still directs the Chinese ministries in the Northern California and Nevada District). Evelyn Hatch died during her fifth term in Malaysia. While conducting her funeral service, current Southwestern President Delmer Guynes said he saw over her coffin a vision of a bill-of-lading with "Paid-in-Full" stamped across it because "Evelyn had paid her debt to a lost world."[30]

Katie Wise and Elizabeth Galley Wilson were forced to leave China during World War II. They were captured by the Japanese in the Philippines and were interned in a prison camp for three hard years.[31]

Probably Southwestern's most famous missionary product was J.W. Tucker. He graduated from Southwestern in 1938 and went to the Belgian Congo (now Zaire). He and his family returned to the Congo again and again until the rebel Simbas murdered him in 1964 and threw his body to the crocodiles. The seeds he planted have grown into a thriving church in Zaire today. The Tuckers' commitment to Africa and the tragedy of his death were the subject of a best-selling book by his widow, Angeline Tucker. *He is in Heaven* was published in 1965. Many missionaries on the field today answered the call after God touched their hearts while reading the story of J.W. Tucker.[32]

The 1940's was an active decade for Oklahoma-sponsored missionaries. V.H. and Eva Shumway arrived in Nigeria in December, 1945. Africa was primitive. Sanitary conditions were terrible. The Shumways lived in a mud house in the middle of an African village until they could build a mission station. They took the gospel to a region filled with 700,000 people who spoke the Boki language. That region had never had a missionary until the Shumways arrived. In 1959 the Shumways pioneered a Pentecostal work in southeastern Nigeria where a secret murder society, the Obudo Odog, ceremonially killed humans and ate the bodies. The pagan area had been avoided by many missionaries. Despite these circumstances, 13 churches, meeting in their own buildings made out of sticks, were started in just one year. Because of the Shumways' faithfulness, many Assemblies of God churches exist in southeastern Nigeria today. V.H. Shumway remembers a trip to a region in northern Nigeria with Oklahoma District Superintendent Robert Goggin:

"Thousands of people would surround our large sound truck with four loudspeakers mounted on it. We preached in village after village, and thousands responded. The people literally mobbed Sister Goggin when she tried to hand out tracts in the native language. She had to be rescued from the natives who were so hungry for anything about this new Jesus they had just learned about."[33]

God used visiting missionary to India Doris Maloney to impact the heart of young Verlin Stewart in 1938. At the end of the missionary service in the country church at Vassar, Oklahoma, Stewart knew he was headed for Latin America. After graduating as valedictorian of his class at Southwestern Assemblies of God College in 1949, he married Pauline Kennedy. They arrived in Havana, Cuba, on Thanksgiving Day, 1951. In 1959 they were called to Colombia, a South American country that only had three Assemblies of God churches. For the next 20 years the Stewarts planted dozens of churches. Every new church was a direct battle against Satan. Rebels ran loose in the country and would stop buses along the road and cut passengers' heads off. In spite of the intense opposition, there are 300-400 Assemblies of God churches in Colombia today. Pauline Stewart died of lung cancer in 1991. Verlin Stewart and his new wife, Wanda, now preach occasional crusades in Latin America even though Brother Stewart is partially paralyzed from a stroke he suffered on the mission field in Ecuador in 1977.[34]

In 1942, 19-year-old Thelma Roark went from Oklahoma to Springfield to a national C.A. conference. One night she saw a vision of black people with their hands outstretched. They were saying, "Come and help us." She asked the Lord where the crowds were and told Him she was willing to go to Africa. She met Leroy Ward who also felt a call to Africa. Thelma went to the field still single but married Leroy in 1953 in Africa. They worked as missionaries for 18 years in Liberia and 15 years in Nigeria. Two and a half years were spent in a leper colony in Liberia where they built the first permanent church.[35] In 1958 the Wards reported that it was a year of revival in Liberia with 650 saved as a result of taking the gospel message to 56 villages.[36]

Robert and Naomi Cobb began their missionary service in 1950 as head of what is now the Central Bible College of Nigeria at Port Harcourt, Nigeria. Living conditions were bleak:

"Everything was mud, mud houses, mud roads, mud tables. Our ceilings were made out of bamboo poles and palm leaves.

There was no electricity. We carried our water from the river. Water had to be boiled for both drinking and bathing."[37]

After Brother Cobb suffered a heart attack in 1961, they were transferred to Accra, Ghana, where they saw the local church grow from 100 to 450. They began Sunday Schools in northern Ghana before transferring to Dar Es Salaam, the capital city of what is now Tanzania. When they arrived, there was only one Assemblies of God church in that major port city. When they left 17 years later, there were 38 churches. Later, Brother Cobb was president of the Swaziland College of Theology in Southern Africa before he retired.[38]

Post-war prosperity allowed Oklahoma Assemblies of God believers to vastly increase missions giving. In 1949 Full Gospel Tabernacle in Tulsa led the state with over $12,000 in missions offerings. Other top missions-minded churches in 1949 were Tulsa Faith Tabernacle, Bartlesville First, Miami Assembly, Sand Springs Assembly, Broken Arrow Assembly, Enid Gospel Tabernacle, Oklahoma City Faith Tabernacle, Tulsa Capitol Hill, and Oklahoma City Capitol Hill. Laverne Assembly led the state that year in per capita missions giving.[39]

In 1951 Oklahoma churches topped the $100,000 mark in missions giving for the first time. Tulsa Full Gospel Tabernacle gave almost $8,000 as the top individual church. Seminole Old Glory Mission was the highest per capita giving church.[40]

Missionary Norma Johanson experienced the inadequate transportation system in Liberia in west Africa in 1953. She walked or was carried by native porters for a full day through the jungle on her way to a national workers convention:

"Late in the afternoon rains came down and beat us hard. Toward dusk we came to a river and hill and heard singing. As we were swinging over the waters in our hammocks [a primitive way of crossing rivers] I looked toward the hilltop and saw actually hundreds of black people singing as they came to meet us... I wept as I listened and felt in my heart, 'Lord this is a semblance of the entrance into heaven through those pearly gates.' To hear such singing by redeemed Africans...and to see their joy was a wonderful experience... Sister Davis and I were the only two white persons at the convention of 1,600."[41]

The June, 1952, edition of the *Assemblies of God News* notified Oklahoma pastors that two new missionary families were seeking services to raise their budgets. The Raymond Brock family from the West Tulsa Assembly had been appointed to Nigeria, and the Clarence Roberts family were new missionaries to India.[42]

Ray Brock wrote from his post at the Nigeria Bible Institute in 1954 that one hundred students had gathered to study God's Word. Some students came from 1,000 miles away—from tribes that had never had a missionary but had heard the gospel and were preparing to take the message back to their own people.[43]

Leaders of the Assemblies of God foreign missions program recognized from its beginning the necessity for training national ministers and workers to carry on the work after missionaries returned to America. Many missions experts attribute the success of Assemblies of God missions to that attitude.

Sickness and disease have always been the enemies of missionary families. Monthly reports from missionaries often contained the bad news of disease hampering the efforts of the missionaries. One report from Brother and Sister Virgil Smith, long-time Oklahoma missionaries to Brazil, talked about "an affliction that has greatly handicapped her," and about lamentable conditions in Brazil due to "disease, heathen worship, plagues, leprosy, and Catholic domination."[44]

Earl and Nelda Taylor arrived in Japan in January, 1956. World War II had destroyed all but two Assemblies of God church buildings in Japan. When the Taylors left 30 years later, there were 125 Assemblies of God churches in the country. When Nelda Taylor was laid to rest in 1990, her funeral was on the same date—35 years later—that she and Earl had stepped off the boat in Japan for the first time.[45]

OKLAHOMA INFLUENCE IN TOGO

Oklahoma missionaries have for many years been attracted to the harvest field in Africa. Murray and Marjorie Brown had gone to Togo in the 1940's as the first Oklahoma missionaries in that country, but still reported heathen conditions in 1958:

"The face of Africa is changing rapidly, but we are still aware of savagery...when we leave the larger governmental centers.

408

Some still make sacrifices of humans... Secret cannibal feasts are held occasionally in certain clans, and one sees bodies mutilated by the sharpening of front teeth and cutting of tribal marks on face and body... [The good news is that] many are turning from dead gods to serving the Living Lord. The most primitive and uncivilized people are receiving the gospel message."[46]

Oklahoma's presence has been felt in Togo for a half century. From the very beginning of the Assemblies of God effort in that country, Oklahoma missionaries have played a key role. After Murray Brown came Ben and Colleen Tipton, David and Claudia Wakefield, Jack and Carmelita Bledsoe, and Melton and Alma Hill.

In the 1950's, other Oklahoma missionaries began their service in foreign lands. The Paul Hutsells went to South America, Florence Bassett was in Liberia, and the Dale Browns arrived in Gold Coast (now Ghana) in west Africa, where they reported a "land of great need."[47]

Paul Hutsell was called to be a missionary during a skit presented by Missionary Adele Flower at the first national Sunday School convention in Springfield, Missouri, in 1951. Hutsell began to weep and told his wife, Dreta, that "God wants us to be missionaries." The Hutsells prayed for God's will. On the sixteenth day of fasting, Jesus literally came to Paul Hutsell:

"As I walked into the kitchen, Jesus was standing there in person. I knelt at His feet, and He placed His hand on my shoulder—a physical touch. He spoke to me in an audible voice... He lifted me up, put His arm around my neck and His hand on my shoulder, and said that if I would obey Him and follow Him wherever He asked me to go, He would make our ministry fruitful... I cannot explain the awe, the wonder, the excitement of the moment... The Lord disappeared, and I went to bed... A vivid picture came to my mind—the continent of South America in three dimensions in color. Toward the southern part a large green area stood out... I arose and wrote down all the instructions I was given by the Spirit."[48]

The Hutsells drove to a library the next day and discovered that the large green area on the map was the Gran Chaco area of Argentina and Peru. Then they knew where God wanted them to take the gospel. The Hutsells served as missionaries in South America for more than 20 years. Paul is presently the area director for the Caribbean nations for the Division of Foreign Missions of the General Council.[49]

In 1956 Melton and Alma Hill made application to go to Africa as teachers—rather than preachers. The application was unusual, and God had to open doors to enable the Hills to be appointed as "teachers" to Togo in 1959. After District Superintendent Goggin visited the Hills in Togo, he returned to Oklahoma and recommended that Melton Hill be ordained since he "was preaching more than he was teaching in Africa."

Melton had spent time in the military in the Seabees learning construction. One day while building a church in Africa he realized how God had divinely prepared him in his youth in the Seabees for the task of constructing new churches in Togo. Presently, Alma Hill teaches at the West Africa Advanced School of Theology, an Assemblies of God school in Lome, Togo. The school serves as a point of advanced training for national pastors in eleven west African countries. Melton continues to plant and build new churches. There are now 250 national pastors for 45,000 Assemblies of God believers in Togo, largely due to the efforts of a string of "Okie" missionaries since 1940.[50]

Charity Harris was called to the mission field in a vision:

"I saw a big mountain, one side of it was a steep cliff. I saw people marching up that mountain, then reaching the crest, and going toward the cliff. I said, 'Lord, is there someone to warn them that there is a cliff there?' He said, 'There is no one.' After I asked two other times, the Lord asked me if I would go and stand on the hill to warn the people. I said I would go."[51]

Charity and Ruth Harris were appointed as missionaries to Tanganyika (now Tanzania) in eastern Africa in 1957. Charity lived in a tent and a brush arbor for three months while he built a primitive house out of handmade bricks and hand-sawed lumber. He learned Swahili out of a book at the rate of 10-15 words per night. At the end of the three months he preached an entire sermon in Swahili.

Sickness plagued the Harris family in Africa. Malaria, dysentery, worms, rashes, and kidney infections took their toll; but God always healed them. Charity was bothered off and on for years with dysentery and almost died with it in 1959.[52]

In 1970 Ruth Harris had been diagnosed with ovarian cancer and was scheduled for a serious surgery in Africa. The day before the operation, a letter arrived from a woman in the state of Washington. The lady had been praying for a year for a strange woman she had never seen except in a vision. When she looked at a missions magazine, she saw Ruth's picture and wrote to the Harrises that God had confirmed His healing of Ruth. The letter concluded with the words "He has met your need." At the last minute the surgeon said he had made a mistake and that Ruth did not need surgery. The intercessory prayers of a stranger halfway around the globe saved Ruth Harris's life.[53]

THE STRAIN ON FAMILIES

Probably the most difficult part of being a missionary is the terrible strain on family relationships. Children often have to be placed in boarding schools—sometimes a thousand miles away from their parents. Alma Hill says one of the loneliest moments in her life was when she had to leave her six-year-old child at a boarding school, knowing that she would not see him for three or four months. Colleen Tipton left her son at the same boarding school at Jos, Nigeria, and was haunted by Jonathan's cries of "Please don't leave me." Americans at home seldom know the intense loneliness suffered by missionaries thousands of miles from their families and friends. In 1957 Ruth Harris wrote to Marie Goggin:

"Brother Harris is away on safari most of the time now. We get lonesome and miss him but that is the way God's work goes. Soon he will be going to Njombe to start the mission house there, so we will be left by ourselves a lot."[54]

The author has seen the tears of many missionaries whose children have grown up in a foreign land and were devastated by culture shock when they returned to America for college. The daughter of an Assemblies of God missionary recently said she was tired of people in Oklahoma asking her if she was glad to be "home." She said her "home" was on the mission field where her parents still served and where she grew up. Assemblies of God missions leaders are keenly aware of the problem and have set up an effective program of counseling and support for missionary kids who suffer problems on their return to this country. Oklahoman Cary Tidwell directs the worldwide missionary family support program from his post at the Division of Foreign Missions in Springfield.

Chapter 34

Missions Support Groups

The missionaries get great support from a number of special groups of men and women, teen-agers, and children, in our Assemblies of God churches.

SPEED-THE-LIGHT

In this program developed by Ralph Harris in 1944, the youth of Assemblies of God churches raise money for transportation and other equipment for missionaries. A goal of $100,000 was announced for 1944. By 1993, America's youth gave more than $5,000,000 to Speed-the-Light.[1]

In Oklahoma, STL was immediately popular among youth groups. In 1950 they raised more than $8,000 for STL. Projects for that year included autos for Virgil Smith in Brazil and Hugh Jeter in Cuba and $1,000 to be applied to the cost of a large motor boat for Alaska.[2] In 1977 Oklahoma raised $138,000 and placed fourth in the nation. Verdigris Assembly was the top fund-raising church with $6,500.[3] By 1983 Oklahoma had climbed into third place nationally in STL giving. Tulsa Woodlake, with $15,000, topped Oklahoma churches that raised over $153,000 that year.[4] Oklahoma churches gave $229,000 to STL in 1988, good for second in the nation. Oklahoma City Crossroads Cathedral gave over $16,000.

In 1992 Oklahoma Assemblies of God youth raised $443,268 (second in the nation) for Speed-the-Light, an 11 percent increase

413

over the previous year. Tulsa Carbondale led the list of seven churches that raised more than $10,000 each for STL. The other six leaders were Oklahoma City Lakeside, Bethany Cornerstone, Chickasha First Assembly, Tulsa Woodlake, Prague First Assembly, and Broken Arrow First Assembly.[5]

The Assemblies of God News has featured photos of dozens of missionaries posing with their Speed-the-Light vehicles. Duane Collins wrote in 1975 that his two STL motor bikes were an indispensable aid to his work in the mountains of Senegal where cars could not travel. Collins said, "Tomorrow I will be making an 80-mile trip by motor bike in the region. Our hands are not tied, because of you."[6] David Newberry, a former Oklahoma pastor, had raised a lot of STL money before going to South Africa. In 1978 he thanked C.A.'s back home:

"I realize I'm on the receiving end of the program now. So please remember, no matter how you raise your Speed-the-Light pledges—washing cars, bake sales, peddling candy, or contributions—each and every dollar is truly appreciated and used to speed the light to a world that desperately needs Christ."[7]

BGMC

The Boys and Girls Missionary Crusade (BGMC), with the help of its famous "Buddy Barrel," has raised millions of dollars to provide Sunday School materials, Bible school books, and songbooks for missions churches. It is a program of the national Christian Education Department. More than two million dollars was raised by BGMC nationally in 1992. Oklahoma has always been near the top in BGMC giving. In 1992 Oklahoma BGMC offerings were $89,862 (6th in the nation), given by 217 churches.[8]

LIGHT FOR THE LOST

Light for the Lost (LFTL) is a program of Men's Ministries to raise money for evangelistic literature for missionaries. Its members are known as "councilmen" who pay $15 monthly for the administrative support of the program. All monies raised by special speakers and at banquets go directly to support the missionaries' evangelistic ministries. California businessman Sam Cochran began LFTL in 1953. It was accepted by the General Council as an official program in 1961. Shortly thereafter, Charles

"Chuck" Freeman got involved with Cochran and about 30 other councilmen.

In 1967 Freeman introduced the program to Oklahoma District Superintendent Robert Goggin, who contributed the first $600. From 1969 to 1974, Freeman introduced LFTL to Oklahoma Assemblies of God men through a series of sectional meetings. LFTL banquets were first held in 1974. By 1979 a dozen annual banquets were held. Jim Holt, from Woodlake Assembly in Tulsa, joined Freeman as the two top LFTL leaders in the state. Holt's church became the second church in the nation to have 100 councilmen. In 1981 Oklahoma became the first district in the fellowship to have 500 councilmen. Oklahoma now has more than 1,000 councilmen (number one nationally) and raised $272,214 in 1992 (third nationally).[9] LFTL contributions totalled over $3,000,000 in the U.S. in 1992.

Chuck Freeman has held about every post in the national Light for the Lost program, including president. In 1993 he served as national vice president.

"Prayer task forces" have been a vital part of Light for the Lost since Freeman led the first one to Mexico in 1974. Target cities around the world are selected where teams of men go for five days. They fast the breakfast and noon meal and pray for four hours every morning. After literature is passed out in the afternoon, another two hours are spent in prayer. At night, special crusade services are held. Amazing revival reports come from the many cities where prayer task forces have been held in recent years.

Chuck Freeman is famous for the ribs that he cooks for LFTL banquets and retreats. Most Oklahoma Assemblies of God believers have eaten Chuck's ribs:

"I became famous for my ribs by accident. We had to have a tool to get into Oklahoma churches. I saw a cooker for sale and thought if I could buy it, I could cook steaks and ribs for men and then present the LFTL program to them. The response has been unbelievable."[10]

WOMEN'S MINISTRIES

An important part of the story of the Oklahoma missions program is the direct participation of lay women through Women's

415

Ministries (formerly Women's Missionary Council). The idea was born in a church in Houston, Texas, in 1925 when a local women's leader, Etta Calhoun, formally organized her group into a "council." Other states, including Oklahoma, were quick to follow even though the General Council did not make the WMC official until 1951.[11]

Oklahoma had an informal WMC program under the leadership of Mrs. W.T. McMullan of Okmulgee and Mrs. George Patterson of Broken Arrow until the first official election of a WMC president, Lola Miles of Collinsville, in 1932. Other early WMC leaders were Eula Linn of Shawnee, Dorothy Ray of Bristow, Louisa Conrad of Waynoka and Ethel Jones of Chickasha.[12]

The purpose of the Women's Missionary Council is stated in its Constitution:

"To stimulate a missionary spirit in the women of the Assembly through prayer, increased knowledge of the Bible, study of mission service for the needy, and regular contributions to both home and foreign fields...supplying clothing for those in need...giving out tracts...visiting the sick and poor...visiting hospitals, jails, county farms... Report of work done should be made so that our light may shine out in the sea of sickness, sin, and despair, so that others may see the heavenly shore."[13]

Oklahoma Assemblies of God women have always been near the top in the national fellowship in giving. In 1992, 8,630 Oklahoma women gave $424,755 in Women's Ministries and Missionettes offerings—ranking fifth nationally. First Assembly in Owasso led the state in 1992 in giving to the W.M. Pledge Fund—for the 28th consecutive year. Other churches in the top five in W.M. giving in 1992 were First Assembly, Chickasha; Calvary Assembly, Lawton; Broken Arrow First Assembly; and Tulsa Woodlake Assembly.[14]

Marie Goggin faithfully served as Oklahoma WMC President from 1954 to 1981. In her monthly column in the *Assemblies of God News*, she kept Oklahoma ministers informed about the missionary force overseas. In the January, 1956, issue, Sister Goggin wrote that Earl and Nelda Taylor had sailed for Japan, that Verlin and Pauline Stewart were glad to be back in Cuba, that

David and Claudia Wakefield were taking care of 26 outstations in Togo and had seen four or five hundred saved, including four chiefs, and that C.W. Roberts was reporting that God was blessing India.[15]

Oklahoma WMC leaders were constantly urging groups to send necessary supplies to missionaries. Practical hints were given on how to ship packages to foreign fields. "Put them in a corrugated box and tie them with a heavy cord, then sew some burlap around the box, and wrap it in brown paper," wrote WMC President "Ma" Steger. Suggested items for the packages going to missionaries were dried prunes, dried beans, powdered milk, dry yeast, hard candy, raisins, and dried apricots.[16]

WMC groups (now called Women's Ministries groups) often sent "drums" (50-gallon steel barrels) of supplies to missionaries. The John Garlock family waited months for cooking utensils and supplies at their station in South Africa. They wrote: "It is worth every moment of waiting... I can't tell you how wonderful it is to open the cupboard door and see all the gleaming cooking utensils." The Ralph Hollandsworths called it a "red letter day" when their barrels arrived.[17]

The value of the Women's Missionary Council in Oklahoma was evident in a letter from Bill and Alberta Roberts, missionaries to South India, in June, 1953:

"If anyone tells you that the WMC is a gossip group, please have them write me... We have talked to other missionaries from other states, and they are all in a dither trying to buy sheets, pillowcases, and other linens. And then we unpacked our Oklahoma linens and thanked God for such fine women as those who make up the Oklahoma District Women's Missionary Council."[18]

Chapter 35

'Til the Whole World Knows

Oklahoma missionaries continued to take the good news to all corners of the globe in the 1960's. V.H. Shumway, Jr., followed in the footsteps of his father but went to India. The senior Shumway described a typical night's service of open-air revivals during the dry season in Nigeria:

"We all climb into the sound truck and away we go. Usually the young people sing choruses all the way... Paul, our assistant, calls to the people walking along the roads or working on their farms, over the loud speaker, inviting them to the meeting. Upon arrival, Mrs. Shumway starts playing Christian records turned up high in order to draw the people... We have prayer, we preach and then show a Christian film... There is much weeping in the audience... We drive home weary but rejoicing that again the Lord has saved precious souls."[1]

Opal Poag arrived in Liberia in 1962 after a 38-day journey as the only passenger on a freighter:

"Most of the time I was seasick, but in spite of this the presence of the Lord was very real. It gave me enough time to realize just what I was doing, even though the enemy did try to magnify the things I had left behind."[2]

Ralph and Rosemary Hollandsworth continued their service in Nigeria to areas never reached by missionaries:

"Though most of the people have seen white men, it is always amusing to watch those who haven't. In one village a young woman was literally dragged by others to force her to shake hands with us. You never saw one so terrified!"[3]

Missionaries had to realize that their "seed-planting" on foreign fields often did not produce immediate results. Paul and Dreta Hutsell reported from Paraguay in 1963:

"During the past three months we have traveled extensively in the interior of the country. One trip we made on motor scooters covering more than 500 miles that took us into new areas in the eastern jungle. We have given out thousands of pieces of literature and we ask you to pray with us that the Word that was sown both in preaching and in tracts bring forth a good harvest. We will return in a few months to gather the fruits."[4]

Ben and Colleen Tipton made the first of many trips to Africa in 1963. Colleen wrote Sister Goggin:

"How happy we are to have finally arrived in the land of our calling... As we stood before our first congregation and looked into the hungry faces we realized that we could give them the greatest thing they have need of, the bread of life."[5]

The Tiptons found that civilization—but not salvation—had come to Cameroon in west Africa:

"In one vast area, 100,000 people live out over the water in houses built on stilts. In many of these huts you would find a Singer sewing machine or a transistor radio, but they have never been reached with the message which is over 2,000 years old. Still they follow their pagan gods in worship, even offering human sacrifices, not knowing that the Son of God has become their supreme sacrifice. Can you imagine the joy that is ours to be privileged to carry the message to these so steeped in darkness who have never heard the good news about Jesus?"[6]

The Glen Reeves family went to Nigeria in 1964, and the David Montgomerys served in Mexico. In 1964 Bobbie Wilkins was appointed as a missionary to Liberia.

In tribal villages, missionaries always wanted to see the chief converted because of his influence. Veteran missionary Murray Brown reported the conversion of the paramount chief in a village in Togo in 1964:

"He was beaming with joy... A thousand people witnessed the old man standing on a balcony to announce to the huge crowd that he was destroying everything he had formerly worshiped and feared... They built a bonfire and the flames destroyed human skulls, horns, and other idols... The ugly clay and cement fertility god that had ruled over the entrance of his home was pounded into small bits and scattered on the garbage heap."[7]

Jack and Carmelita Bledsoe began their service in Togo, Dahomey (now Benin), and Senegal in 1968.[8]

Arlie and Jennie Teske spent 50 days at sea on their first trip to Korea as Oklahoma missionaries in 1965. The Teskes count their greatest victory in Korea over the last three decades as "seeing many students, prisoners, military and ordinary people acclaiming Christ as Savior through correspondence courses, citywide tent crusades, and literature distribution, and then seeing these people continue to grow and mature in Christ."[9]

Oklahoma passed the half million dollar mark in annual foreign missions offerings in 1968. Miami First Assembly gave over $12,500, tops in the state, while 116 other Oklahoma churches gave more than $1,000 each.[10]

Otis Keener Jr. was granted special recognition by the Division of Foreign Missions as a missionary-evangelist in 1962. *The Pentecostal Evangel* featured the story of a two-week revival held by Keener in Samoa. It was entitled, "Oklahoma Adopts Pago Pago." A band led a procession from the church to the palm-lined shore of Pago Pago where Keener baptized 59 new believers, including the police captain's daughter and the daughter of the speaker of the House of Representatives.[11]

Oklahoma kept sending out new missionaries in the 1970's. Duane and Ruth Collins left for language school in Switzerland in August, 1972, on their way to Senegal in Africa.[12] Al Perna, Jr., and Cary and Faye Tidwell worked with Continental Teen Challenge in Europe. The Tidwells also served in Ghana. Ben and Darlene Odell ministered in a strong Muslim area of Togo beginning in 1973.[13]

421

An unusual foreign missions effort was begun in West Germany in 1974 by Darrel and Dosha Delozier. Darrell had retired from the Air Force and saw the need for a hospitality house for military personnel in Germany. They named it "Berea House" to identify with the Berean Fellowship of military personnel in Europe.[14]

David and Cheryl Newberry began tent crusades in South Africa in 1978. Money for the tent came from a special fund for Good News Crusades, a program of church-planting evangelistic campaigns around the world.

Oklahoma veteran missionary Ben Tipton was given special status as a missionary-evangelist to conduct revivals and crusades in Africa rather than be stationed in one location.[15] Tipton's new status has paid off tremendously. More than 100 churches have begun as a result of his tent crusades. Ben and Colleen Tipton do not overlook followup of new converts. Teams of evangelists follow them into an area where a tent crusade has been held to teach the new converts and establish a local church.[16]

Tipton once gave a unique altar call in the African country of Benin. He began preaching under a tree in an area where the gospel had never been heard. For several weeks, no one responded. Finally, Ben drew a line in the sand and told the natives, "All of us on this side of the line know Jesus and are ready to go. You have not received Jesus and are not ready to die. Will you step across the line with us?" The village chief was the first to cross the line. Soon others followed. Within a few months, a thriving Assemblies of God mission was established.[17]

In 1978 Oklahoma churches gave $1,274,361 to foreign missions, a 100 percent increase over 1968. Tulsa Woodlake led the list with $68,715 followed by Bethany Parkview, Bartlesville First, Tulsa Eastland, Oklahoma City Capitol Hill, and Ponca City First.[18]

Three Oklahoma missionary families were added in 1979: Quentin and Elizabeth McGhee for Kenya, Gary and Wilma Davidson for Ireland, and Don and Linda Stamps for Brazil.

Even in the 1990's, missionaries continue to have major logistical problems. In Kenya, Quentin McGhee is trying to produce Christian textbooks in 40 native languages at the East Africa School of Theology:

"It is a huge task in a country that is so slow. It might take 15 trips to the printer to get a simple cover done for a textbook.

Computers break down. Parts don't fit. Just about the time you get to know the right people in the government, a coup or an election takes place and you start the process again. We who have been raised in America do not realize the backward condition of most of the peoples of the earth."[19]

In the past decade, Oklahoma has continued to send many new missionary families into countries around the world. A complete list of Oklahoma Assemblies of God missionaries from 1914 to 1994 appears in the Appendix.

Missions giving has risen dramatically. In 1992 Oklahoma Assemblies of God churches gave $4,658,483 to Foreign Missions (4th in the nation) out of a total of $8,006,590 to World Ministries (6th in the nation).

Crossroads Cathedral in Oklahoma City was the top church in the entire Assemblies of God fellowship in 1992 in giving to Foreign Missions with offerings of $853,616. Woodlake Assembly in Tulsa was 6th with $417,354. Three other Oklahoma churches placed among the top 100 churches in the nation: Tulsa Carbondale Assembly, 41st; Oklahoma City Faith Tabernacle, 61st; and Tulsa Christian Chapel, 67th.[20]

The Oklahoma District had nine churches in 1992 that ranked in the top 100 churches nationally in per capita giving to Foreign Missions. Leedey Assembly was 5th in the nation. Others in the top 100 were Glencoe Assembly, Bethany Cornerstone, Tulsa Carbondale, Tulsa Woodlake, Roosevelt Assembly, Purcell Memorial Assembly, Verdigris Assembly, and Tulsa Christian Chapel.[21]

WHAT ONE CHURCH CAN DO FOR MISSIONS

Crossroads Cathedral in Oklahoma City is at the center of one of the most spectacular stories in the history of Foreign Missions. That one church is literally changing the face and destiny of an entire African nation.

Malawi is a small scenic country in the eastern part of southern Africa. It is slightly larger than the state of Pennsylvania. Most of its eight million people are poor and live in small villages. British Missionary David Livingstone reached the area in 1859. He found it torn by tribal wars and saw the suffering caused by slave-traders. After existing as a British protectorate for decades, Malawi became an independent republic in 1966.[22]

Crossroads Cathedral Pastor Dan Sheaffer felt a burden for Malawi in the early 1980's. He had converts in the nation even

423

before he set foot on Malawi soil. Sheaffer sent a taped sermon to Malawi. A postal official was curious and wanted to hear the tape. He listened to the tape, was converted, and wanted all of his workers to hear the message. As a result, they were all saved.

Malawi was a spiritually bankrupt country when Crossroads Cathedral began sending financial help and large groups of workers in 1982. When the massive effort began, there was only a handful of Assemblies of God churches in the country with adequate facilities. There are now more than 800 churches. Crossroads Cathedral's Decade of Harvest goal of building 1,000 churches in Malawi will be reached long before the end of the decade.

The time for harvest in Malawi is short for many people. Missionaries Bill and Reita Moore concluded a four-year term in Malawi in 1993. Bill Moore explains the time problem:

"The World Health Organization predicts that AIDS will reduce the population in Malawi to two million by the year 2,000. There literally will be millions of souls dying in the country within the next few years. We must do everything possible to give every person caught up in the AIDS epidemic in Malawi the chance to accept Jesus."[23]

The rapid expansion of the Assemblies of God in Malawi has caused a severe shortage of Christian workers. Crossroads Cathedral is providing the funding for a new $3,000,000 Bible school to train new pastors and workers. Pastor Sheaffer says the goal of his church is—that by the year 2,000, every person living in Malawi will be able to walk or ride a bus to an Assemblies of God church.

For almost a century, the divine purpose of the Pentecostal movement has been to evangelize the entire world. The words of J.W. Welch in the June 17, 1916, issue of the *Weekly Evangel* are even more pertinent today than they were then:

"These are the last days... The harvest is here now... We ought to be busy in the vineyard of service... There is a field of certain fruitage. It is the field of soul-saving evangelism. Anything that hinders the church today from being a soul-saving institution is a work of evil."[24]

Oklahoma missionaries and their supporters throughout the state continue this soul-saving evangelism, knowing their task is not done 'til the whole world knows Jesus.

424

◄ *Lola Miles, Womens Mission-ary Council President from 1932 to 1935.*

▲ *Bobbie Wilkins and her Speed-the-Light pickup in Liberia.*

▲ *Leroy and Thelma Ward and family.*

▲ *Ernestine, Hugh, and Louise Jeter in Peru, c. 1934.*

▼ *Alva and Louise Walker and children, Peru, 1940.*

▲ *Ralph and Rosemary Hollandsworth.*

▼ *Stella, George, Warren and George Flattery Jr., leaving for Africa, 1945.*

▲ *Missionary Murray Brown (center) receives keys to Speed-the-Light truck from DCAP L.B. Keener, 1947. J.L. McQueen looks on.*

Robert Cobb ▶
in Nigeria, 1954.

428

▲ *The Verlin Stewarts, 1957.*

▲ *Marie Goggin and sectional WMC representatives, c. 1957.*

▲ *WMC Day, 1957. (l to r) Murray Brown, Marjorie Brown, Everett Phillips (Field Secretary for Africa), Marie Goggin, Margaret Holleman, Carl Holleman.*

▲ *The Robert Cobbs, 1957.*

430

▲ *The Hugh Jeters, Morocco, 1958.*

▲ *1959 WMC convention in Oklahoma City.*

1959 Speed-the-Light rally.

▲ *The Virgil Heddlestons.*

▲ *(l to r) Dreta Hutsell, Paul Hutsell, Ruth Harris, Charity Harris, Mrs. Raymond Brock, Raymond Brock, Thelma Ward, Ted Vassar, Estelle Vassar, Carl Holleman, Ruth Holleman.*

437

▲ *The Melton Hill family, 1971.*

▲ *The V.H. Shumways.*

438

▼ *The Darrel Deloziers.*

▲ *Cary and Faye Tidwell, 1973.*

▲ *The Earl Taylors.*

439

Duane, David, ▶
and Ruthie Collins,
1975.

▲ *Thelma Cox and Kate Osage, Longdale Indian Church, 1975.*

440

▶ *District Missions Director Lindell Warren (l) gives world missions award to Jim Holt of Woodlake Assembly in Tulsa, 1988.*

▲ *Rev. and Mrs. Marion Clark, home missionaries.*

▲ *Jennie, Rebecca, and Arlie Teske, South Korea, 1989.*

▲ *1986 Indian camp at Wright City.*

▲ *Gary, Wilma, Kristi, Mark, and Dana Davidson, missionaries to Ireland.*

446

▲ *Men of Cathedral of the Hills in Edmond built a 30 x 70 church in Madrid, Mexico, in six days in 1991.*

◄ *North Rock Creek Indian Church near Shawnee.*

447

▲ *The Quentin McGhees, Nairobi, Kenya, 1993.*

▲ *The national Light for the Lost convention in Oklahoma City, April, 1993.*

448

Chapter 36

Revive Us Again!

It is refreshing to compare the first issue of the monthly newsletter sent to Oklahoma District ministers in 1944 with the latest issue. The name of the publication has been changed from the *Assemblies of God News* to *The Outlook*. Full-color covers have replaced simple black and white typesetting. But the content of the newsletter is the same. There is still emphasis on soul-winning, divine healing, on the baptism in the Holy Spirit, on holy living, and on prayer. Monthly columns contain information on conversions and infillings of the Holy Spirit. Prayer requests and testimonies of God's answers are reported.

Eight decades of progress have not dimmed our leaders' strong defense of the Pentecostal message. We still believe that "receiving the baptism of the Holy Spirit doesn't make you Pentecostal. It's what you do after you receive the baptism that makes you Pentecostal."[1]

Should we expect mighty, supernatural acts of God to occur in Assemblies of God services today as in "the good old days"? Evangelist Jim King has a simple, forthright answer:

"Yes, God has not changed. The mighty revivals recorded in the Book of Acts were often birthed by a miracle. God is a 'signs and wonders' God. He wants to do the same today as He did in the early and middle years of our movement. I believe in these last days we will see the supernatural if we will hunger and pray for it and give God the opportunity to manifest His mighty power.

He promised He would pour His Spirit out on all flesh. I believe that day is not coming...it's here now! My prayer is that God will put a desire in our hearts to see Him 'do exceeding abundantly above all that we ask or think, according to the power that works in us' (Ephesians 3:20)."[2]

RISE AND WALK

God's power to heal and restore is just as strong in 1994 as it was on the Day of Pentecost or in the early part of the twentieth century. In 1993 an Oklahoma Assemblies of God professional football player, Dennis Byrd, became a highly visible spokesman for the awesome power of God.

Byrd played football at Mustang and the University of Tulsa before being drafted by the New York Jets of the National Football League in 1989. Byrd and his wife Angela were active at Woodlake Assembly of God in Tulsa during the off-season. Dennis was a good witness of his Christian commitment. He and Angela led a Bible study group for the Jets players and wives.

Dennis' life as a pro football player ended when he collided with a teammate in a game against the Kansas City Chiefs on November 29, 1992. The injury shattered his neck. Dennis was paralyzed from the neck down. During the next year, Dennis and Angela were in the national spotlight because of their amazing faith and trust in God and because of Dennis' miraculous recovery from his devastating injury. The Byrds were featured on the most popular television talk-shows and programs. The testimony appeared in both sports and religious publications. Dennis' autobiography was a best-seller. And, a movie of the Byrds' trials and triumphs was made. Dennis credits his recovery to the Lord:

"I'm grateful to Jesus Christ, who was there when no one else could be. I thank Him for my salvation and for the strength He gave me in my darkest hour. Because of Christ...I now stand in the bright light of day—in triumph."[3]

There is an amazing thread of eternal truth that runs from early-day Pentecost in Oklahoma to the Dennis Byrd story in the 1990's. God is faithful. When no one else can help in life's darkest hour, God is there. Nothing is impossible with Him!

At the 1993 General Council, the Assemblies of God fellowship was challenged by the question, "Are we remaining true to the course laid out for us in the original call which formed our fellowship?" We must face this question and seek the Holy Spirit's help to be all God wants us to be. We have been challenged by the goals of the Decade of Harvest. God wants us to hunger to be part of the greatest revival He has ever sent to this earth.

In conclusion, I present to you "A Call to Revival," by Oklahoma District Superintendent Armon Newburn, under whose leadership and by whose outstanding cooperation this book was written.

A CALL TO REVIVAL

"O Lord, revive thy work in the midst of the years, in the midst of the years make known; in wrath remember mercy." (Habakkuk 3:2)

What is revival? Revival is a mighty spiritual awakening among the people of God that will turn their hearts toward God, earnestly seeking His divine will for their lives. This turning to God and seeking God will produce sanctified, set apart, holy living, and complete obedience to the Word of God. This obedience to the will and Word of God will cause the Church to thrust in the sickle and reap the ripened harvest of lost souls for whom Christ gave His precious blood.

CONDITIONS DEMAND REVIVAL

The Scripture says, "Righteousness exalteth a nation: but sin is a reproach to any people" (Proverbs 14:34). It is time we should look at conditions and circumstances exactly as they are and not hide from the brutal, disturbing facts we find today in America.

Abortion on demand has devalued life. The breakdown of marriages is bringing tragic results to our society. Prosperity has dulled our sense of dependence on God. We are preoccupied with material things. The moral fabric of our society is decaying before our eyes. Sexual permissiveness and unnatural lifestyles have pro-

451

duced AIDS—the plague of our generation. Our beloved America is tearing apart at the seams both spiritually and morally. Our nation is going to pieces morally because we have gone to pieces spiritually.

Let's face it, the Church is not without blame. The Church has a flirtation going with the world; and as a result the Church is the weakest in an hour when it should be the strongest. Thus, we have ritual without power, prayer without answers, worship without the Spirit. Prayerlessness, worldliness, and unconcern have robbed us of the power and presence of God. Is it any wonder our nation is crumbling?

As we see our nation so reproached by sin, it is high time that we should cry out to God for a spiritual awakening. I believe there is a remnant of dedicated, concerned people in our churches who realize this is the only answer to our dilemma in America. This remnant of believers is beginning to cry out, "Wilt thou not revive us again: that thy people may rejoice in thee." (Psalm 85:6). Yes, conditions demand revival.

GOD HAS A FORMULA

God has clearly defined His formula for revival in His holy book. "If my people, which are called by my name, shall humble themselves, and pray, and seek my face, and turn from their wicked ways; then will I hear from heaven, and will forgive their sin, and will heal their land." (2 Chronicles 7:14).

Here are four conditions for revival of spiritual life. If my people will...

1. *Humble themselves*

We are full of pride and self-righteousness. We must recognize we are nothing, and God is everything. Without Him, we can do nothing. Without His anointing and presence, we are in abject spiritual poverty. If we will humble ourselves enough to confess our sins of unbelief, omission, and pride, and earnestly repent, we can touch the heart of God and hear from heaven.

2. *Pray*

We must once again be people of prayer. God answers prayer. We must get back to our personal altars. We must get our churches back to the altar. There is no substitute for prayer.

452

"The effectual fervent prayer of a righteous man availeth much" (James 5:16).

3. *Seek my face*

We must diligently turn to God and seek His presence. To seek God's face is a far different matter than to just say a prayer. This seeking denotes waiting before God. It means a time of deep soul searching. It means an agony of desire for revival, renewal, and holy living. It denotes intercessory prayer. Intercessory prayer is preliminary to any great move of God. Intercessory prayer will precede revival in this last hour.

4. *Turn from their wicked ways*

God's people must lay aside every weight and the sin that doth so easily beset us (Hebrews 12:1). We must turn from idols of our own making. Let us turn from our conformity to this sinful world, asking God to forgive and cleanse us and make us in the image of His dear Son. Oh, for the sensitivity of days gone by! How lightly we regard and look upon sin! Our pioneers in days gone by feared sin more than death. We desperately need a new sense of the awfulness of sin. May God help us somehow to understand just how horrible sin is in His sight; then we will turn to Him with a burning desire for sanctified, holy living.

If we are serious about revival, we cannot play-act with God. It is humility God wants. It is brokenness and contrition God wants. It is intercessory prayer God wants. It is turning from our wicked ways that God wants. Nothing else, absolutely nothing else, will meet God's approval. When these conditions are met, we can expect revival. Wherever these conditions are being met today...revival fires are burning brightly.

> *Lord, as of old at Pentecost*
> *Thou didst thy power display,*
> *With cleansing, purifying flame,*
> *Descend on us today.*

> *Come, Holy Spirit, Heavenly Dove,*
> *With all thy quickening power;*
> *Kindle a flame of sacred love*
> *On these cold hearts of ours.*

453

Lord, let revival come once again upon Your Church! With agony of desire we will seek Your face!

THE RESULTS WILL BE GLORIOUS

God will hear and answer our prayers. God will forgive and cleanse from sin, and He will restore His favor upon us. Our churches will be renewed, and God will bring healing to our land. This healing will be evidenced by an outpouring of the Holy Spirit upon the people so that sinners will be converted as "Whosoever shall call upon the name of the Lord shall be delivered" (Joel 2:32).

The Lord has said, "Call unto me, and I will answer thee, and show thee great and mighty things, which thou knowest not" (Jeremiah 33:3). As we call upon the Lord, the Book of Acts will come alive, and we will see conversions, healings, and miracles. We will rediscover that Jesus Christ is "the same yesterday, and today, and forever" (Hebrews 13:8).

LET US FACE THE CHALLENGE

We are in the final decade of this century, and the closing years of another millennium. As people of God, we must sense the urgency of the hour and our awesome responsibilities to affect the eternal destiny of judgment-bound souls. This is serious business. This is our generation, and it is either heaven or hell. Do we have preachers desperate enough to pay the price for revival? Do we have deacons and teachers who will pay the price for revival? Do we have mothers and fathers who are concerned enough about broken homes and broken lives to pay the price for revival? Do we have youth desperate enough to seek God and change this generation? If so, then revival is on the way! Praise God, I believe we do!

Let us begin to express our heartfelt desire with the words of the old song:

> *Revive us again,*
> *fill my heart with thy love;*
> *May each soul be rekindled*
> *with fire from above.*

And when this happens, we can sing:

All glory and praise
  To the Lamb that was slain,
Who has borne all our sins,
  And has cleansed every stain!
Hallelujah! Thine the glory!
Hallelujah! Amen!
Hallelujah! Thine the glory!
Revive us again.

As we humble ourselves, and pray, and seek God's face, and turn from wicked ways, let's begin to live in the expectation of revival, because God will send it. He will respond to the effectual fervent prayers of His people.

I conclude with the soul-searching prayer recorded in Psalm 51. This was the prayer of David as he cried out for revival and renewal in his own soul:

"Purge me with hyssop, and I shall be clean; wash
  me, and I shall be whiter than snow.
Make me to hear joy and gladness; that the bones
  which thou hast broken may rejoice.
Hide thy face from my sins, and blot out all
  mine iniquities.
Create in me a clean heart, O God; and renew
  a right spirit within me.
Cast me not away from thy presence; and take
  not thy Holy Spirit from me.
Restore unto me the joy of thy salvation; and
  uphold me with thy free Spirit.
Then will I teach transgressors thy ways;
  and sinners shall be converted unto thee."
                                                      (Psalm 51: 7-13)

∴ Footnotes ∾

CHAPTER 1 — Oh, What Singing! Oh, What Shouting!

1. Ethel E. Goss, *The Winds of God* (New York: Comet Press, 1958), 208-210.
2. Carl Brumback, *Suddenly...From Heaven* (Springfield, Missouri: Gospel Publishing House, 1989), 131.
3. Edith Waldvogel Blumhofer, *The Assemblies of God* (Springfield, Missouri: Gospel Publishing House, 1989), 144-145.
4. Goss, 108-109.
5. Ibid., 188-189.
6. Ibid., 184-185.
7. Ibid., 80-81.
8. Brumback, 142-143.
9. Goss, 235-236.
10. Stanley Burgess and Gary McGee, ed., *Dictionary of Pentecostal and Charismatic Movements* (Grand Rapids: Zondervan, 1988), 812-813.

CHAPTER 2 — How It All Began

1. Brumback, 2-3.
2. Ibid. 3.
3. Stanley H. Frodsham, *With Signs Following* (Springfield: Gospel Publishing House, 1946), 19-20.
4. Brumback, 12.
5. J. Roswell Flower, "Historical Review of the Pentecostal Movement", *Assemblies of God Heritage*, Fall, 1985, 11.
6. Goss, 40.
7. Klaude Kendrick, *The Promise Fulfilled* (Springfield: Gospel Publishing House, 1961), 60.
8. *A Portion of Carter, Oklahoma History*, various authors, privately published, 1975, 45.
9. Brumback, 67.
10. Personal interview with Paul L. Ferguson, April 20, 1990, Assemblies of God Archives.
11. Handwritten notes of Paul L. Ferguson, Assemblies of God Archives.
12. Goss, 213.
13. Ibid., 213.

CHAPTER 3 — Azusa Street and Beyond

1. Brumback, 36.
2. Frodsham, 32-34.
3. Ibid., 32-34.

4. *The Apostolic Faith*, January, 1907, 1.

5. Ibid., 4.

6. Blumhofer, 176.

7. Gerald S. Pope, *75th Anniversary Celebration*, privately published, 1982, 2-4.

8. *The Latter Rain Evangel*, February, 1909, 19.

9. "The River Still Flows", *The Pentecostal Evangel*, 5 February 1967, 15.

10. Leroy Hawkins, *A History of the Assemblies of God in Oklahoma: The Formative Years, 1914-1929*, Unpublished dissertation, 1964, 20.

11. Ibid., 21-22.

12. *Lincoln County, Oklahoma History* (Claremore, Oklahoma: Country Lane Press, 1988), 917.

13. Ibid., 280.

14. Dan Morgan, *Rising in the West* (New York: Alfred A. Knopf Inc., 1992), 27-29.

15. Ibid., 27-30.

CHAPTER 4 — The Fire Spreads in All Directions

1. Hawkins, 32-33 and personal interview with Ossie Jones, August 17, 1993.

2. Brumback, *Suddenly...From Heaven*, 170.

3. *The Pentecostal Evangel*, 29 May 1966, 7.

4. Ibid.

5. Ethel Music, *Life and Testimony of Evangelist Ethel Music*, privately published, undated, 8.

6. Written notes of Paul Ferguson, Assemblies of God Archives.

7. Local church history.

8. Personal interview with Bertie Roberts, May 26, 1993.

9. Hawkins, 35.

10. Brumback, 296-297.

11. Ibid., 165-166.

12. Goss, 249.

13. Pope, 5.

14. Local church history.

15. Bob Eskridge, privately published history of Broken Arrow Assembly, undated, 12.

16. Brumback, 168.

17. *Broken Arrow Ledger*, 22 August 1912, 1.

18. Ibid., 29 August 1912, 1.

CHAPTER 5 — Pentecost Everywhere

1. The Assemblies of God Archives in Springfield owns a marvelous collection of old copies of *Word and Witness*.

2. Douglas Barley letter to author, April, 1993.

3. *Word and Witness*, 20 September 1913, 1.

4. Ibid.

CHAPTER 6 — Oklahomans at Hot Springs

1. William Menzies, *Anointed to Serve* (Springfield, Missouri: Gospel Publishing House, 1971), 87.

2. *Word and Witness*, 20 December 1913, 4.

3. Menzies, 80.

4. *Word and Witness*, 20 March, 1914, 1.

5. Brumback, 181.

6. Personal interview with Allie Hughes, March 10, 1993.

7. Personal interview with Ossie Jones, September 10, 1993.

8. Hawkins, 45, and Personal interview with Ernest Strong, March 24, 1993.

9. Allie Hughes interview.

10. *The Pentecostal Evangel*, 20 March 1955, 10.

11. *Tulsa Daily World*, 22 July 1914, 5.

12. *The Christian Evangel*, 19 September 1914, 1.

13. *Tulsa Democrat*, 24 July 1914, 3.

14. *Tulsa Daily World*, 30 July 1914, 10.

15. *The Christian Evangel*, 22 August 1914, 1.

16. Ibid.

CHAPTER 7 — New Growth Despite Controversy

1. Menzies, 115.

2. Brumback, 202.

3. Ibid., 197.

4. Menzies, 118.

5. Blumhofer, 239-242.

6. Ibid., 242-243.

CHAPTER 8 — The Sick Are Healed

1. *Assemblies of God Heritage*, Winter 91-92, 21, 28.

2. *Weekly Evangel*, 17 June 1916, 15.

3. Ibid., 4 November 1916, 7, and 8 September 1917, 16.

4. Ibid., 24 November 1917, 14.

5. Ibid., 16 February 1918, 16.

6. *The Pentecostal Evangel*, 15 November 1919, 11, and *Christian Evangel*, 19 April 1919, 14.

7. Local church history.

8. Unpublished history of Fifth and Peoria, 5.

9. *The Pentecostal Evangel*, 8 February 1919, 4.

459

10. Ibid., 14 June 1919, 9.
11. Local church history.
12. Eskridge, 7.
13. *Christian Evangel*, 19 April 1919, 13.
14. Ibid., 7 November 1914, 1.
15. *Word and Witness*, September 1915, 1.
16. *Weekly Evangel*, 10 April 1915, 1.
17. *Word and Witness*, 20 May 1914, 3.
18. *Weekly Evangel*, 7 April 1917, 6.
19. Ibid., 19 May 1917, 15.
20. Ibid., 27 March 1915, 2.
21. *Christian Evangel*, 8 March 1919, 14.
22. *Word and Witness*, October 1915, 8.
23. *Weekly Evangel*, 6 January 1917, 16.
24. *Word and Witness*, July 1914, 2.
25. Jewell Nicholson Cunningham, *Covered Wagon Days of Evangelism* (Tyler, Texas, privately published, 1984), 50-51.
26. Ibid., 53-57.
27. Ibid., 58.
28. *Weekly Evangel*, 22 May 1915, 3.

CHAPTER 9 — A Fertile Field for Pentecost

1. Personal interview with Allie Hughes, March 10, 1993.
2. Lincoln County History, 281.
3. Letter from Otto Goins to Cynthia Wilson, August 18, 1993.
4. *Weekly Evangel*, 5 May 1917, 14.
5. Lincoln County History, 85.
6. Ibid., 64-64.
7. *Weekly Evangel*, 4 May 1915, 4.
8. Ibid., 17 March 1917, 14.
9. *Christian Evangel*, 28 June 1919, 14.
10. Ibid., 10 October 1914, 4.
11. *Weekly Evangel*, 17 March 1917, 14.
12. *Christian Evangel*, 23 January 1915, 4.
13. *Weekly Evangel*, 24 July 1915, 2.
14. *Word and Witness*, October 1915, 7.
15. Local church history.
16. *Word and Witness*, September 1915, 5.
17. Ibid., 19 September 1915, 3.
18. *Christian Evangel*, 19 April 1919, 14.
19. Ibid., 28 June 1919, 14.

20. *Word and Witness*, 20 October 1914, 4.
21. *Weekly Evangel*, 31 July 1915, 3.
22. Phonograph record, Assemblies of God Archives.
23. *Weekly Evangel*, 12 June 1915, 4.
24. Ibid., 11 August 1917, 14.
25. *The Pentecostal Evangel*, 13 December 1919, 14.
26. *Christian Evangel*, 31 October 1914, 4.
27. *Weekly Evangel*, 24 October 1914, 2.
28. Cunningham, 44.
29. Hawkins, 74.
30. *Weekly Evangel*, 18 December 1915, 3.
31. Ibid., 11 September 1915, 12.
32. Ibid., 27 March 1915, 2.
33. Ibid., 31 July 1915, 2.
34. Ibid., 29 September 1915, 16.
35. Ibid., 18 December 1915, 4.
36. Ibid., 26 June 1915, 1.
37. Ibid., 17 November 1917, 14.
38. *Christian Evangel*, 31 October 1914, 4.
39. Hawkins, 73.
40. *Oklahoma City Times*, 12 October 1963, 12.
41. Personal interview with Ossie Jones, September 10, 1993.
42. Local church history.
43. *Christian Evangel*, 31 October 1914, 4.
44. *Weekly Evangel*, 12 June 1915, 4.
45. Ibid., 12 June 1915, 4.
46. *Christian Evangel*, 28 June 1919, 14.
47. Hawkins, 79.

CHAPTER 10 — The Roaring Twenties

1. Flowers, 13.
2. Menzies, 143.
3. Ibid., 134-135.
4. Brumback, 295.
5. Blumhofer, 258.
6. Ward, 40.
7. Brumback, 241.
8. Hawkins, 85.
9. *The Pentecostal Evangel*, 13 November 1920, 14.
10. Ibid., 15 November 1924, 9.
11. 1924 District Council Minutes, 9, and 1925 Minutes, 6.

12. Hawkins, 94.

13. E.R. Winter, *Thirty-Five Years on the Range for Jesus*, Privately printed, 1960, 21-22.

14. Personal interview with Melvin Lynn, September 7, 1993.

15. Ossie Jones interview.

16. Ibid.

17. Ibid.

18. *The Pentecostal Evangel*, 23 November 1929, 20.

19. Personal interview with Gordon Millard, September 9, 1993.

20. *The Pentecostal Evangel*, 19 March 1921, 14.

21. Ibid., 19 February 1921, 22.

22. Ibid., 22 January 1921, 15.

23. Ibid., 28 May 1921, 14.

24. Local church history.

25. *The Pentecostal Evangel*, 21 April 1923, 10, and 1924 District Council Minutes, 8.

26. Local church history.

27. Hawkins, 100-101.

28. Ibid., 103-104.

CHAPTER 11 — Praying for Rain

1. Local church history.

2. *The Pentecostal Evangel*, 16 May 1925, 6-7.

3. Local church history.

4. *The Assemblies of God Heritage*, Spring 1992, 13.

5. *The Pentecostal Evangel*, 30 October 1920, 14.

6. Ibid.

7. Ibid., 12 November 1921, 14.

8. Martin Perryman, "Beginnings: Early Days of Pentecost and the Assemblies of God In and Around the Area of Anadarko, Oklahoma", unpublished dissertation, May 2, 1986.

9. *Assemblies of God News*, May 1966, 3.

10. Blanche McClure, 50-year anniversary pamphlet of Stecker Assembly of God.

11. Perryman, 8-12.

12. Ibid., 14-16.

13. Local church history.

14. Personal interview with Vesta Bice, June 24, 1993.

15. Ibid.

16. Rex Humbard, *My Father*, privately published, 1953, 53.

17. *The Pentecostal Evangel*, 29 October 1921, 15.

18. Personal interview with Birdie Rackley, May 10, 1993.

19. Personal interview with Bert Webb, March 18, 1993.

20. Dexter Collins, "When the Fire Fell", *The Pentecostal Evangel*, 13 November 1966, 6.

21. *The Pentecostal Evangel*, 22 October 1927, 13.

22. Glenn Gohr, "Bert Webb, A Man Used by God", *The Assemblies of God Heritage*, Fall 1991, 9.

23. Bert Webb interview.

24. Ibid.

25. Blumhofer, 255.

26. Gohr, 10.

27. Personal interview with N.B. Rayburn, July 15, 1993, and letter to Cindy Wilson, July 21, 1993.

28. *The Pentecostal Evangel*, 22 September 1923, 11.

29. Ibid., 21 April 1923, 10.

30. Letter from Connie Walker to author, June 7, 1993.

CHAPTER 12 — Churches Springing Up Everywhere

1. Local church history.

2. Local church history.

3. Personal interview with A.R. Donaldson, September 15, 1993.

4. *The Pentecostal Evangel*, 3 May 1924, 12.

5. Local church history.

6. Local church history.

7. Local church history.

8. Local church history.

9. Local church history.

10. Local church history.

11. Local church history.

12. Local church history.

13. Local church history and personal interview with Pearl Roberts, September 21, 1993.

14. Hawkins, 107.

15. *The Pentecostal Evangel*, 4 August 1923, 8.

16. Ibid.

17. Ibid, 5 June 1970, 5-8.

18. Local church history.

19. Perryman, 7-8.

20. Ibid.

21. Lee Sheaffer, *The Story of Faith Tabernacle*, privately published, 1962, 5-7.

22. *Golden Grain*, April 1928, 29.

23. Sheaffer, 9.

24. Personal interview with Laverne Hanigan, May 26, 1993.

25. *Golden Grain*, June 1928, 14.

26. Ibid., November 1928, 59.

27. Sheaffer, 5-7.

28. *Dictionary of Pentecostal and Charismatic Movements*, 883-884.

29. Ossie Jones interview.

Chapter 13 — Great Depression Brings Expansion

1. Bob Burke and Von Creel, *Lyle Boren: Rebel Congressman* (Oklahoma City: Western Heritage Books, 1991), 30-31.

2. Ibid., 32.

3. Personal interview with Forrest Murray, June 3, 1993.

4. Local church history.

5. Local church history.

6. Eskridge, 15.

7. Sheaffer, 12-13.

8. Menzies, 145.

9. Local church history.

10. Local church history.

11. Personal interview with Ethel and Allen Wade, May 26, 1993.

12. Personal interview with Matt Goss, April 15, 1993.

13. *The Pentecostal Evangel*, 15 May 1966, 30.

14. Local church history.

15. *Reflections of Faith* (Springfield: Assemblies of God Benevolences Department, 1992), Volume III, 7.

16. 1930 District Council Minutes, 2.

17. 1931 District Council Minutes, 23.

18. 1932 District Council Minutes, 22-24.

19. Perryman, 7.

20. *The Pentecostal Evangel*, 5 December 1936, 17.

21. Personal interview with Vivian McCormick, April 29, 1993.

22. Local church history.

23. Local church history.

24. Local church history.

25. Letter from Helen Lusby to author, October 26, 1993.

26. Local church history.

27. Local church history and personal interview with Bertie Roberts, June 17, 1993.

28. *The Pentecostal Evangel*, 30 December 1956, 13.

29. Personal interview with James Dodd, October 1, 1993.

CHAPTER 14 — Revivals in the Thirties

1. *The Pentecostal Evangel*, 10 December 1938, 17.
2. Ibid., 7 August 1937, 12.
3. Letter from Otto Goins to Cynthia Ruth Wilson, August 18, 1993.
4. Personal interview with Marvin McElhannon, August 15, 1993.
5. Personal interview with Boyd Tucker, August 15, 1993.
6. Personal interview with Rufus Strange, July 15, 1993.
7. Ida May Graham, *Hitherto Hath The Lord Led Us* (Tulsa, Oklahoma: Vickers Printing Company, 1947), 24.
8. 1930 District Council minutes, 6.
9. Wayne Warner, ed., *Touched by Fire* (Plainfield, New Jersey: Logos International, 1978), 131-132.
10. Blumhofer, 263.
11. Forrest Murray interview.
12. Menzies, 147.
13. Personal interview with Paul Sharpe, September 13, 1993.
14. Personal interview with Bob Eskridge, September 10, 1993.
15. Songbook file, Assemblies of God Archives.
16. *Dictionary of Pentecostal and Charismatic Movements*, 692.
17. Blumhofer, 261.
18. Menzies, 266.

CHAPTER 15—Heroes of the Faith

1. *C.A. Herald*, November 1956.
2. Personal interview with J.W. Reddick, August 1, 1993.
3. *Reflections of Faith* (Springfield: Assemblies of God Benevolences Department, 1983).
4. Personal interview with Joe Stumbaugh, September 1, 1993.
5. Mary Ruth Chamless, *Behold God's Handmaid* (Chatham, Illinois: Paprus Book Printers, 1988), 48.
6. Ibid., 48, 88.
7. Ibid., 121.
8. Alpha Henson, *Clyde* (Stow, Ohio: Cre-Com Publishers, Inc., 1976), 15.
9. Ibid., 16.
10. Glenn Gohr, "Devoted to Ministry", *The Pentecostal Evangel*, 26 February 1989, 12.
11. Ibid., 13.
12. Personal interview with Leenetta Scott, March 11, 1993.
13. Local church history.
14. Personal interview with Leenetta Scott, March 11, 1993.
15. Glenn Gohr, "Pioneering in Oklahoma", *Assemblies of God Heritage*, Spring 1992, 7.

16. Samuel Scott file of Assemblies of God Archives.
17. Files of Samuel and Leenetta Scott.
18. Personal interview with Carol Pierce, April 29, 1993.
19. Personal interview Vesta Bice, June 24, 1993.
20. Personal interview with W.C. and Katherine Drain, June 15, 1993.
21. Ibid.
22. Carole Heckard interview with Leslie and Ida Moore.

CHAPTER 16 — Southwestern Bible School

1. Menzies, 141.
2. Blumhofer, 322.
3. *The Pentecostal Evangel*, 2 January 1936, 4.
4. Ibid.
5. Autobiography of P.C. Nelson from files of Southwestern Assemblies of God College, P.C. Nelson Library, Waxahachie, Texas, 4.
6. Ibid., 5.
7. Ibid., 6.
8. Ibid., 10.
9. *The Pentecostal Evangel*, 27 November 1920, 8.
10. P.C. Nelson autobiography, 32.
11. Ibid., 41, and *The Pentecostal Evangel*, 15 May 1983, 25.
12. P.C. Nelson autobiography, 42-43.
13. Ibid., 43.
14. *The Pentecostal Evangel*, 27 June 1927, 13.
15. Newspaper clippings from Nelson files at Southwestern Assemblies of God College. The college also has on display the desk and typewriter used in Enid by P.C. Nelson.
16. Lloyd Conditt, unpublished paper on P.C. Nelson, April 26, 1949, Southwestern Assemblies of God College.
17. Blake L. Farmer, *Southwestern Assemblies of God College: Founding, Growth and Development 1927-1965*, unpublished dissertation, Baylor University, Waco, Texas, August, 1965, 16.
18. *The Pentecostal Evangel*, 10 March 1928, 13.
19. Personal interview with Hugh Jeter, June 15, 1993.
20. Ibid.
21. Ibid.
22. Farmer, 22.
23. Alumni booster brochure, files of Southwestern Assemblies of God College.
24. Charles Blair, *The Man Who Could Do No Wrong* (Lincoln, Virginia: Chosen Books, 1981), 60-61.
25. Personal interview with Matt Goss, April 15, 1993.
26. Personal interview with Lillie Bennett, May 6, 1993.

27. *The Southwesterner*, 1934 yearbook of Southwestern Bible School, 48-49.

28. Personal interview with Louise Unruh, May 6, 1993.

29. Personal interview with Connie Walker, May 5, 1993.

30. *The Pentecostal Evangel*, 23 November 1929, 20.

31. 1931 SBS yearbook, 53.

32. 1936 SBS yearbook, 55.

33. Farmer, 26.

34. Faye Farmer (Bertelmann), *The History of Southwestern Assemblies of God in Waxahachie*, unpublished, University of Texas, December 16, 1971, 2.

35. Personal interview with Klaude Kendrick.

36. Personal interview with Ron McCaslin, August 7, 1993.

CHAPTER 17 — War Brings More Hard Times

1. *Assemblies of God Heritage*, Winter 91-92, 13. U.S. Grant later pastored First Assembly of God in Kansas City, Missouri. He was recognized as one of the outstanding pastors in the Assemblies of God movement.

2. Menzies, 326.

3. Ibid., 326-327.

4. 1943 District Council Minutes, 46.

5. 1944 District Council minutes, 43.

6. 1944 District Council Minutes, 57.

7. 1941 District Council Minutes, 51.

8. 1943 District Council Minutes, 49.

9. Ibid., 55-56.

10. Ibid., 56.

11. *Assemblies of God News*, 1 June 1945, 1.

12. 1945 District Council Minutes, 43.

13. *Reflections of Faith*, 1983, 8.

14. Ibid., 39.

15. Rufus Strange interview.

16. Interview with H.L. Walker, July 15, 1993.

17. Carole Heckard interview with Leslie Moore.

18. Ibid.

19. Personal interview with Cleo and Viaretta Johnson, July 7, 1993.

20. *Vinita Daily Journal*, 28 April 1987, 5.

21. Local church history.

22. *Assemblies of God News*, June 1966, 3.

23. Ibid., July 1966, 3.

24. *The Pentecostal Evangel*, 7 June 1953, 14.

25. *Assemblies of God News*, July 1967, 3.

26. Lincoln County History, 207-208.

CHAPTER 18 — Progress in the Forties

1. *Assemblies of God Heritage*, Spring 1993, 9.
2. Interview with Gordon Speed, November 19, 1993.
3. 1941 District Council Minutes, 49.
4. 1946 District Council Minutes, 42.
5. 1940 and 1949 District Council Minutes.
6. *Assemblies of God News*, June 1945, 3.
7. Ibid., October, 1946, 4.
8. Interview with JoAnn Newburn, October 11, 1993.
9. Interview with Armon Newburn, June 28, 1993.
10. Personal files of Samuel and Leenetta Scott.
11. 1943 District Council Minutes, 54.
12. *Assemblies of God News*, 1 September 1947, 3.
13. Ibid., 1 January 1947, 3.
14. Personal interview with A.K. and Vadie Davis, August 17, 1993.
15. 1946 District Council Minutes, 62.
16. 1940 and 1949 District Council Minutes.
17. *Assemblies of God Heritage*, Winter 91-92, 19.
18. 1940 District Council Minutes, 59.
19. Ibid., 57.
20. 1941 District Council Minutes, 67.
21. 1946 District Council Minutes, 42, 58.
22. *Assemblies of God News*, 1 November 1947, 2.
23. 1948 District Council Minutes, 80.
24. 1949 District Council Minutes, 91.
25. 1946 District Council Minutes, 63-64.
26. 1947 District Council Minutes, 46.
27. Ibid., 46-47.
28. 1949 District Council Minutes, 80.
29. Ibid.
30. Menzies, 254-255.
31. *Assemblies of God Review*, November 1945, 1.
32. *The Pentecostal Evangel*, 7 July 1957, 15.
33. *Reflections of Faith*, 66.
34. Eskridge, 7.
35. 1940 District Council Minutes, 44.
36. Ibid., 50.
37. *The Pentecostal Evangel*, 27 April 1940, 14.
38. 1941 District Council Minutes, 55.
39. 1946 District Council Minutes, 55.

40. Ibid., 58.
41. 1947 District Council Minutes, 63.
42. Ibid., 46.
43. 1940 District Council Minutes, 43.
44. Ibid., 51.
45. 1941 District Council Minutes, 47.
46. *C.A. Herald*, August 1943, 7.
47. 1943 District Council Minutes, 50.
48. 1949 District Council Minutes, 74.

CHAPTER 19 — Facing Doctrinal Differences

1. Blumhofer, Vol. 2, 10-11.
2. Brumback, 332-333.
3. Ibid.
4. 1932 District Council Minutes, 53.
5. Personal interview with Carl McCoy, June 15, 1993.
6. Blumhofer, Vol. 2, 50, 63.
7. Brumback, 333.
8. Personal interview with Earl Oliver, May 20, 1993.
9. Personal interview with Lawrence Langley, June 22, 1993.
10. Personal interview with Lois Burke, June 22, 1993.
11. Personal interview with Kenneth Stafford, July 18, 1993.
12. Personal interview with Cleo Johnson.
13. *Dictionary of Pentecostal and Charismatic Movements*, 759-60.
14. Wayne E. Warner, *Kathryn Kuhlman* (Ann Arbor, Michigan: Servant Publications, 1993), 163.
15. *Dictionary of Pentecostal and Charismatic Movements*, 760.
16. Ibid., 7-8.
17. Ibid., 8.
18. Ibid., 345, and personal interview with E.W. Swift, September 15, 1993.
19. Ibid., 222.
20. Menzies, 335.
21. Ibid.
22. Ibid.

CHAPTER 20 — Strong District Leadership

1. 1952 District Council Minutes, 55.
2. 1951 and 1959 District Council financial reports.
3. 1955 District Council Minutes, 68-69.
4. 1956 District Council Minutes, 59.
5. 1952 District Council Minutes, 93-94.

6. *Assemblies of God News*, May 1953, 1.

7. 1954 District Council Minutes, 54.

8. 1955 District Council Minutes, 53-54.

9. 1953 District Council Minutes, 55.

10. *Assemblies of God News*, July 1953, 3.

11. *Assemblies of God News*, May 1955, 3.

12. Ibid., January 1959, 8.

13. 1957 District Council Minutes, 61-62.

14. *Assemblies of God News*, May 1953, 3.

15. Ibid., November 1953, 3.

16. Ibid., March 1958, 2.

17. Personal interview with Eugene Burke, June 22, 1993.

18. 1953 District Council Minutes, 91, and *Assemblies of God News*, December 1953, 3.

19. Ibid., October 1959, 8.

20. Blumhofer, Vol. 2, 204.

CHAPTER 21 — Special Ministries

1. Personal interview with John McPherson, May 10, 1993.

2. W.W. Hays, *Delivered From Alcohol, Dope, and Death*, privately published and undated.

3. Edith Hays, *Please, God Help Me*, privately published and undated.

4. Personal interview with W.W. Hays, May 30, 1993.

5. *Assemblies of God News*, July 1953, 2, and November 1953, 6.

6. Ibid., December 1953, 6.

7. 1951 District Council Minutes, 75-76.

8. 1953 District Council Minutes, 75.

9. *Assemblies of God News*, May 1954, 5.

10. 1950 District Council Minutes, 73.

11. 1951 District Council Minutes, 78.

12. 1952 District Council Minutes, 79.

13. 1956 District Council Minutes, 87.

14 . *Assemblies of God News*, September 1957, 6.

15. Ibid.

16. 1958 District Council Minutes, 86.

17. 1959 District Council Minutes, 84.

CHAPTER 22 — Challenged by Social Change

1. Menzies, 348.

2. 1952 District Council Minutes, 98.

3. *Assemblies of God News*, February 1958, 8.

4. Menzies, 227.

CHAPTER 23 — Going On with God

1. Letter from Paul Hutsell to author, October 26, 1993.
2. *Reflections of Faith*, 34.
3. *Assemblies of God News*, November 1951, 2.
4. 1950 and 1959 District Council Minutes.
5. *The Pentecostal Evangel*, 17 June 1962, 12.
6. *Assemblies of God News*, March 1966, 3.
7. *The Pentecostal Evangel*, 5 November 1950, 20.
8. 1950 District Council Minutes, 55-61.
9. 1951 District Council Minutes, 59-64.
10. 1952 District Council Minutes, 60-65.
11. Local church history.
12. *Assemblies of God News*, August 1966, 3.
13. Letter from Robert Rider to author, November 1, 1993.
14. Local church history.
15. *Assemblies of God News*, March 1955, 4, and June 1955, 4.
16. Ibid., February 1955, 4.
17. Ibid., June 1966, 3.
18. Personal interview with Franklin Blair, July 15, 1993.
19. Personal interview with H.A. Brummett, August 4, 1993.
20. 1959 District Council Minutes, 58-63.
21. *The Pentecostal Evangel*, 9 September 1950, 2; 29 November 1953, 11; 24 January 1954, 5; 1 August 1954, 10; 28 November 1954, 11; 13 July 1958, 25.

CHAPTER 24 — "Not Conformed to This World"

1. Menzies, 340.
2. Ibid., 342.
3. Ibid.
4. Assemblies of God News, February 1961, 3.
5. Ibid., March 1961, 5.
6. Blumhofer, Vol. 2, 166-168.
7. Menzies, 349-350.
8. Blumhofer, Vol. 2, 103.
9. *Dictionary of Pentecostal and Charismatic Movements*, 159.
10. Ibid., 600.
11. Blumhofer, Vol. 2, 105.
12. *Assemblies of God News*, March 1961, 5.
13. Ibid., February 1971, 3.

CHAPTER 25 — The Great Pickens Revival

1. Personal interview with Walter Spradling, June 30, 1993.
2. Personal interview with Don Holmes, June 29, 1993.

471

3. Walter Spradling interview.

4. The Pickens revival story was compiled with interviews of Walter Spradling, Don Holmes, Odell Stuart, Don Burke, and Gary Davidson.

5. *The Pentecostal Evangel*, 12 October 1969, 39.

6. Personal interview with Eugene Howeth, August 17, 1993.

7. *The Pentecostal Evangel*, 24 November 1968, 24.

8. *The Pentecostal Evangel*, 8 October 1972, 30.

9. Ibid., 12 March 1972, 23.

10. Ibid., 22 July 1973, 12.

11. Personal interview with Bill Weaver, August 13, 1993.

12. Personal interview with Dan Sheaffer, July 6, 1993.

13. Ibid.

CHAPTER 26 — More Members, Fewer Churches

1. 1959-1969 Oklahoma District Annual Reports.

2. Personal interview with Herbert Wharton, June 12, 1993.

3. 1959-1969 District Council Minutes.

4. 1959-1979 District Council Minutes.

5. 1965 District Council Minutes, 66-67.

6. *Assemblies of God Courier*, August 1962.

7. *Assemblies of God News*, October 1963, 5.

8. 1964 District Council Minutes, 67.

9. 1979 District Council Minutes, 86.

10. 1963 Minutes, 73, 1973 Minutes, 83.

11. 1960 Minutes, 70.

12. 1963 Minutes, 74.

13. Personal interview with Armon Newburn, June 28, 1993.

14. Ibid.

15. Ibid.

16. Ibid.

17. Personal interview with Roger Mattox, November 19, 1993.

18. 1968 Minutes, 68.

19. *Assemblies of God News*, September 1964, 6.

20. 1970 Minutes, 76.

21. 1979 Minutes, 88.

22. Personal interview with Pam King, November 15, 1993.

23. Personal interview with Jim McNabb, August 30, 1993.

CHAPTER 27 — New Programs Added

1. Menzies, 278.

2. *Assemblies of God News*, February 1972, 6.

3. Ibid., September 1966, 6.

4. 1975 Minutes, 83.

5. 1962 Minutes, 62.

6. 1979 Minutes, 76-77.

7. Personal interview with Phil Taylor, June 30, 1993.

8. Personal interview with Curtis Owens, August 15, 1993.

9. Personal interview with Terry and Sue Davidson, August 27, 1993.

10. 1979 Minutes, 86.

11. 1966 Minutes, 61.

12. 1979 Minutes, 78.

13. 1965 Minutes, 65.

14. 1979 Minutes, 80-81.

15. *Assemblies of God News*, July 1961, 7.

16. Menzies 283 and 1971 Minutes, 82.

17. *Assemblies of God News*, May 1966, 4.

18. Ibid., July 1972, 5.

19. Ibid., October 1963, 6.

20. Menzies, 278-279 and *The Pentecostal Evangel*, 22 November 1970, 18, 19.

CHAPTER 28 — Raised from His Deathbed

1. Personal interview with W.G. and Doris Baker, July 23, 1993.

2. 1968 District Council annual report, 2.

3. 1962 and 1964 Minutes.

4. *Assemblies of God News*, November 1968, 8.

5. 1979 Minutes, 77.

6. 1980 District Council annual report and financial statement.

7. 1960 and 1980 Minutes.

8. *Assemblies of God News*, March 1963, 5.

9. H.A. Brummett interview.

10. *The Assemblies of God at 75* (Springfield: Gospel Publishing House, 1989), 20.

CHAPTER 29 — Oklahoma Leads the Way

1. 1981 Minutes, 73.

2. 1984 Minutes, 64.

3. 1989 Minutes, 74.

4. 1992 ACMR.

5. *Assemblies of God Courier*, October 1993.

6. 1982 Minutes, 76.

7. *Oklahoma Outlook*, September 1986, 6.

8. *The Council Today*, General Council daily newspaper, 13 August 1993.

9. *Oklahoma Outlook*, December 1986, 6.

10. 1992 Minutes, 99-103.

11. Ibid.

12. 1991 Minutes, 106.

13. 1981 Minutes, 73.

14. 1992 Minutes, 104-105 and 1993 Minutes, 16.

15. *The Pentecostal Evangel*, 8 June 1991, 24.

16. *Oklahoma Outlook*, December 1985, 9; February 1986, 10; February 1987, 8.

17. Ibid., July 1987, 8.

18. Ibid., September 1988, 7.

19. *The Pentecostal Evangel*, 31 March 1991, 29.

20. 1988 Minutes, 79.

21. Personal interview with Lindell Warren, 18 July, 1993.

22. *The Pentecostal Evangel*, 10 March 1991, 28.

23. *Assemblies of God News*, July 1982, 4.

24. *Oklahoma Outlook*, May 1992, 4.

25. *Assemblies of God News*, August 1984, 4.

26. *Oklahoma Outlook*, October 1992, 4.

27. Ibid., November 1992, 4.

28. 1993 District Council Annual Report, 28-29.

29. 1986 Minutes, 72.

30. 1990 Minutes, 80.

31. Blumhofer, Vol. 2, 168.

32. Ibid., 186.

33. Ibid., 187.

34. Ibid., 188-189.

35. Ibid., 189-190.

36. Armon Newburn sermon delivered at Cathedral of the Hills, Edmond, Oklahoma, January, 1989.

CHAPTER 30 — Okies in Print

1. Richard Exley, *Abortion: Pro-Life by Conviction, Pro-Choice by Default* (Tulsa, Oklahoma: Honor Books, 1989), xi.

2. Personal interview with Raymond T. Brock, August 10, 1993.

3. John G. Hall, *God's Dispensational and Prophetic Plan* (Newcastle, Oklahoma: privately published, 1965), Introduction.

4. Grady Adcock, *I Love Poetry* (Tulsa, Oklahoma: privately published, 1992), 21.

5. Personal interview with Loren Triplett, December 5, 1992.

6. Back cover of *The Full Life Study Bible* (Grand Rapids: Zondervan, 1992).

7. *Assemblies of God News*, March 1984, 8.

8. *Oklahoma Outlook*, April 1987, 8.

9. Personal interview with JoAnn Newburn, November 7, 1993.

CHAPTER 31 — Looking Back—Looking Ahead

1. 1993 Oklahoma District Council Annual Report, 4.
2. 1992 Annual Church Ministries Report, Oklahoma.
3. Ibid.
4. Perkins is a typical small church where members of one family make up a large part of the congregation. In a Wednesday night service in the summer of 1993, Associate Pastor Lynn Hazelbaker led the praise and worship, Lynn Hazelbaker Jr. played the drums, Mary Hazelbaker sang in a trio, and Katrina Hazelbaker taught Missionettes. Four other members of the family fill positions ranging from Sunday School teacher to W.M. President.
5. *The Pentecostal Evangel*, 15 June 1986, 26.
6. Ibid., 25 May 1986, 28.
7. Ibid., 31 January 1988, 29.
8. Ibid., 16 December 1984, 29.
9. *The Pentecostal Evangel*, 27 November 1988, 27.
10. Ibid., 24 November 1985, 28.
11. *Oklahoma Outlook*, September 1991, 4.
12. Edgar McElhannon interview.
13. Dan Sheaffer interview.
14. H.A. Brummett interview.
15. *The Pentecostal Evangel*, 5 September 1993, 7.
16. *Oklahoma Outlook*, April 1992, 2.
17. *Assemblies of God News*, August 1980, 3.
18. James Dodd interview.
19. *Assemblies of God News*, June 1983, 3.
20. Ibid.
21. Ibid.
22. Personal interview with Greg Whitlow, July 19, 1993.
23. *The Assemblies of God at 75*, 94-95.
24. 1988 Minutes, 81.
25. Lindell Warren, Information sheet presented to the 1993 District Council.
26. *The Pentecostal Evangel*, 16 June 1991, 29.

CHAPTER 32 — Home Missions

1. Local church history.
2. Cunningham, 155-156.
3. Gordon Speed interview.
4. *Assemblies of God News*, February 1959, 7.
5. Ibid., September 1963, 7.
6. Ibid., September 1967, 4.
7. *The Pentecostal Evangel*, 17 February 1974, 20-21.

8. Ibid.

9. *Oklahoma Outlook*, March 1986, 4.

10. *Assemblies of God News*, January 1959, 7.

11. Ibid.

12. Ibid., July 1961, 7.

13. Ibid., August 1966, 7.

14. Ibid., March 1958, 7.

15. Personal interview with Don Ramsey, August 12, 1993.

16. *Oklahoma Outlook*, September 1987, 3.

CHAPTER 33 — To the Ends of the Earth

1. Blumhofer, 290.

2. Brumback, 337.

3. *Weekly Evangel*, 17 June 1916, 1.

4. Menzies, 242.

5. Ibid., 243-244.

6. Hawkins, 64.

7. Ibid., 108-109.

8. Pope, 5.

9. *The Pentecostal Evangel*, 16 September 1922, 11.

10. Ibid., 12 January 1924, 14.

11. Ibid.

12. Ibid., 22 August 1925, 12.

13. Ibid., 20 November 1926, 20.

14. 1930 Minutes, 41.

15. Blumhofer, 298.

16. *The Pentecostal Evangel*, 8 October 1927, 8.

17. Letter from Louise Jeter Walker to author, July 19, 1993.

18. Ibid.

19. Ibid.

20. Hugh Jeter interview.

21. *Good News*, Southwestern Assemblies of God College, Spring/Summer 1993, 2.

22. 1936 Southwestern Bible School yearbook.

23. Personal interview with Carl Holleman, June 25, 1993.

24. Ibid.

25. 1939 Minutes, 45.

26. Carl Holleman interview.

27. *Assemblies of God News*, July 1953, 7.

28. Carl Holleman interview.

29. Ibid.

476

30. *Good News*, 3.
31. Ibid.
32. Ibid. and *Dictionary of Pentecostal and Charismatic Movements*, 854.
33. Personal interview with V.H. Shumway, April 20, 1993.
34. Personal interview with Verlin Stewart, April 13, 1993.
35. Personal interview with Thelma Ward, April 22, 1993.
36. *Assemblies of God News*, February 1958, 7.
37. Personal interview with Robert Cobb, June 22, 1993.
38. Ibid.
39. *Assemblies of God News*, February 1950, 2.
40. Ibid., April 1952, 3.
41. Ibid., March 1953, 6.
42. Ibid., June 1952, 3.
43. Ibid., January 1954, 7.
44. Ibid., June 1950, 6.
45. Personal interview with Earl Taylor, July 21, 1993, and letter from Taylor to C.R. Wilson, July 23, 1993.
46. *Assemblies of God News*, May 1958, 7.
47. Ibid., May 1956, 7.
48. Personal interview with Paul Hutsell, November, 1993.
49. Ibid.
50. Personal interview with Melton and Alma Hill, July 30, 1993.
51. Personal interview with Charity and Ruth Harris, May 1, 1993.
52. Ibid.
53. Ibid.
54. Alma Hill interview and *Assemblies of God News*, July 1957, 7.

CHAPTER 34 — Missions Support Groups

1. Menzies, 274.
2. 1951 Minutes, 77.
3. *Assemblies of God News*, March 1978, 6.
4. Ibid., March 1984, 6.
5. 1993 District Council annual report, 12.
6. *Assemblies of God News*, August 1975, 6.
7. Ibid., November 1978, 6.
8. 1993 District Council annual report, 16.
9. Ibid., 22.
10. Personal interview with Charles "Chuck" Freeman, June 29, 1993.
11. Menzies, 278-279.
12. 1932 Minutes, 42.
13. 1933 Minutes, 42.

14. 1993 Minutes, 18-21.
15. *Assemblies of God News*, January 1956, 7.
16. Ibid., July 1953, 7.
17. Ibid., September 1959, 7.
18. Ibid., June 1953, 7.

CHAPTER 35 — 'Til the Whole World Knows Jesus
1. *Assemblies of God News*, June 1961, 4.
2. Ibid., November 1962, 7.
3. Ibid., November 1962, 4.
4. Ibid., June 1963, 4.
5. Ibid., August 1963, 7.
6. Ibid., October 1967, 4.
7. Ibid., November 1964, 8.
8. Personal interview with Jack Bledsoe, April 27, 1993.
9. Letter from Arlie Teske to author, June 2, 1993.
10. *Assemblies of God News*, May 1969, 4.
11. *The Pentecostal Evangel*, 2 September 1962, 14-15.
12. *Assemblies of God News*, August 1972, 4.
13. Ibid., November 1972, 6, and March 1973, 7.
14. Ibid., December 1974, 4.
15. Ibid., November 1978, 6.
16. Personal interview with Colleen Tipton, September 10, 1993.
17. Ibid.
18. *Assemblies of God News*, April 1979, 4.
19. Letter from Quentin McGhee to author, July 7, 1993.
20. 1993 District Council annual report, 10.
21. Ibid.
22. "Malawi," *World Book Encyclopedia*, 1985, Vol. 13, 79-80.
23. Bill Moore in sermon delivered at Cathedral of the Hills, Edmond, Oklahoma, November 28, 1993.
24. *The Pentecostal Evangel*, 18 July 1993, 16-17.

CHAPTER 36 — Revive Us Again!
1. Blumhofer, Vol. 2, 190, quoting W.I. Evans.
2. Personal interview with Jim King, October 15, 1993.
3. Natalie Nichols, "Rise and Walk, The Trial and Triumph of New York Jet Dennis Byrd", *Charisma*, December 1993, 48-50.

Appendix A

Officers of the Oklahoma District Council of the Assemblies of God, 1914-94

DISTRICT SUPERINTENDENT*

W.T. Gaston	1914-1915	James S. Hutsell	1927-1938
Willard H. Pope	1915-1916	George W. Hardcastle	1938-1943
J.R. Evans	1916-1917	F.C. Cornell	1943-1947
S.A. Jamieson	1917-1920	V.H. Ray	1947-1951
Fred Eiting	1920-1921	Robert E. Goggin	1951-1980
Paul H. Ralston	1921-1922	James C. Dodd	1980-1983
Oscar Jones	1922-1927	Armon Newburn	1983-

*The position was known as district chairman until 1927.

ASSISTANT DISTRICT SUPERINTENDENT*

John Linn	1916-1917, 1937	Roy L. Steger	1946-1953
		James C. Dodd	1953-1980
Berl Dodd	1938-1943	Armon Newburn	1980-1983
George W. Hardcastle	1943-1946	Frank Cargill	1983-

*The position was known as assistant chairman until 1927.

WOMEN'S MISSIONARY COUNCIL PRESIDENT*

Mrs. W.T. Mcmullan	1930	Harriette Beaty	1935-1948
Mrs. George Patterson	1931-1932	Dorothy Ray	1948-1950
Lola Miles	1932-1935	Trudy Steger	1950-1953

Grace Murrell	1953-1954	Marie Goggin	1954-1981
Edna Grace	1954	Rosie Yandell	1981-

*The title became Women's Ministries director in 1986.

DISTRICT SECRETARY-TREASURER*

Vache A. Hargis *(secretary)*	1914-1915	Wallace S. Bragg	1939-1942
Willard H. Pope *(treasurer)*	1914-1915	V.H. Ray	1942-1947
S.L. Shockey	1917-1920	Robert E. Goggin	1947-1951
D.E. Collins	1920-1922	V.H. Ray	1951-1953
Glenn Millard	1922-1926	Floyd L. Poag	1953-1958
James S. Hutsell	1926-1927	L.H. Arnold	1958-1972
Glenn Millard	1927-1932	Elmer T. Watkins	1972-1986
R.H. Hoyer	1932-1939	James C. Girkin	1986-

*Secretary and treasurer were separate positions until 1917.

DISTRICT CHRIST'S AMBASSADORS PRESIDENT*

Bert Webb	1925-1928	Samuel J. Scott	1942-1944
Glenn Millard	1928-1930	William C. Shackelford	1944
Clarence Gordon	1930-1931	T.C. Burkett	1944-1946
Glenn Millard	1931-1932	L.B. Keener	1946-1949
Albert Ogle	1932-1933	Carl McCoy	1949-1953
Wallace S. Bragg	1933-1935	T.A. McDonough	1953-1962
Earl F. Davis	1935-1936	Armon Newburn	1962-1966
Albert Ogle	1936-1939	Eugene Meador	1966-1970
William C. Shackelford	1939-1941	John Gifford	1970-1975
Samuel J. Scott	1941	Frank Cargill	1975-1983
Harvey Mitchell	1941-1942	Tom Greene	1983-

*The position became known as district youth director in 1985.

DISTRICT SUNDAY SCHOOL SUPERINTENDENT

J.E. Wilson	1944-1945	W.M. Rumbaugh	1953-1960
Paul Copeland	1945-1948	Leslie Moore	1960-1972
W.M. Rumbaugh	1948-1950	W.G. Baker	1972-1990
L.B. Keener	1950-1953	Jack Salkil	1990-

*The position was combined with district C.A. president from 1936 to 1944. The present position was created in 1944. In 1979 the title was changed to Christian education director.

DISTRICT MISSIONS DIRECTOR* HOME MISSIONS SECRETARY

John Grace	1953-1972	W.L. Miles	1945
James C. Girkin	1972-1986		
Lindell Warren	1986-		

*The position was created in 1953.

480

Appendix B

District Officers by Year of Election

KEY

DS	District Superintendent
AS	Assistant District Superintendent
SEC	Secretary-Treasurer
SSS	District Sunday School Superintendent
CED	District Christian Education Director
DCAP	District Christ's Ambassadors President
WMCP	Women's Missionary Council President
MIS	District Missions Director
YOUTH	District Youth Director
WMD	Women's Ministries Director
EP	Executive Presbyters
GP	General Presbyters
SP	Sectional Presbyters

1. Tulsa—July 24-30, 1914
   Chairman—W.T. Gaston; Secretary—Vache A. Hargis; Treasurer—Willard H. Pope.

2. Tulsa—1915
   Chairman—Willard H. Pope

3. Pawhuska—November 26-December 2, 1916
   Chairman—J.R. Evans; Assistant Chairman—John Linn.

4. Pawhuska—November, 1917
   Chairman—S.A. Jamieson; Assistant Chairman—Fred Eiting; Secretary-Treasurer—S.L. Shockey; Presbyters—T.J. O'Neal, Oscar Jones, J.J. Grobbs.

481

5. Wellston—April 2-7, 1918
   All officers reelected.

6. Claremore—April 1, 1919
   All officers reelected.

7. Panama—October, 1919
   (Two District Councils were held in 1919.)
   All officers reelected.

8. Chickasha—October, 1920
   Chairman—Fred Eiting; SEC—D.E. Collins; Presbyters—Paul H. Ralston, A.B. Harmon, W.H. Whelchel, J.C. Thomas, J.E. Chambers.

9. 1921
   Chairman—Paul H. Ralston; all other officers reelected.

10. 1922
    Chairman—Oscar Jones; SEC—Glenn Millard.

11. Collinsville—November 12-17, 1923
    All officers reelected.

12. Shawnee—October 14-18, 1924
    All officers reelected.

13. Sand Springs—October 27-30, 1925
    Chairman and SEC reelected. Presbyters—E.M. Adams, James Hutsell, J.W. Hudson, F.E. Conrad, S.M. Padgett, Gordon Millard.

14. Shawnee—October 19-22, 1926
    Chairman reelected; SEC—James Hutsell; Presbyters—E.M. Adams, F.F. Conrad, S.M. Padgett, C.E. Shields, Walter Higgens.

15. Woodward—August, 1927
    District Superintendent (DS)—James Hutsell; SEC—Glenn Millard; all other officers reelected.

16. Tulsa—October 23-26, 1928
    DS—James Hutsell; SEC—Glenn Millard; Presbyters—E.M. Adams, Gordon Millard, F.E. Conrad, J.W. Hudson, Fred Eiting, A.R. Colbert, Oscar Jones.

17. Enid—October 29-31, 1929
    All officers reelected.

18. Enid—October 14-17, 1930
    DS and Secretary reelected; District C.A. President (DCAP)—Clarence Gordon (Previous DCAP's had been elected at the state youth convention.); Presbyters—Adams, Millard, Eiting, Hudson reelected, John Linn, R.H. Hoyer.

19. Seminole—October 20-23, 1931
    DS and Secretary reelected; DCAP—Glenn Millard; Presbyters—Hudson, Hoyer, Millard, Linn reelected, Thomas Gray, Oscar Jones.

20. Shawnee—October 3-6, 1932
    DS reelected; SEC—R.H. Hoyer; Presbyters—Gray, Hudson, Linn, Jones reelected, A.J. Wilcox, Wallace Bragg; DCAP—Albert Ogle; WMC President (WMCP)—Lola Miles (previous WMCP had been elected at a separate meeting).

482

21. Tulsa—October 3-6, 1933
    DS, Secretary, and WMCP reelected; DCAP—Wallace Bragg; Presbyters—E.M. Adams, Berl Dodd, F.E. Conrad, R.L. Steger, T.S. Miles, W.T. McMullan.

22. 1934—Minutes not available.

23. Enid—October 1-4, 1935
    DS, SEC, and WMCP reelected; DCAP—Earl Davis; Presbyters—L.D. Roberts, T.E. May, Berl Dodd, F.E. Conrad, E.C. Tobey, R.L. Steger.

24. Bartlesville—October 5-9, 1936
    DS, DCAP, WMCP, reelected; SEC—Wallace Bragg; General Presbyters—P.C. Nelson, John Linn; SP—Preston Roberts, John Linn, T.E. May, C.J. Brown, P.C. Nelson, F.E. Conrad, Berl Dodd, Ed Bice, W.L. Fortenberry, E.C. Tobey, R.V. Carter, T.K. Davis.

25. Chickasha—October 5-7, 1937
    DS, WMCP, SEC and General Presbyters reelected; Assistant Superintendent—John Linn; SP—H.T. Owens, George W. Hardcastle, Berl Dodd, F.E. Conrad, Frank Postelle, T.K. Davis; DCAP—Albert Ogle.

26. Ada—October 3-6, 1938
    DCAP and WMCP reelected; DS—George W. Hardcastle; SEC—Wallace Bragg; AS—Berl Dodd; EP—Hardcastle, Dodd, Bragg, H.T. Owens, F.C. Cornell; GP—P.C. Nelson, James Hutsell; SP—H.T. Owens, V.H. Ray, Roy Steger, Frank Conrad, Frank Postelle, T.K. Davis.

27. Oklahoma City—September 25-28, 1939
    (*Author's Note*: In 1939, the annual District Council was designated as the "24th annual council." However, it was the 27th meeting of the District Council, which had not received a numerical designation in the official minutes before 1939. Also, beginning in 1939, sectional presbyters were elected at sectional meetings by pastors of the section. The sectional presbyters listed hereafter are those contained in the official minutes of the various District Councils.)

    DS and SEC reelected; Assistant Superintendent (AS)—Berl Dodd; Executive Presbyters (EP)—Hardcastle, Dodd, Bragg, F.C. Cornell, John Linn; General Presbyters (GP)—Hardcastle, P.C. Nelson, Bragg; Sectional Presbyters (SP)—M.D. Hartz, V.H. Ray, R.L. Steger, Frank Conrad, Frank Postelle, T.K. Davis; DCAP—William Shackelford; WMCP—Harriette Beatty.

28. Tulsa—September 23-26, 1940
    DS, SEC, AS, DCAP, WMCP, EP, GP reelected; SP—Hartz, Steger reelected, L.H. Arnold, Willie Davis, S.J. Scott, William Lowder, James S. Murrell, Rufus Strange, W.C. Gilbert.

29. Shawnee—October 6-10, 1941
    DS, AS, SEC, WMCP reelected; DCAP and Sunday School Superintendent (SSS)—S.J. Scott; EP—Hardcastle, Dodd, Bragg, Cornell, R.L. Steger; GP—Hardcastle, Bragg, W.C. Shackelford; SP—Hartz, Arnold, Davis, Lowder, Steger, Strange, Murrell reelected, R.A. Work, C.J. Brown.

30. Seminole—October, 1942
    All officers reelected.

483

31. Tulsa—October 4-8, 1943
    DS—F.C. Cornell; AS—George W. Hardcastle; SEC—V.H. Ray; DCAP, SSS, and WMCP reelected; EP—Cornell, Hardcastle, Ray, M.D. Hartz, W.C. Shackelford; GP—Cornell, Hardcastle, Ray; SP—Hartz, Arnold, Work, Steger, Murrell reelected, H. Ross Davis, C.A. Snodgrass, R.W. Newby, Henry C. Humphrey.

32. Shawnee—October 2-6, 1944
    DS, AS, SEC, WMCP, EP, GP reelected; DCAP—T.C. Burkett; SSS—J.E. Wilson; SP—Hartz, Arnold, Davis, Work, Murrell, Humprhey reelected, V.J. Boutwell, C.J. Brown, Orville J. Painter.

33. Tulsa—October 1-5, 1945
    DS, AS, SEC, WMCP, DCAP, GP reelected; SSS—Paul Copeland; EP—Hardcastle, Ray, Shackelford, R.L. Steger; SP—Hartz, Arnold, Davis, Work, Painter, Murrell, Brown reelected, A.H. Monroe, Albert D. Pyle; Home Missions Secretary—W.L. Miles.

34. Ardmore—October 7-10, 1946
    DS, SEC, WMCP, SSS reelected; AS—R.L. Steger; EP—Cornell, Steger, Ray, Shackelford, Glenn Millard; GP—Cornell, Steger, Ray; DCAP—L.B. Keener; SP—Hartz, Arnold, Davis, Work, Monroe, Murrell reelected, Leslie Moore, John Grace, Olen Cossey.

35. Tulsa—October 6-9, 1947
    DS—V.H. Ray; SEC—Robert E. Goggin; AS, SSS, DCAP, WMCP reelected; EP—Ray, Steger, Goggin, Shackelford, and Millard; GP—Ray, Steger, Goggin; SP—Davis, Arnold, Work, Hartz, Grace, Murrell, Cossey, Moore reelected, Homer Boyd, Neil Webb, R.L. Brooks, Floyd Poag, Haskell Rogers, William Lowder, Willis Stafford, Carl McCoy.

36. Shawnee—October 4-6, 1948
    DS, AS, SEC, DCAP, EP, GP reelected; WMCP—Dorothy Ray; SSS—W.M. Rumbaugh; SP—Boyd, Arnold, Grace, Poag, Murrell, Cossey, Moore reelected, L.J. Choate, W.F. Gilchrist, John R. Keith, David Roper.

37. Oklahoma City—October 3-6, 1949
    (All District Councils have been held in Oklahoma City since 1949)

    DS, AS, SEC, WMCP, SSS, GP all reelected; DCAP—Carl McCoy; EP—Ray, Goggin, Steger, Shackelford, F.C. Cornell; SP—Gilchrist, Boyd, Choate, Arnold, Keith, Grace, Poag, Roper, Cossey, Murrell reelected, Olen T. Craig, F. Virgil Claxton.

38. October 2-5, 1950
    DS, AS, SEC, DCAP, GP reelected; SSS—L.B. Keener; WMCP—Trudy Steger; EP—Ray, Steger, Goggin, Cornell, W.M. Rumbaugh; SP—all reelected.

39. October 1-4, 1951
    DS—Robert E. Goggin; SEC—V.H. Ray; AS, SSS, DCAP, WMCP reelected; EP—Goggin, Steger, Ray, Cornell, Rumbaugh; GP—Goggin, Steger, Ray; SP—Gilchrist, Boyd, Choate, Arnold, Grace, Poag, Craig, Cossey, Murrell, Roper reelected, James C. Dodd.

40. October 6-8, 1952
   DS, AS, SEC, SSS, DCAP, WMCP, GP reelected; EP—Goggin, Steger, Ray, Rumbaugh, M.D. Hartz; SP—Boyd, Choate, Arnold, Dodd, Grace, Poag, Craig, Claxton, Cossey, Murrell, Roper reelected, George A. Brannon.

41. October 5-8, 1953
   DS reelected; AS—James C. Dodd, SEC—Floyd L. Poag; DCAP—T.A. McDonough; SSS—W.M. Rumbaugh; WMCP—Grace Murrell; EP—Goggin, Dodd, Poag, Hartz, J.R. Keith; GP—Goggin, Dodd, Poag; SP—Boyd, Arnold, Claxton, Cossey, Murrell, Roper reelected, C.O. Haymaker, H.A. Medford, Joe Stumbaugh, Leo Swicegood.

42. October 4-7, 1954
   DS, AS, SEC, SSS, DCAP, EP, GP reelected; WMCP—Marie Goggin; Missions Director (MIS)—John Grace; SP—Boyd, Claxton, Haymaker, Medford, Stumbaugh, Swicegood, Roper, Cossey reelected, Leslie Moore, Olen T. Craig, W.H. Kennemer, A.N. Burns.

43. October 3-5, 1955
   All officers reelected except for SP—L.H. Arnold replaced Burns.

44. October 1-3, 1956
   All officers reelected except for SP—L.J. Choate replaced Haymaker, W.T. McFarland replaced Medford.

45. October 7-9, 1957
   All officers reelected except for SP—Haskell Rogers replaced Roper; G.A. Brannan replaced Craig.

46. October 6-8, 1958
   DS, AS, MIS, DCAP, SSS, WMCP reelected; SEC—L.H. Arnold; EP—Goggin, Dodd, Arnold, Cornell, Steger; GP—Goggin, Dodd, Arnold; SP—All reelected except Olen T. Craig replaced McFarland, Carl McCoy replaced Brannan.

47. October 5-7, 1959
   DS, AS, MIS, DCAP, SSS, WMCP, SEC, GP reelected; EP—Goggin, Dodd, Arnold, Cornell; SP—Choate, Craig, Kennemer, Stumbaugh, Moore, Swicegood, Claxton, Cossey, and McCoy reelected; Walter Swaim, W.T. McFarland, William Lowder.

48. October 3-5, 1960
   DS, AS, SEC, MIS, DCAP, WMCP, GP reelected; SSS—Leslie Moore; EP—Goggin, Dodd, Arnold, Cornell, R.L. Steger; SP—All reelected except Walter Leppke replaced Choate.

49. October 2-4, 1961
   All officers reelected except SP—Lawrence Langley replaced McFarland, W.R. Davis replaced Moore.

50. October 1-3, 1962
   All officers reelected except Armon Newburn replaced T.A. McDonough as DCAP.

51. October 7-9, 1963
   All officers reelected.

485

52. October 6-8, 1964
    All officers reelected except SP—Franklin D. Blair replaced Lowder.

53. October 5-7, 1965
    All officers reelected except SP—George A. Brannan replaced Langley.

54. October 4-6, 1966
    All officers reelected except Eugene Meador replaced Armon Newburn as DCAP.

55. October 3-5, 1967
    All officers reelected except SP—J.E. Frady replaced Davis, J.W. Newby replaced Claxton, Ernest L. Rolland replaced Blair.

56. October 1-3, 1968
    All officers reelected.

57. October 7-9, 1969
    All officers reelected.

58. October 6-8, 1970
    DS, AS, SEC, SSS, MIS, WMCP, GP reelected; DCAP—John Gifford; EP—Goggin, Dodd, Arnold, Armon Newburn, Elmer T. Watkins; SP—All reelected except L.A. Haymaker replaced Leppke.

59. October 5-7, 1971
    All officers reelected except SP—Marvin K. McElhannon replaced Craig.

60. October 3-5, 1972
    DS, AS, WMCP reelected; SEC—Elmer T. Watkins; MIS—James C. Girkin; SSS—W.G. Baker; EP—Goggin, Dodd, Watkins, Newburn, John W. Newby; GP—Goggin, Dodd, Watkins; SP—All reelected except Grady Adcock replaced Kennemer, M. Russell Herndon replaced Newby.

61. October 2-4, 1973
    All officers reelected except SP—H.L. Morrison replaced Brannan.

62. October 1-3, 1974
    All officers reelected.

63. September 30-October 2, 1975
    All officers reelected.

64. October 5-7, 1976
    All officers reelected except Frank Cargill replaced John Gifford as DCAP and SP—James E. Mabry replaced Leo Swicegood.

65. October 4-6, 1977
    All officers reelected.

66. October 3-5, 1978
    All officers reelected.

67. October 2-4, 1979.
    All officers reelected.

68. October 7-9, 1980
    DS—James C. Dodd; AS—Armon Newburn; SEC, MIS, DCAP, WMD (The Women's Missionary Council President was changed to Women's Ministries

486

Director in 1976), CED (Sunday School Superintendent was changed to District Christian Education Director in 1979), reelected; EP—Dodd, Newburn, Watkins, Newby, Joe Stumbaugh; GP—Dodd, Newburn, Watkins; SP—All reelected except Robert P. Rider replaced Joe Stumbaugh and Ervin A. Donaldson replaced M. Russell Herndon.

69. October 6-8, 1981

All officers reelected except Rosie Yandell replaced Marie Goggin as WMD and SP—All reelected except Ralph Reddout replaced L.A. Haymaker, Bernard Escalante replaced H.E. Morrison, Lloyd Winkle replaced Marvin McElhannon, Lindell H. Warren replaced Olen F. Cossey.

70. October 5-7, 1982

All officers reelected except SP—T.C. Burkett replaced Bernard Escalante.

71. October 4-6, 1983

(*Author's Note*: Another numerical correction. Both 1982 and 1983 District Councils were designated the "70th annual council session," which is correct. 1983 was the 71st meeting but 70th annual meeting.)

DS—Armon Newburn; AS—Frank Cargill; SEC, WMD, MIS, CED reelected; DCAP—Tom Greene; EP—Newburn, Cargill, Watkins, Ervin A. Donaldson, Tom Goins; GP—Newburn, Watkins; SP—All reelected except Greg Whitlow replaced Ervin A. Donaldson and John E. Brown replaced Ernest L. Rolland.

72. October 2-4, 1984

All officers reelected except SP—Bobby L. Minick replaced Walter Swaim and Frankie Pollard replaced Carl McCoy.

73. November 11-13, 1985.

DS, AS, WMD, YOUTH (DCAP changed to District Youth Director in 1985), EP, GP, CED, MIS, SEC reelected; SP—All reelected except W.O. Hatley replaced Bobby L. Minick and Herbert Wharton replaced T.C. Burkett. (In the January, 1986 Executive Board meeting, James Girkin replaced E.T. Watkins as secretary-treasurer and Lindell Warren replaced Girkin as missions director.)

74. November 10-12, 1986

All officers reelected except EP—John Brown replaced Ervin A. Donaldson; SP—H.A. Brummett replaced Grady Adcock, Charles Dean replaced J.E. Frady, Jim McNabb replaced Greg Whitlow and Paul Sharpe replaced Lindell Warren.

75. November 9-11, 1987

All officers reelected except SP—Curtis Owens replaced Ralph Reddout and Dwain Jones replaced John Brown.

76. November 14-16, 1988

All officers reelected.

77. November 13-15, 1989

All officers reelected.

78. November 12-14, 1990

All officers reelected except CED—Jack Salkil replaced W.G. Baker; SP—David

Stuart replaced James E. Mabry, Eugene Howeth replaced Dwain Jones and T.D. Gifford replaced Frankie Pollard.

79. November 11-13, 1991
All officers reelected except SP—Roger Mattox replaced W.O. Hatley, Bill Weaver replaced H.A. Brummett and Doyle Seeley replaced Robert P. Rider.

80. November 9-11, 1992
All officers reelected except SP—Robert Adams replaced Lloyd Winkle.

81. November 8-10, 1993
All officers reelected.

$\mathcal{Appendix}\ C$

Biographical Sketches of Officers of the Oklahoma District Council, 1994

Armon and JoAnn Newburn

ARMON NEWBURN
District Superintendent

Armon Newburn was born November 16, 1932, at Grandma Newburn's house at Wister, Oklahoma. During his sophomore year he was saved at First Assembly in Spiro, where the family had moved. He received the baptism in the Holy Spirit about six months later.

From the time he was filled with the Spirit, Newburn felt he needed to preach. He played the piano and occasionally spoke at youth meetings, but did not move into full-time ministry until after he graduated from high school in 1950. He was licensed to preach in February, 1952, and married JoAnn Boyd, the daughter of longtime Poteau Pastor Homer Boyd, in June, 1952.

The Newburns' first pastorate was in Wister, beginning the month after they were married. In 1953 they moved to First Assembly in Muldrow where they pastored for six years until they were elected as pastors of First Assembly in Duncan.

In 1962 Brother Newburn was appointed Oklahoma District Christ's Ambassadors president. During his term as DCAP, Newburn spearheaded the purchase and development of property at Turner Falls for youth camps and other district functions.

In 1966 Capitol Hill Assembly in Tulsa called Armon Newburn to be pastor. Under his leadership, the church grew rapidly. In 1974 a new building was constructed in the Woodlake area of Tulsa, so the church was renamed Woodlake Assembly of God.

The Newburns pastored Woodlake for 17 years, during which time it became one of the leading churches in the Assemblies of God fellowship. While pastoring, Newburn also served as an executive presbyter of the Oklahoma District.

Newburn was elected Oklahoma assistant district superintendent in 1980 but continued to pastor Woodlake. In 1983, upon the retirement of James Dodd, Newburn was elected Oklahoma's 14th district superintendent.

Newburn has degrees from Oklahoma City Southwestern College, Southwestern Assemblies of God College, Evangelical Bible College and Seminary, Luther Rice Seminary, and Carl Albert Junior College. In 1980 he also received a Doctorate of Letters from International Bible Institute and Seminary.

He serves on the governing boards of Evangel College in Springfield, Missouri, and Southwestern Assemblies of God College in Waxahachie, Texas. In 1993 Newburn was granted an honorary doctorate degree from Southwestern and was named chairman of the Southwestern Board of Directors. He also has served on the boards of the American Indian Bible College and Hillcrest Children's Home, as well as on the Northeast Urban Church Planning Board.

At the 1993 General Council, Newburn was elected as a non-resident executive presbyter. In this capacity he is one of the 14 men who govern the national Assemblies of God fellowship.

Armon and JoAnn Newburn have two children—Greg and Lisa—and three beautiful granddaughters.

Brother Newburn has a dream for the Oklahoma fellowship:

"We need a new freshness. I want to see a real move of the Holy Spirit like we had at the turn of the century. Our kids need to experience Pentecost in our homes and churches. We all need to get ready for the trumpet sound."

FRANK CARGILL
Assistant District Superintendent

The pastor's wife and an elderly doctor brought Frank Cargill into this world in 1949 on an oil-field lease in Drumright, Oklahoma. His parents attended First Assembly in Drumright, where M.A. Malone was pastor. Cargill's maternal grandfather was D.C. Callahan, who founded First Assembly in Sallisaw and pastored there for 25 years.

Cargill was saved at a youth rally at Skiatook on December 7, 1959, at age 10. He received the baptism in the Holy Spirit three months later.

During his teen years, Cargill felt God was calling him to preach the gospel. He taught

Frank and Linda Cargill

490

In December, 1945, Brown married fellow Central Bible College student Olive "Polly" Kellner. They began their ministry in 1946 by pastoring Elm Grove, a small church that met in a schoolhouse near Muskogee, Oklahoma. The Browns pastored several churches in New York for 23 years, and pastored in Boston from 1968 to 1974 before returning to Oklahoma. Brown was elected senior pastor at Central Assembly in Tulsa in 1974. Three heart attacks prevented him from asking for reelection in 1977. The Browns traveled in evangelism from 1977 to 1981, when they accepted their present pastorate at First Assembly in Lawton.

They have two daughters—Sue and Linda—and four grandchildren.

Brother Brown says the key to a successful pastorate is a complete trust in God:

"A pastor must give himself to God and say, 'Here I am. I'm your employee. You put me where you want me to be and then give me the grace to be there if I find it difficult.' I have no special talents. If He has used me, it's because He used the talent He gave me. I'm His employee and He has commanded me to work for Him. I recognized a long time ago that I couldn't do anything without Him."

TOM GOINS
Executive Presbyter

Tom Goins was born October 26, 1936, in Okmulgee, Oklahoma. His father was pioneer Oklahoma Assemblies of God preacher Otto Goins.

Tom was saved at about age five in the church at Haydonville—a church built by his father and his future father-in-law, O.W. Johnston. He married Darlene Johnston in 1958. After graduating from Oklahoma State University with a degree in electrical engineering, Goins signed on with Montgomery Ward and became the local store manager in Trinidad, Colorado. It was there God began dealing with him about the ministry. He says, "It

Tom and Darlene Goins

wasn't the big light flashing...it was just the inward desire to serve God the best I could." Under the guidance of his local pastor, Simon J. Peters, Goins started ed a church in Aguilar, Colorado.

Goins served a year as associate pastor of First Assembly in Wichita, Kansas. In 1963 he was elected pastor at First Assembly in Wilburton, Oklahoma. He pastored at First Assembly in Sapulpa from 1966 to 1971; First Assembly in Bartlesville from 1971 to 1976; and at First Assembly in Lakewood, Colorado from 1976 to 1978.

Goins was elected pastor of Broken Arrow Assembly in August, 1978. The Goinses have three children—Kari, Kelly, and Kevin—and two grandchildren.

Here is Tom Goins' ministerial philosophy:

"I believe strongly that the local assembly has its first responsibility to the local community. The church must minister to the whole family as well as reach out to all who are without God and have no knowledge of salvation. I must be a pastor to all age groups and all people of my city. I must lead my church to have a strong vision for the work of God that ranges from help of the needy of our community to a great foreign missions program."

∽

Tom, Pam, Andy, and Bridgette Greene

TOM GREENE
District Youth Director

Thomas Wayne Greene was born in Oklahoma City on March 13, 1953, into an Assemblies of God home. He was reared in Faith Tabernacle where he was called to preach at age 19.

It was no surprise to the Greene family that Tom became a preacher. One of Tom's grand-mothers had predicted when he was a small child that he would some day preach the gospel. Tom's paternal grandfather was S.N. Greene, an Okla-homa songwriter who was famous for writing Pentecostal hymns such as "Job's God Is True."

Tom married Pam Martin in Oklahoma City on June 9, 1973. After preaching at every opportunity for two years, he became associate pastor at First Assembly in Woodward in 1975. He served as youth pastor at Oklahoma City Faith Tabernacle and Bartlesville Tuxedo Assembly until God called him to his first pastorate, First Assembly in Henryetta, in June, 1981.

The Greenes pastored the Henryetta church until Tom was elected district Christ's Ambassadors president in October, 1983. In 1985 the position title was changed to district youth director.

Tom and Pam have two children—Bridgette and Andrew.

After directing the Oklahoma District's youth programs for a decade, Greene recognizes more than ever the importance of young people being active in a local Assemblies of God church:

"It is terribly incorrect to refer to our youth as the 'church of tomorrow.' Unless we encourage and allow youth to be an active part of the church *today*...there will be no church of *tomorrow*."

Appendix D

Foreign and Home Missionaries of the Oklahoma District, 1914-1994

Randy and Brenda Anoatubby
Almyra Aston
Betty Ayers
James and Ramona Banks
James W. Banks
Forrest and Ethel Barker
Florence Bassett
John and June Bellamy Jr.
Jack and Carmelita Bledsoe
Gary and Shirley Bohanon
Harry E. Bowley
O.S. Boyer
Bill Boyles
Raymond T. Brock
Dale and Betty Brown
Murray and Marjorie Brown
Franklin and Doris Burns
Mike and Debbie Caldwell
Marion Clark
Rose Clark
Gertrude Clonce

Robert and Naomi Cobb
Duane and Ruth Collins
Thelma Cox
Gary and Wilma Davidson
Sylvia Davidson
Dorothy Davis
W.E. and Helen Davis
Roger Davis
Darrel and Dosha Delozier
Charles Dennis
John and Ernestine Jeter Doan
Mack and Merlene Dolchok
Terry and Leonna Dorsey
Dewain and Naomi Duck
Bill and Jean Everitt
Robert and Norene Feller
Mike and Nancy Ferguson
Ada Fesler
Mark and Nancy Fitzgerald
George and Stella Flattery
V.L. Fullerton

Jonathan Gainsbrugh
John Garlock
Gary and Nancy Gibson
Ardith and Dottie Graves
Mark and Diane Guest
Joseph and Patricia Habibi
Stephen and Gale Hadden
Phyllis Hammerbacker
Charity and Ruth Harris
W.W. and Edith Hays
Virgil Heddelston
Eldon and Gloria Hicks
Melton and Alma Hill
Ralph and Rosemary Hollandsworth
Carl and Margaret Holleman
Wayne Hunter
Paul and Dreta Hutsel
Dean and Lucille Jackson
Hugh and Gertrude Jeter
Hugh and Theola Jeter
Norma Johanson
Dale and Nancy Johnson
Eric Johnson
Mabel Kennedy
Shirley Kenslow
Hazel Kinslow
Dessie Knight
Bill and Barbara Kuert
Jennie and Annie Kulka
Mark and Helba Lemos
Willa B. Lowther
James and Linda Martin
Edgar McElhannon
Quentin and Elizabeth McGhee
Larry and Dee McNeil
James and Lynn Menge
Joni Middleton
Robert and Gioia Mihuc
Norman and Helen Moffatt
David Montgomery
Stephen and Vicki Mooney
Bill and Reita Moore
Byron T. Moore
Lula Morton
Merlin Neely
Roy and Mary Lou Nelson
David and Cheryl Newberry

Ben and Darlene Odell
Charley and Jan Odell
Rodger and Alma Perkins
Al and Emanuela Perna Jr.
Pearl Pickel
Elmo and June Pierce
Opal Poag
Vernon and Geraldine Poncho
Harold and Georgene Powell
Don and Virginia Ramsey
Glen Reeves
John Reynolds
Fari Rider
Bill and Alberta Roberts
Clarence Roberts
James and Norma Scott
Leon Seaton
John and Sherrill Seibold
Marguerite Shaw
Lois Shelton
Harry Shumway
V.H. and Eva Shumway
Randy and Peggy Sims
Agnes Sloan
Grady and Janet Smalling
Caleb Smith
Virgil Smith
Ronnie and Katherine Snow
Bill and Wenda Snyder
Don and Linda Stamps
Verlin and Pauline Stewart
Edgar Stone
Dwayne Suit
Earl and Nelda Taylor
Arlie and Jennie Teske
Cary and Faye Tidwell
Greg and Susan Tiffany
Terry and Naomi Tipps
Ben and Colleen Tipton
A.N. and Blanche Trotter
Kevin and Eunice Tyler
Kenneth and Sheila Vance
Ted and Estelle Vassar
Berta Vaughn
David and Claudia Wakefield
Jonathan Wakefield
Rick and Glenda Walden

Alva and Louise Jeter Walker
Leroy and Thelma Ward
Bobby and Karen Welch
Billy Wheeler
Loretta Wideman

Bobbie Wilkins
Milton Williams
Fred and Nelda Wright
J.W. and Wilma Wyckoff

Appendix E

Assemblies of God Statistics

Churches, USA	11,689	Teen Challenge Staff	1,141
Church Membership, USA	1,337,321	DHM/MAPS Personnel	1,071
Constituency, USA		**Foreign Missions**	
(persons of all ages who		Missionaries	1,677
identify with an A/G church)	2,257,846	Countries Served	133
Ministers *(total)*	30,893	National Ministers/	
Ordained	18,366	Lay Workers	141,440
Christian Education		Churches and Outstations	141,935
Sunday Schools	11,249	Members and Adherents	22,570,692
Enrollment	1,410,579	Bible Schools	417
Private Christian Schools	1,053	Enrollment	52,476
Enrollment	116,379	**Men's Ministries**	
Endorsed Colleges/Seminaries	18	Groups	5,915
Student Enrollment	11,542	Members	128,755
Youth Group Members	289,785	Royal Rangers Outposts	5,637
Revivaltime Weekly Releases	601	Royal Rangers	129,801
Home Missions		**Women's Ministries**	
Total Appointed Missionaries	3,207	Groups	8,795
Military/VA chaplains	185	Members	232,084
New Church Missionaries	77	Missionette Clubs	21,548
Intercultural Missionaries	400	Missionette Members	172,281
Campus Ministers	233	**World Ministries Giving**	$187,692,971
Industrial/Institutional Chaplains	100	**Gospel Publishing House**	
		Literature Printed Daily	24 Tons

Appendix F

Churches Established in the 1940's and 50's

FROM OFFICIAL DISTRICT COUNCIL MINUTES

1940
- Cherokee
- Eagle Grove *(Nash)*
- Earlsboro
- Edmond
- Eufaula *(Artussee School)*
- Green Chapel *(near Wright City)*
- Leach
- Mounds
- Oak Grove *(south of Curtis)*
- Orlando
- One Creek *(near Findley)*
- Perkins
- Pond Creek
- Race Track *(Spiro)*
- Stigler
- Strang
- Summerfield

1941
- Bethel *(near Colcord)*
- Bluejacket
- Camargo
- Cardin
- Catoosa

- Centerview *(near Shawnee)*
- Central Assembly *(near Wolf)*
- Chandler
- Crystal
- Durant
- Granite
- Honobia
- Indian Assembly *(near Canton)*
- Latham
- Little
- Marland
- Meeker
- Nelagoney
- Norman
- Oklahoma City *(South Side)*
- Oklahoma City *(Faith Tabernacle)*
- Oklahoma City *(Ninth and Phillips)*
- Oklahoma City *(Rockwood)*
- Oak Grove *(near Soper)*
- Okmulgee East Side
- Pleasant Hill *(near Haworth)*
- Pryor
- Reydon
- Roosevelt

Sugdon
Taloga
Valliant
Watonga
Webb City
Wister

1943

Cade
Chappel (at Enid)
Chouteau
Eldorado
Farris
Lone Grove
Phillips Plant
Ramona
Saddle Mountain
Tryon

1944

Dawson
Hobart
Madill
Midway *(near Ada)*
Okmulgee Revival Tabernacle
Owasso
Tussy
Waurika
Weatherford

1945

Aztec
Ft. Gibson
Granite
Midwest City
Ninnekah
Oklahoma City *(Southwest Assembly)*
Oklahoma City *(Northeast Assembly)*
Oleta
Sulphur

1946

Corum
Faith Mission
Jay
Marlow
Timber Ridge
Tulsa *(Glad Tidings)*

1947

Achille
Evans *(near Welch)*
Frederick
Mountain Park
Oak Grove *(near Oklahoma City)*
Oklahoma City
      (Assembly of God Mission)
Randlett
Stroud
Verdigris

1948

Blanchard
Burbank
Carnegie
Carney
Coyle
Dewey
Eagletown
Kingfisher
Kingston
Luther
Oakhurst
Pauls Valley
Powell *(near Madill)*
Tulsa *(Silent Sheep Assembly)*

1949

Chickasha *(12th Street)*
Crowder *(Lakeside Assembly)*
Enid *(House of Prayer)*
Fonda
Grandfield
Inola
Lawton *(Bethel Assembly)*
Leflore
Lindsay
McAlester *(North)*
Mingo
Mulhall
Oklahoma City *(Bethel Assembly)*
Oklahoma City *(Fellowship Assembly)*
Purcell
Row *(near Colcord)*
Tishimingo
Topsy
Wayside *(near Miami)*

504

1950
Baum
Cartwright
Crossroads *(near Stratford)*
Dustin
Elmore City
Hollis
Locust Grove
Maysville
Mazie
Oakdale
Oklahoma City Putnam City
Oklahoma City University Heights
Pleasant Hill *(near Ardmore)*
Prague
Skyview
Spavinaw
Spiro
Union Chapel

1951
Braden
Dog Creek
Duncan Bethel Assembly
Marietta
Muskogee Second Assembly
Oak Grove *(near Bristow)*
Roebuck
Temple
Warner
Westville

1952
Bartlesville Tuxedo
Carney
East Side *(near Miami)*
Gage
Hockerville
Leedy
Macomb
Meeker
Oklahoma City Lighthouse
Tulsa North Harvard
Tulsa Philadelphia
Yanush

1953
Bristow
County Line
Gans
Mounds
Newkirk
Oklahoma City S.W. 59th
Simpson Tyler
Tecumseh

1954
Carter
Keefeton
Keystone
Okesa
Oklahoma City Trinity
Perkins
Tamaha

1956
Keota
Oklahoma City Faith Chapel
Tulsa Bellaire
Tulsa Glenwood
Tulsa Suburban
Sapulpa
Wagoner

1957
Jenks Airview
Midwest City Soldier Creek
Stillwater Calvary
Wann
Washington
Wyandotte

1958
Duncan Glad Tidings
Enid Spaulding Assembly
Wilson Fellowship Mission
Wynnewood

1959
Broken Arrow Alsuma
Bokchito
Chickasha Grand Avenue
Davis

*The above list is incomplete because of the unavailability of records or District Council minutes for specific years.

∴ Index ∾

508

509